IMAGES
of Rail

Rails in Rochester and Monroe County

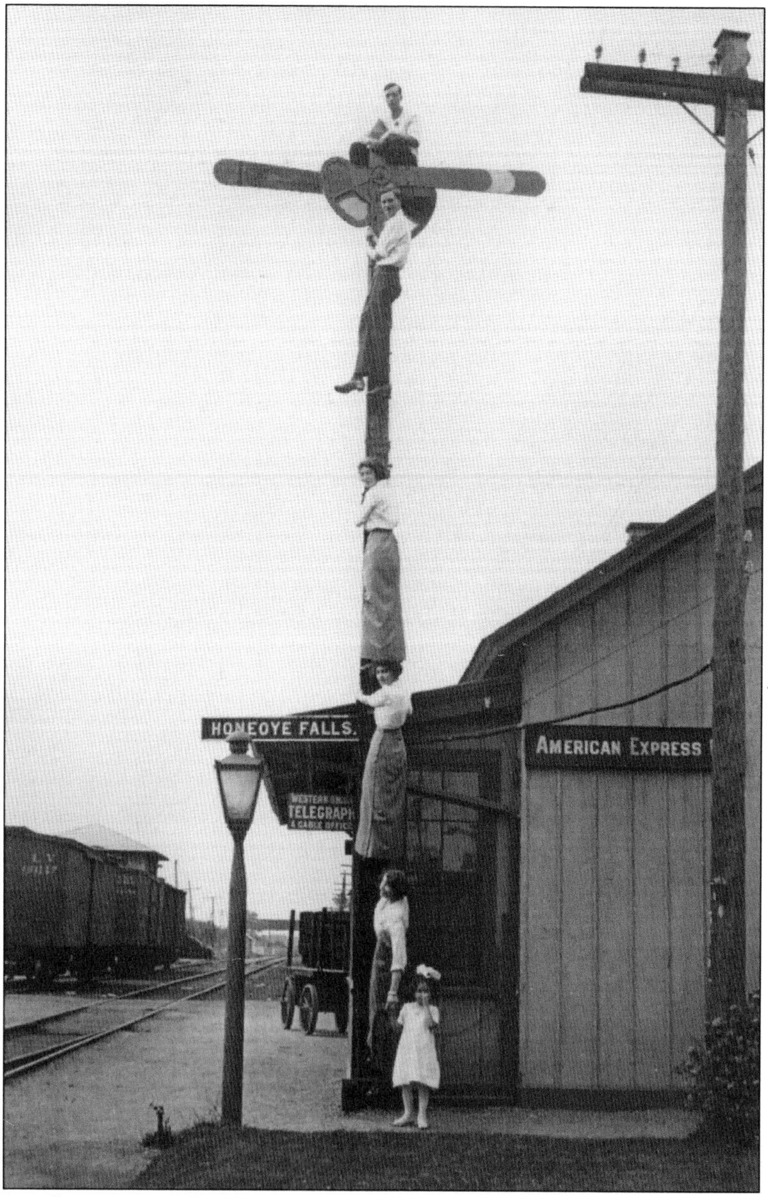

In the village of Honeoye Falls in the town of Mendon, there was not only the Lehigh Valley branch line that ran south from Rochester Junction but also the New York Central (NYC) "Peanut Line" that ran east-west from Tonawanda in Niagara County across southern Monroe County to Canandaigua in Ontario County. People in this c. 1920 photograph seemed to be happy to oblige the photographer and have their picture taken on the semaphore signal at the NYC Honeoye Falls depot. Passenger service on this line ended in 1933. (Courtesy of Town of Mendon historian.)

On the Cover: A New York Central 4-8-2 Mohawk passes the former freight station in the village of East Rochester. Located near the site of the Merchants Despatch Transportation Company, known locally as "the carshops," this mid-1800s building was home to the popular hobby shop Despatch Junction. Sadly, the building and the hobby shop were destroyed by fire in 2014. (Courtesy of Jeff Hands.)

IMAGES
of Rail

RAILS IN ROCHESTER AND MONROE COUNTY

Richard "Dick" Chait

ARCADIA
PUBLISHING

ISBN 978-1-4671-3437-8

Published by Arcadia Publishing
Charleston, South Carolina

Printed in the United States of America

Library of Congress Control Number: 2015936988

For all general information, please contact Arcadia Publishing:
Telephone 843-853-2070
Fax 843-853-0044
E-mail sales@arcadiapublishing.com
For customer service and orders:
Toll-Free 1-888-313-2665

Visit us on the Internet at www.arcadiapublishing.com

This book is dedicated to my mother, who introduced me to the joy of train travel, and to Shiloh, Benning, Theo, Hunter, Eve, Harry, Sam, Freya, Anna, Moira, Lindsey, and Megan, in the hopes that they will have pleasure "riding the rails" just like their grandfather.

Contents

ACKNOWLEDGMENTS

An undertaking like this would not have been possible without the help, cooperation, and encouragement of many people. First and foremost is my immediate family. My wife, Carol Anne, son, Michael, and daughters, Elisa and Jennifer, were supportive beyond measure. Also, I was very fortunate to have had the assistance of the following historians: Lynn Barton, Jim Burlingame, Barbara Chapman, David Crumb, Judy DeRooy, Leanna Hale, Diane Ham, Maureen Kingston, Robert Kruger, Alan Mueller, Bill Poray, Christine Ridarsky, Sue Mee, Pat Wayne, and Peter Widener.

Most cooperative were Karen Dunn, of the American Automobile Association; Pat McKnight, of the Steamtown National Historic Site; Michele Rowe, of the City of Rochester; and Elizabeth Sikorski, of the Rochester Museum & Science Center.

Subject matter experts Ron Amberger, Jim Dierks, Tom Gerbrecht, Jeff Hands, Allen Hilborn, Terry Klee, Scot Lawrence, Richard Margolis, Jim Middleton, Andrea Reithmayr, Duncan Richards, David Staplin, Rich Stoving, John Virgilio, and Otto Vondrak were there to answer the many questions I had and willingly shared their knowledge and resources with me. I am deeply grateful to them all. Lastly, Ken Wingate gave freely of his time to drive an old friend to many of the sites presented in the book. Many thanks, Ken.

It is my hope that the above list of acknowledgments is complete. If there is anyone that I have inadvertently forgotten, I offer my sincere apologies.

INTRODUCTION

Like other major cities in New York State, Rochester and the county in which it resides, Monroe County, owe their economic development from the mid-1800s to the mid-1900s in large measure to rail transportation. Major railroads included Rochester and Monroe County in their expanding rail networks. Long-distance passenger travel became available. Raw materials could be brought in, and manufactured goods could be efficiently shipped out. Companies flourished. Farming communities along Lake Ontario and in the Genesee River valley could be assured that their products could get to market. Rochester and Monroe County were known for their many recreational sites and resorts along Lake Ontario and Irondequoit Bay. Using one of the many electric streetcar routes ensured that these places were within reach. Truly, Rochester and Monroe County enjoyed the reputation of being a great place to work, live, and raise a family. The rail mode of transportation that contributed so greatly to these qualities makes an interesting story

Presented first are depots of the major railroads that appeared on the scene in Rochester. Through acquisitions and consolidations, the New York Central Railroad (NYC) expanded into Central and Western New York State. Its first railroad station in Rochester was built in 1854. NYC went on to build two other railroad stations in Rochester, the last of which was the well-known and beautiful Bragdon Station, designed by Claude Bragdon. In the 1880s, several other railroads realized the potential of the Rochester and Monroe County market and soon established footholds. These railroads included the Buffalo, Rochester & Pittsburgh (BR&P), which eventually became part of the Baltimore & Ohio (B&O), the Lehigh Valley, the Erie, and the Pennsylvania. Both the NYC and the BR&P/B&O extended their lines to Charlotte where the Genesee River flowing north empties into Lake Ontario.

The book also presents important aspects of additional rail activity in Rochester and Monroe County. Railroads that went through the towns of Chili, Henrietta, Mendon, Rush, and Wheatland, located south of Rochester in the Genesee River valley, were especially busy. The village of Scottsville on the Rochester branch line of the BR&P/B&O saw many a coal train bound for the Genesee Docks (coal docks) at Charlotte. East Rochester, a village southeast of the city of Rochester on the NYC main line, was home to the Merchants Despatch Transportation Company, also known locally as the carshops. It was here that all types of freight cars and cabooses were fabricated. Locomotives of all types were seen at Rochester's Goodman Street Yards, a major classification yard on the NYC main line. The yards with its roundhouse, water tower, and coaling tower bristled with activity. Watching the activity at not only Goodman Street Yards, but also at Bragdon Station and at various other locations, rail enthusiasts could see steam engines from J1s to S1s and diesel locomotives from F3s to RS-3s.

The Goodman Street Yards are still very active albeit under CSX. However, the Bragdon Station is gone, as are many of the other sites presented in the book—replaced by running trails, parking lots, and other businesses. It is hoped that what has been presented here will bring back fond memories of these sites and what the rails meant to Rochester and Monroe County.

Some Acronyms and Short Definitions

Alco: American Locomotive Company
BLW: Baldwin Locomotive Works
Bulldog: Nickname for the cab design of Electro-Motive Division (EMD) of General Motors' E and F series diesel locomotives
CCC&StL: Cleveland, Cincinnati, Chicago & St. Louis Railway, known as the "Big Four"
C424: Designation for Alco Century road-switch engine
C-Liner: Designation for the Fairbanks-Morse (FM) diesel road locomotive
Conrail: Consolidated Rail Corporation
CSX: CSX Transportation
Doodlebug: Nickname for a self-propelled baggage/coach car
E7/E8: Designations for EMD diesel passenger locomotives
FA: Designation for Alco diesel road freight locomotives
FT/F3/F7: Designations for EMD diesel road freight locomotives
Geep: Nickname for EMDs GP diesel road-switch engines
GP7/GP9: Designations for EMD diesel road-switch engines
H Class: Designation for NYC's Mikado type 2-8-2 steam locomotive
Hojack: Nickname for NYC's Ontario Division along Lake Ontario's southern shore
Hudson: Name for NYC's J class steam passenger locomotive
J Class: Designation for NYC's Hudson type 4-6-4 steam locomotive
K Class: Designation for NYC's, Erie's, and Lehigh Valley's Pacific type 4-6-2 steam locomotive
LAL: Livonia, Avon & Lakeville Railroad
L Class: Designation for NYC's Mohawk type 4-8-2 steam locomotive
Mikado: Name for NYC's H class steam freight locomotive
Mohawk: Name for NYC's L class steam freight locomotive
NH: New York, New Haven & Hartford Railroad
Niagara: Name for NYC's S class passenger steam locomotive
OMID: Ontario Midland Railroad
PA: Designation for Alco diesel passenger locomotives
Pacific: Name for K and P class steam passenger locomotives
P&LE: Pittsburgh & Lake Erie Railroad
P Class: Designation for B&O's Pacific 4-6-2 steam locomotive
Peanut Line: Nickname for NYC's Tonawanda-to-Canandaigua branch line
Piano Works: Nickname for American Piano Corporation (AMPICO)
PRR: Pennsylvania Railroad
R&SL: Rochester & State Line Railroad
Reefer: Nickname for refrigerated freight car
RF-16: Designation for BLW diesel road locomotive
RG&E: Rochester Gas & Electric Company
RSR: Rochester & Southern Railroad
RS-3/RS-11/RS-32: Designations for Alco diesel road-switch engines
RW&O: Rome, Watertown and Ogdensburg Railroad
S Class: Designation for Niagara type 4-8-4 passenger steam locomotive
S-4: Designation for Alco diesel switch engine
Shark: Nickname for cab design of BLW road diesel locomotives
SW 1500: Designation for EMD road diesel switch engine
U-Boat: Nickname for General Electric's U-25B diesel locomotive
West Shore Line: New York, West Shore & Buffalo Railroad
Whyte notation: Numerical description of the configuration of the steam engine's wheels, for example 4-8-4

One

Major Railroads Come to Town

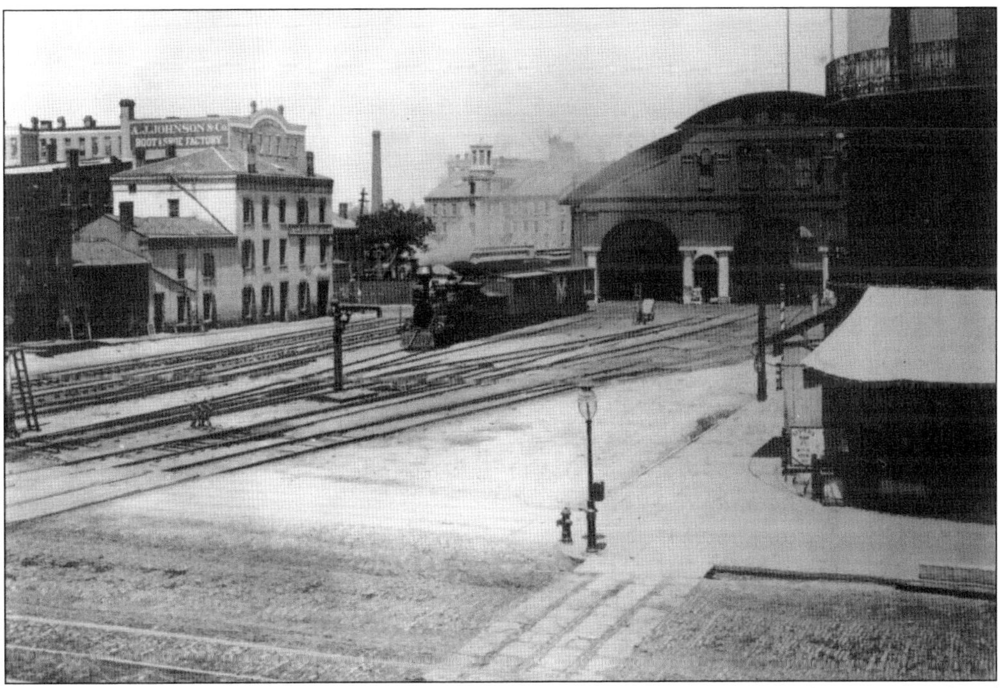

By the 1850s, the New York Central Railroad had consolidated and expanded into Central and Western New York. In 1852, it built its first railroad station in Rochester on Mill Street, west of the Genesee River. By 1870, when this photograph was taken, NYC had merged with the Hudson River Railroad to form the New York Central & Hudson River Railroad (NYC&HR). To the left, in front of the boot and shoe factory building in the photograph, are the NYC&HR offices, and to the right is the balcony of an adjacent hotel. Of note is the fact that President Lincoln stopped here in 1861 before his inauguration. Four years later, in the early hours of April 26, a large crowd gathered at the station to meet the Lincoln funeral train. (Photograph from the William R. Gordon Collection, courtesy of Jeff Hands.)

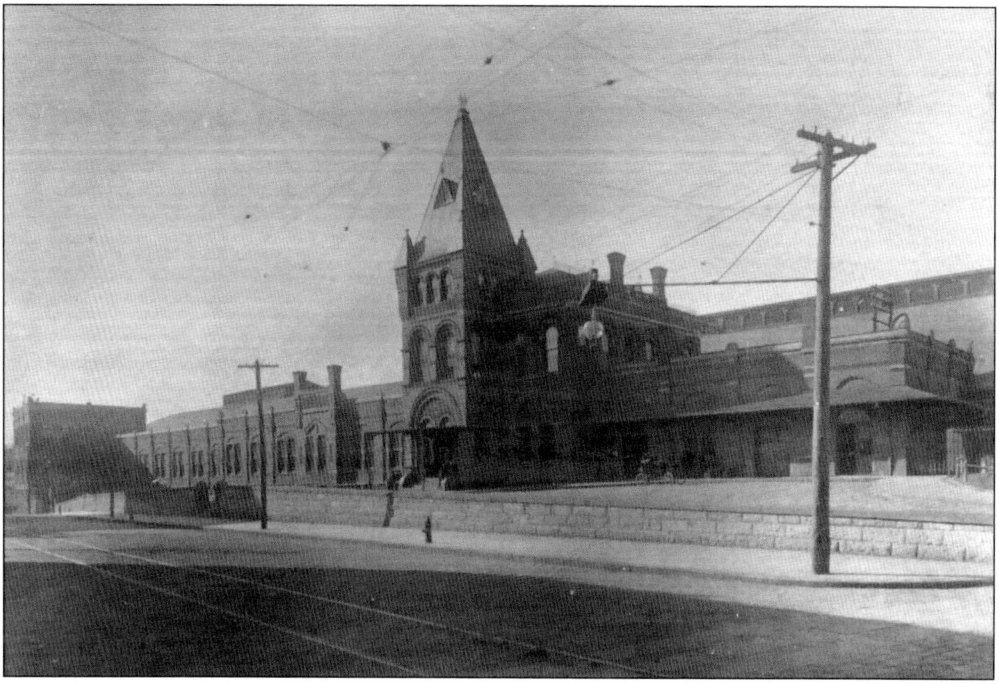

NYC&HR replaced the Mill Street station in 1883 with a larger structure located along Central Avenue between Clinton Avenue and St. Paul Street, east of the Genesee River. It was recognizable by its Victorian architecture as well as its elevated tracks and new train shed. (Courtesy of *Rochester Images*: Rochester Public Library Local History Division.)

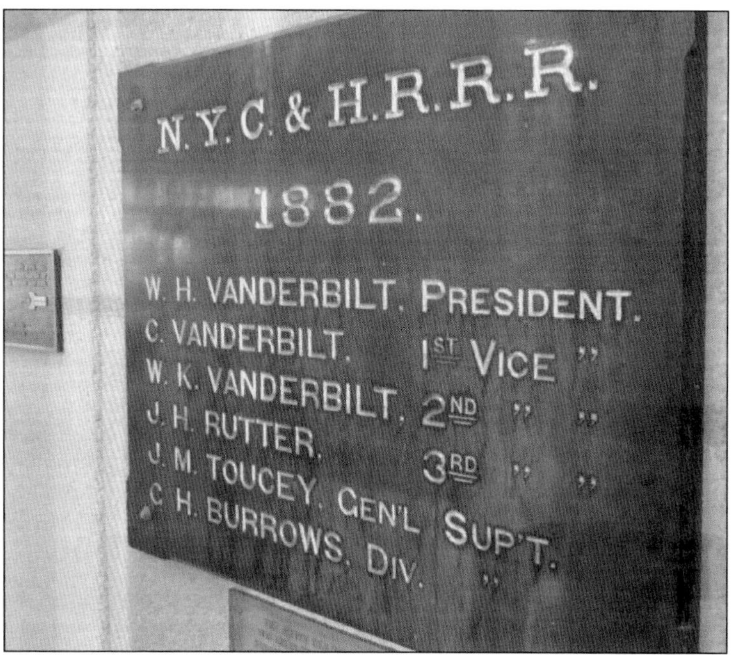

Today, this plaque appears in Rochester's Amtrak (National Railroad Passenger Corporation) station. It lists the officers of the NYC&HR at the time the second Rochester station was built. Note the smaller plaque to the left commemorating the building of the Amtrak station in the 1979. (Author's collection.)

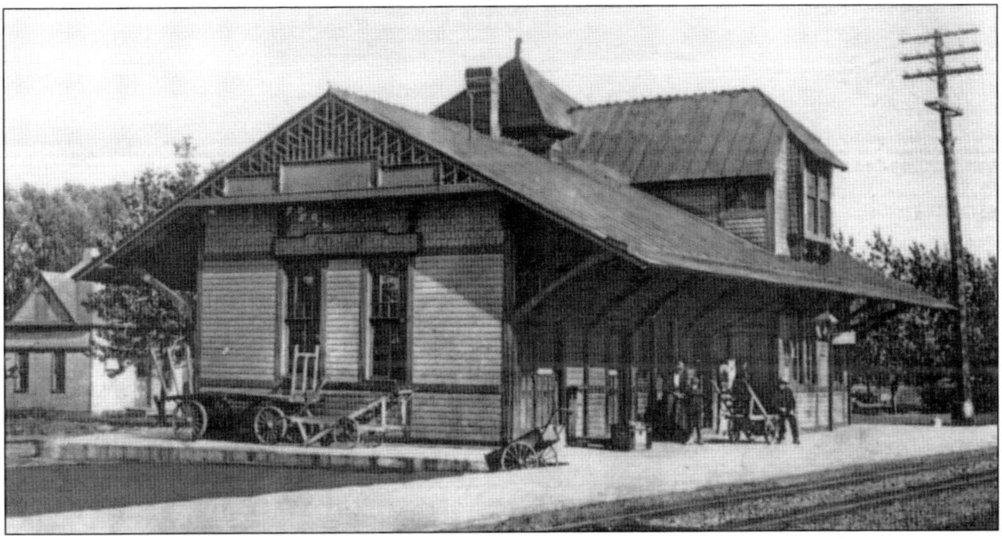

During the 1880s, smaller stations were also constructed along the NYC main line in Monroe County. An example, shown in this photograph, is the depot in the village of Fairport, town of Perinton. The building, in use until the 1950s, was demolished in the early 1960s. (Courtesy of *Rochester Images*: Town of Perinton.)

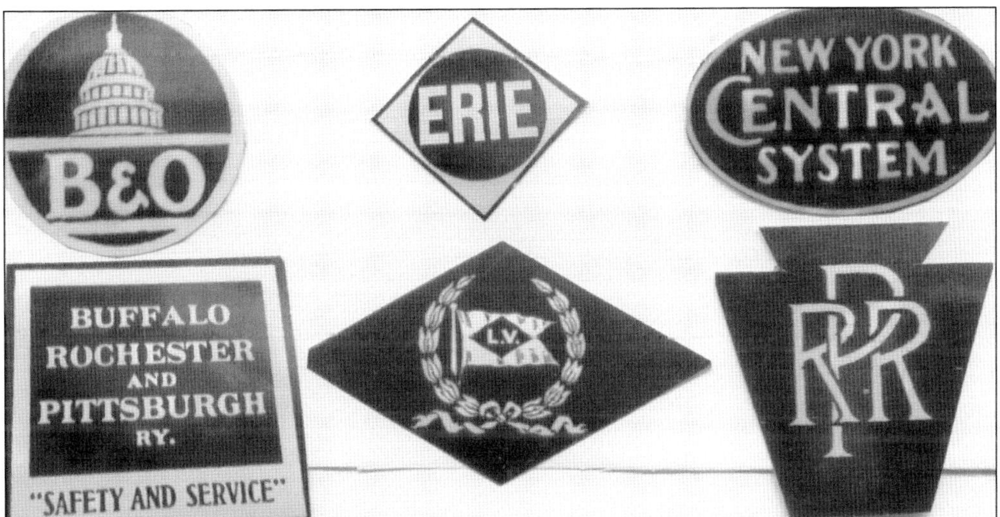

By the time the NYC&HR built the second station in 1883, other major US railroads (logos above) had their eyes on the Rochester market. These railroads were the Buffalo, Rochester & Pittsburgh/Baltimore & Ohio, Erie, Pennsylvania, and Lehigh Valley. (Author's collection.)

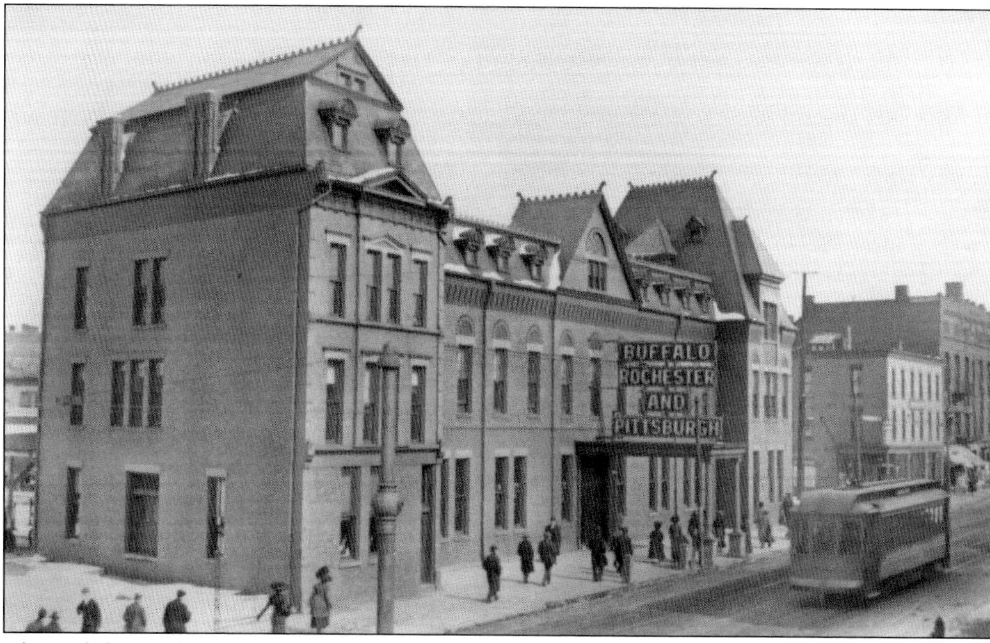

The Buffalo, Rochester & Pittsburgh Railroad (BR&P) occupied this Gothic-style station on West Main Street in 1881. The Baltimore & Ohio (B&O) railroad, which purchased the BR&P in the 1930s, ran connecting passenger service south through the Genesee River valley to Salamanca (Cattaraugus County) and then on to the main line at Pittsburgh. While passenger service was curtailed in the early 1950s, the B&O continued to haul coal to the Charlotte harbor for transport to Canada. Today, the former B&O terminal houses a popular eatery. (Courtesy of *Rochester Images*: Rochester Public Library Local History Division.)

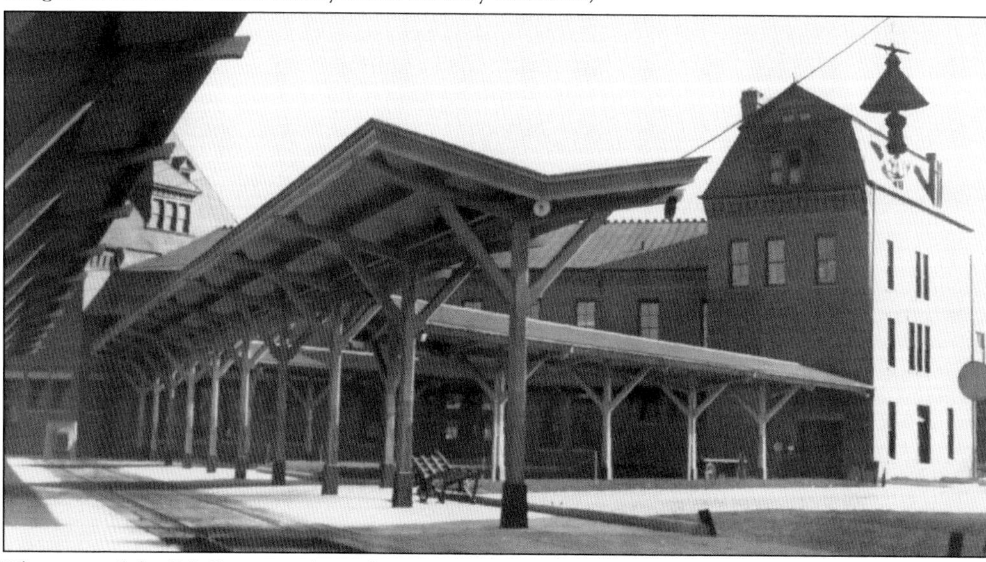

The view of the B&O station from the train platform shows an interesting feature. There appear to be different designs on the structure indicating that the building may have been constructed in sections, possibly at different times. This seems plausible since the site was also used by the BR&P before it was part of the B&O. (Courtesy of *Rochester Images*: Rochester Public Library Local History Division.)

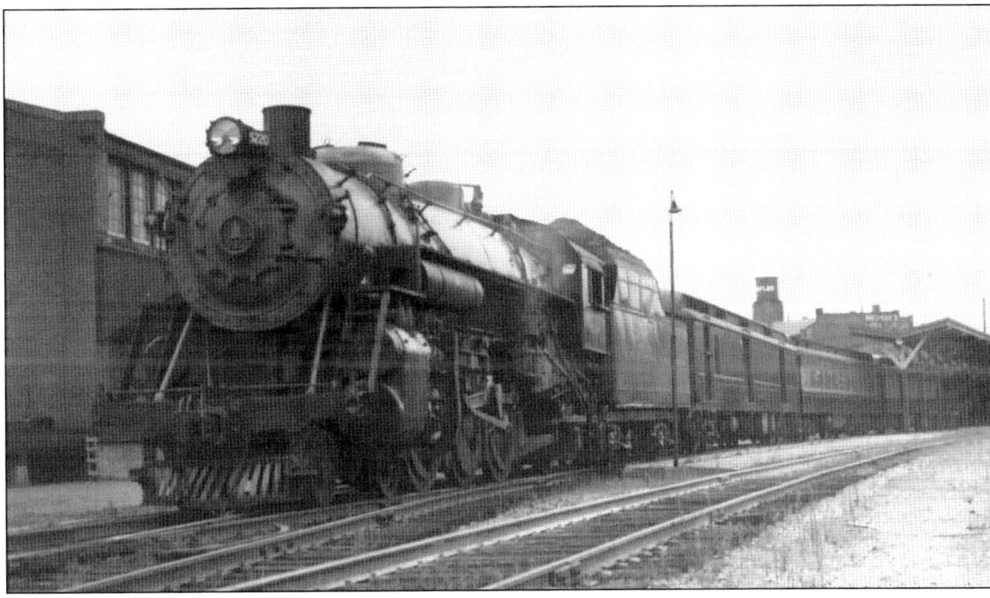

The passenger train shown in this 1940s photograph is about to leave Rochester's B&O station headed to Salamanca. Engine No. 5220 on the headend is a class P-5a Pacific loaded with coal and ready to go. With the Whyte notation system used throughout this book, this steam engine is also known as a 4-6-2, meaning four wheels up front, six large drivers, and two trailing wheels. (Courtesy of *Rochester Images*: Rochester Public Library Local History Division.)

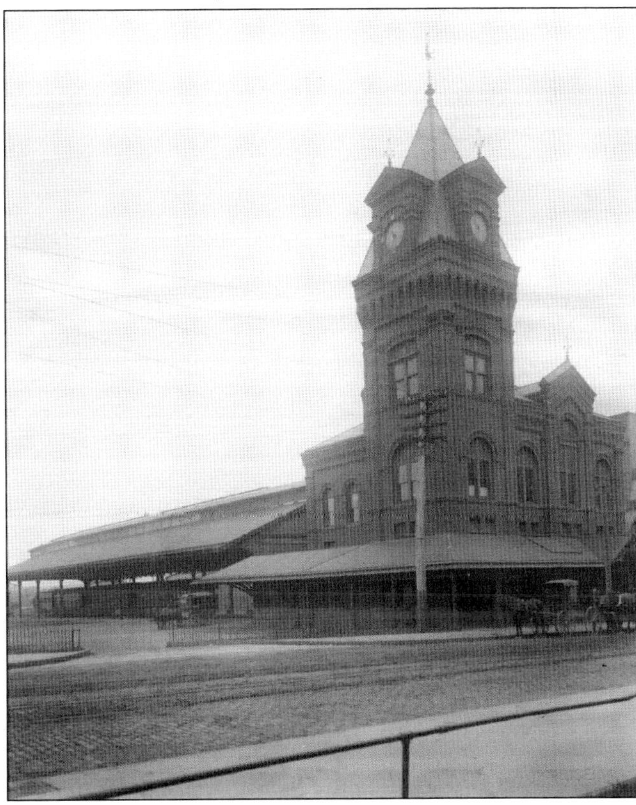

The Erie Railroad also served Rochester. The Rochester branch connected with Erie's main line at Corning in Steuben County. Built in 1887, this Victorian station with its beautiful clock tower stood between Exchange Street and the Genesee River in downtown Rochester. (Courtesy of *Rochester Images*: Rochester Public Library Local History Division.)

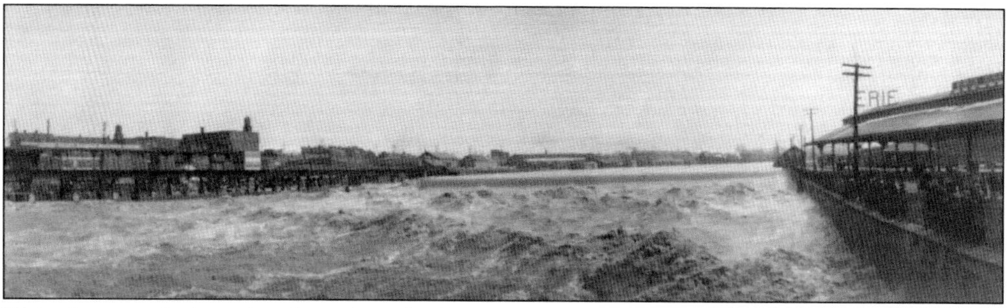

This photograph shows just how close the Erie station was to the west bank of the Genesee River as it flowed north to Charlotte and its meeting with Lake Ontario. (Courtesy of *Rochester Images*: Rochester Public Library Local History Division.)

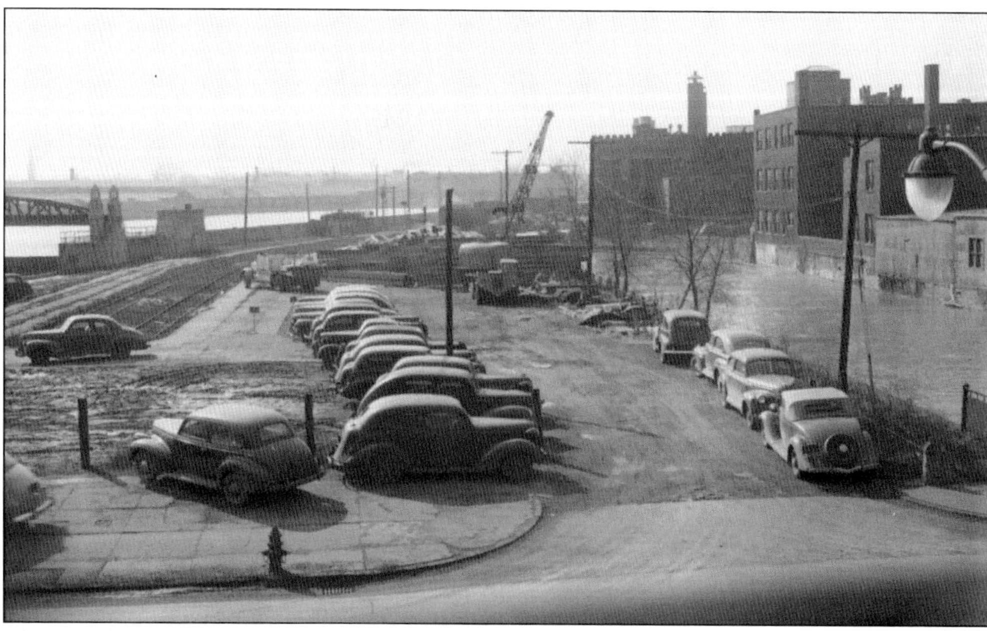

The Erie depot in Rochester was demolished around 1947. The tracks that remained are shown in this photograph. Today, both the tracks and station are gone and the former site of the station is a parking lot in downtown Rochester. (Courtesy of the City of Rochester, New York.)

By the early 1950s, the Erie had begun its dieselization program. Most likely using the Exchange Street tracks that remained after the station was taken down, a new F3 diesel freight locomotive, shown in the photograph, was brought to Rochester as evidence of Erie's commitment to modernize. Visitors to the exhibit can be seen to the left. F3 diesels were built by EMD, a division of General Motors, and are commonly referred to as EMD F3s. (Author's collection.)

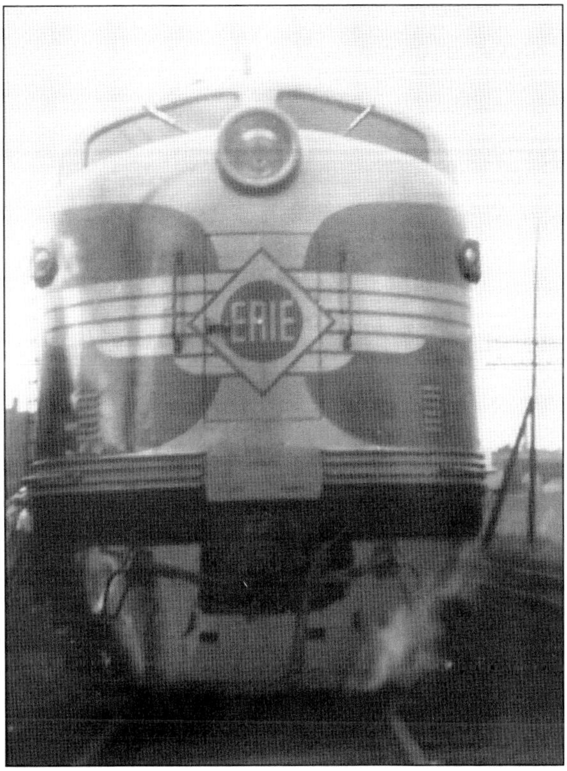

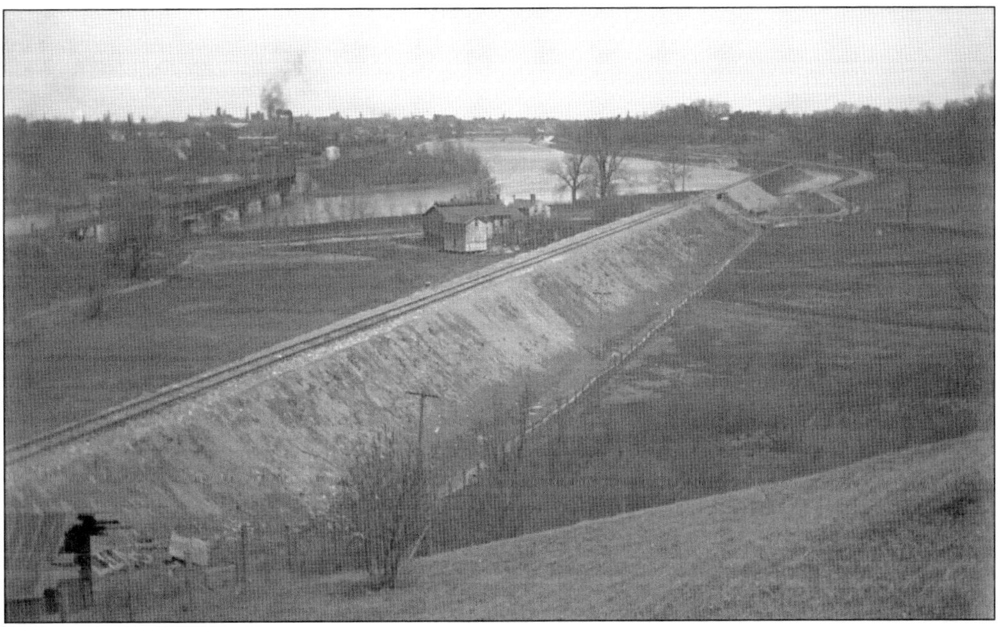

With downtown Rochester in the background, the Lehigh Valley makes its entry into the city on east side of the Genesee River, as seen from Mount Hope Cemetery in this c. 1900 photograph. The track in the background is that of the Erie Railroad crossing the Genesee River headed north to downtown Rochester. (Courtesy of *Rochester Images*: Rochester Public Library Local History Division.)

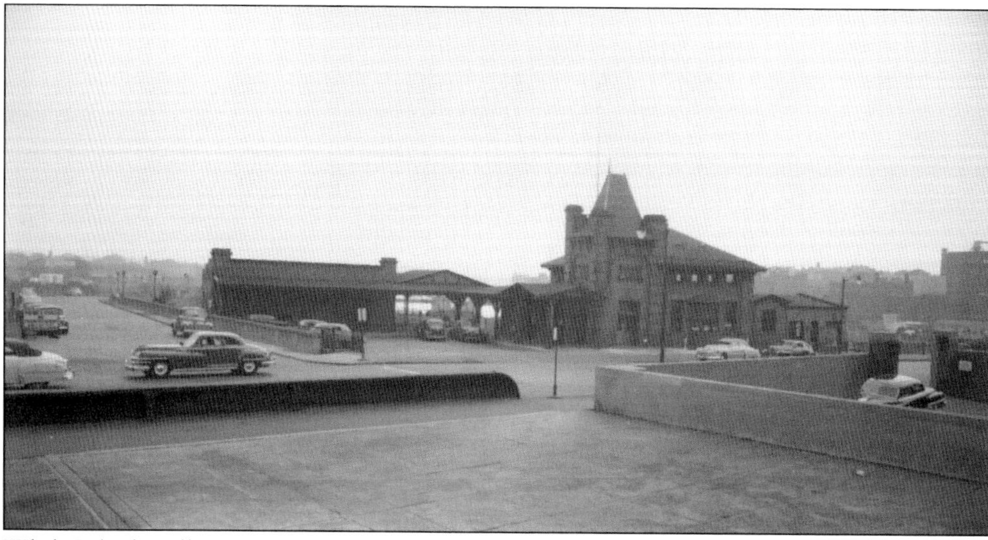

While Lehigh Valley's Rochester station was abandoned in the early 1970s, the Victorian building remains today as an attractive part of downtown Rochester. This 1951 photograph, taken from the Rundel Memorial Library, shows the depot on the south side of Court Street. (Courtesy of the City of Rochester, New York.)

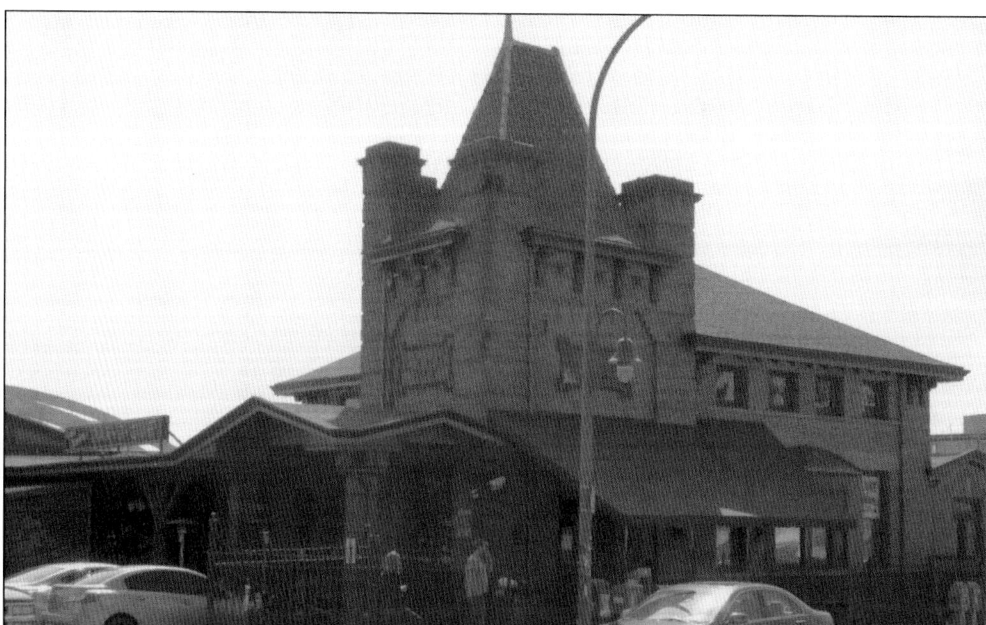

A recognizable feature of the Lehigh Valley station is the 1905 construction date seen along the front and side of the terminal. Like the former B&O station, the former Lehigh Valley station is today home to a popular eatery. (Author's collection.)

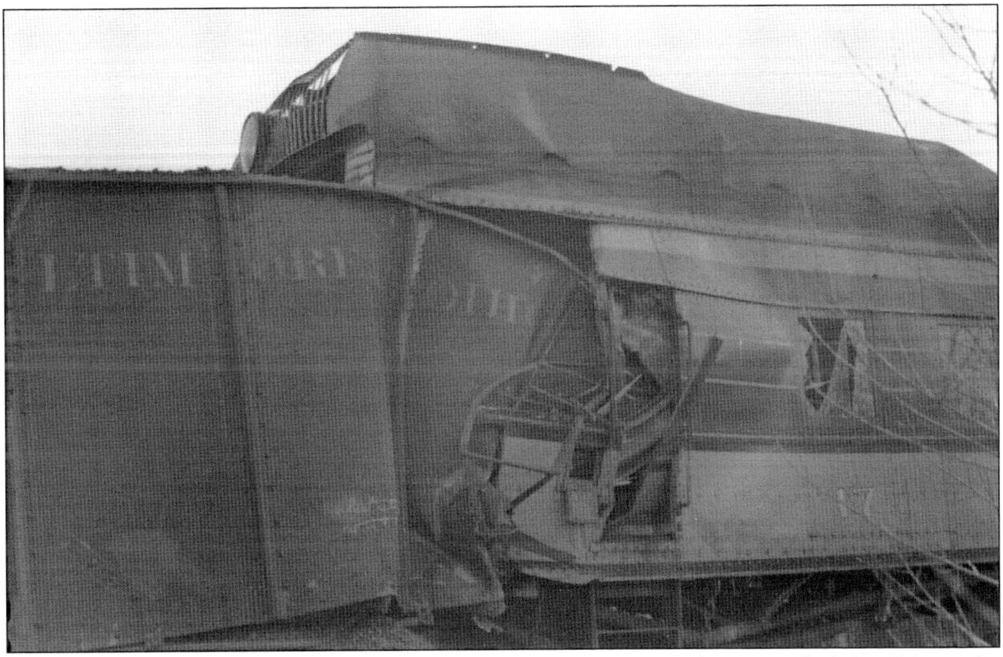

The Lehigh Valley utilized self-propelled gas-electric baggage-coach cars, called doodlebugs, for its Rochester branch line and the trips south to Rochester Junction (town of Mendon) and the interchange with Lehigh Valley's main line. This 1940 photograph shows doodlebug No. 17 after it had collided with a hopper car near the University of Rochester. The Lehigh Valley ended doodlebug service to and from Rochester in 1950. (Courtesy of the City of Rochester, New York.)

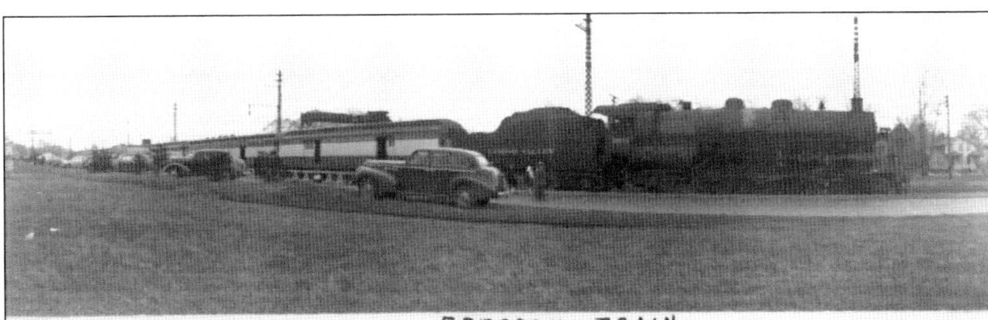

The Lehigh Valley brought the touring New York State Freedom Train to Rochester in 1948. Shown in the photograph is the six-car train, with its 4-6-2 class K-3 Pacific, ready to receive visitors at Lehigh Valley's Mount Hope Avenue Yards. The interior of the cars was modified to house exhibits of interest to the public following World War II. (Courtesy of *Rochester Images*: Rochester Public Library Local History Division.)

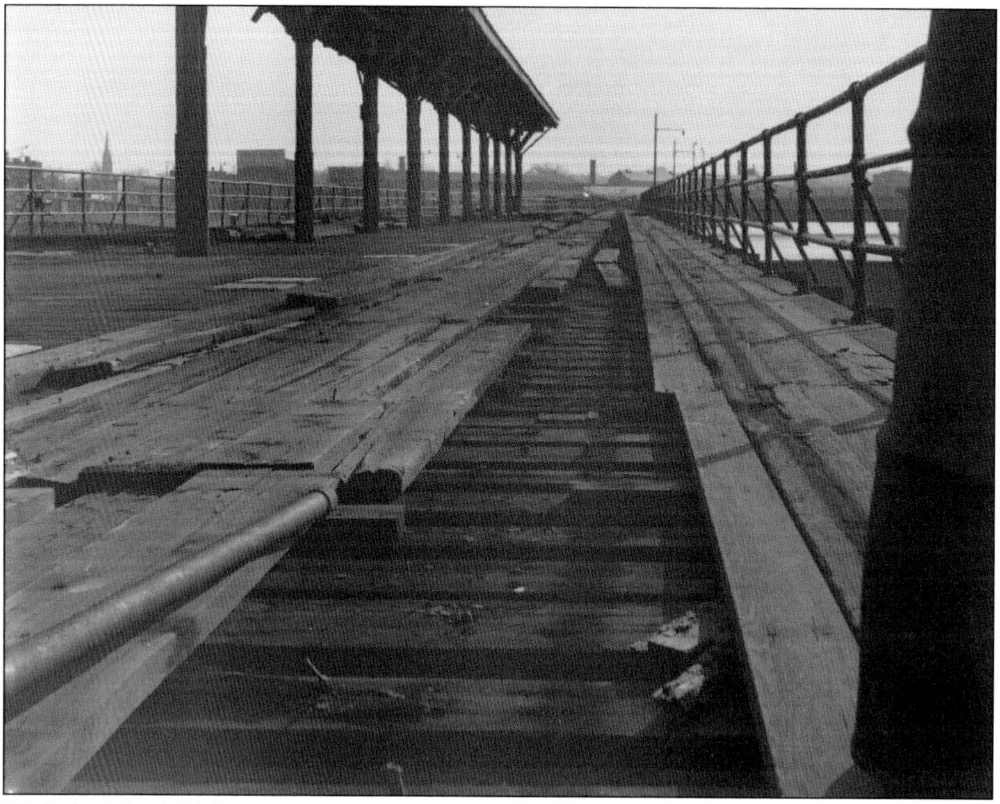

With the Lehigh Valley passenger train service to Rochester ending in 1950, the railroad saw no need to maintain the platforms at its station. While the station was not touched, the platforms were torn up, as shown in this 1955 photograph. (Photograph by Robert Carper, courtesy of Jeff Hands.)

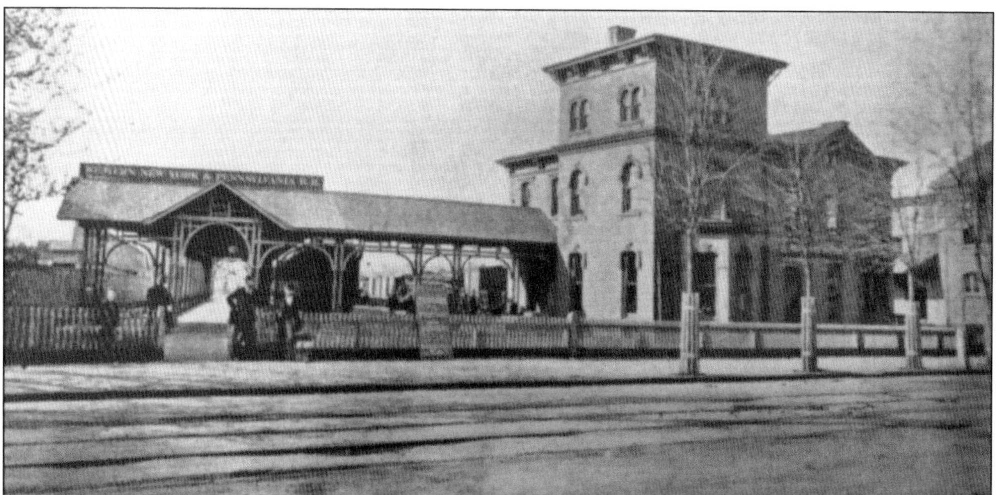

To gain entry into Rochester, the Pennsylvania Railroad (PRR) acquired the Western New York & Pennsylvania Railroad around 1900. Along with the purchase came a large house on West Main Street. The building was converted into the railroad station shown in this c. 1920 photograph. (Courtesy of *Rochester Images*: Rochester Public Library Local History Division.)

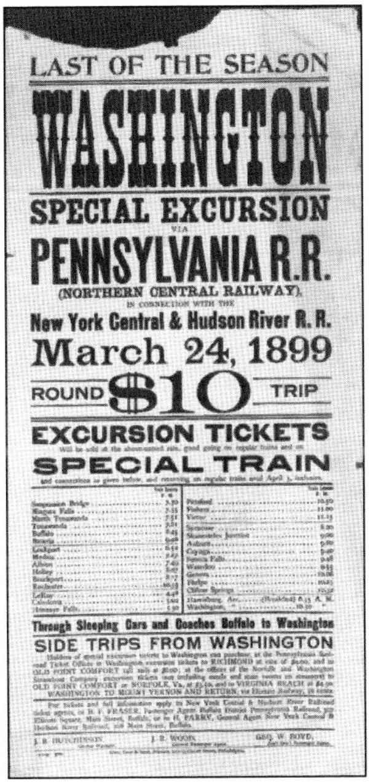

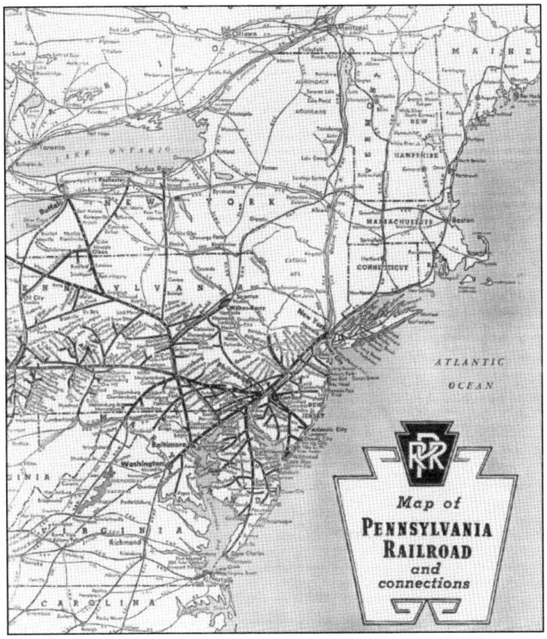

In the late 1800s, the excursions that PRR offered to Rochester sometimes involved other railroads. As an example, this 1899 poster announcing an excursion to Washington seems to be very much a cooperative venture between PRR and NYC. From the West Main Street station, however, it was possible for passengers to use the PRR to get from Rochester to Olean in Cattaraugus County, as shown on this PRR map. In Olean, they could board trains en route from Buffalo to Harrisburg and Washington. Connections in Harrisburg completed the circuitous route from Rochester to New York City. In 1941, due to a lack of ridership, PRR stopped passenger service on the Rochester branch line. (Left, courtesy of *Rochester Images*: Rochester Public Library Local History Division; right, author's collection.)

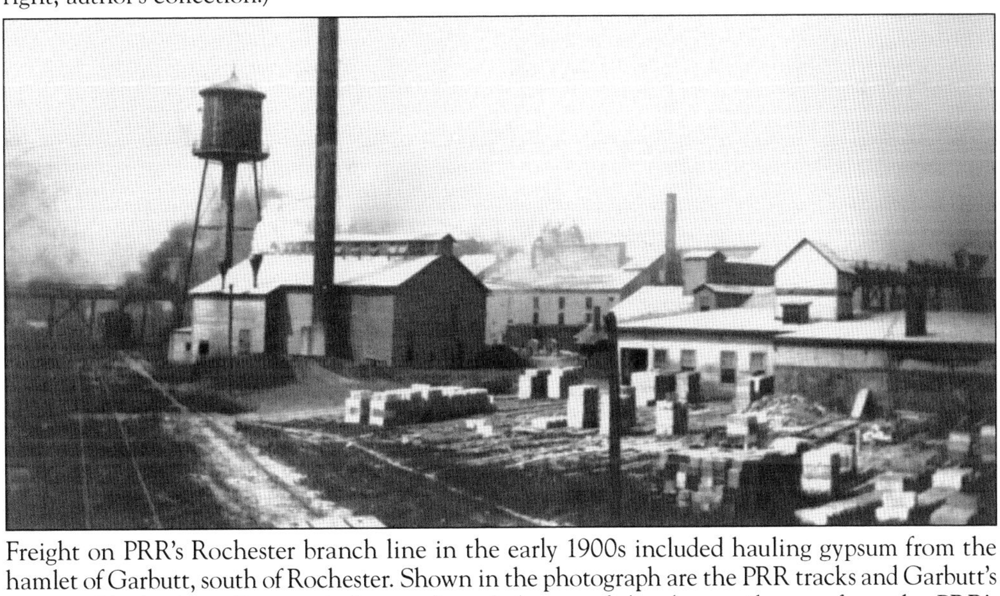

Freight on PRR's Rochester branch line in the early 1900s included hauling gypsum from the hamlet of Garbutt, south of Rochester. Shown in the photograph are the PRR tracks and Garbutt's gypsum block plant. Economic factors forced closure of the three-mile spur from the PRR's Rochester branch to Garbutt in 1944. (Courtesy of Town of Wheatland historian.)

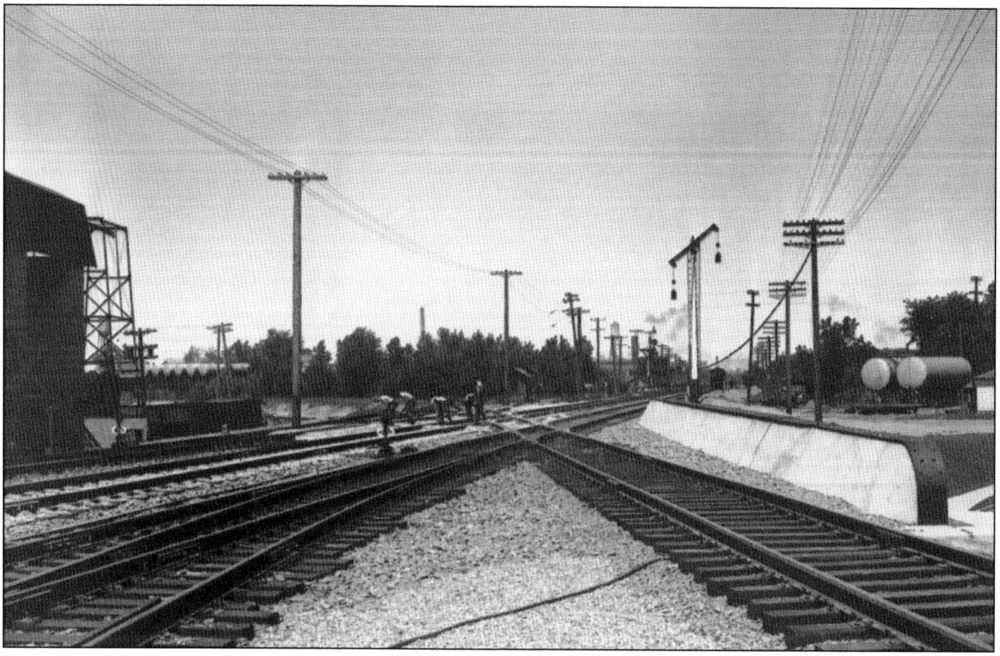

Major railroads that served Rochester in the early to mid-1900s intersected in several locations. In this 1941 photograph, PRR's Rochester branch line is seen crossing the B&O tracks near Chili Avenue heading northwest. (Courtesy of the City of Rochester, New York.)

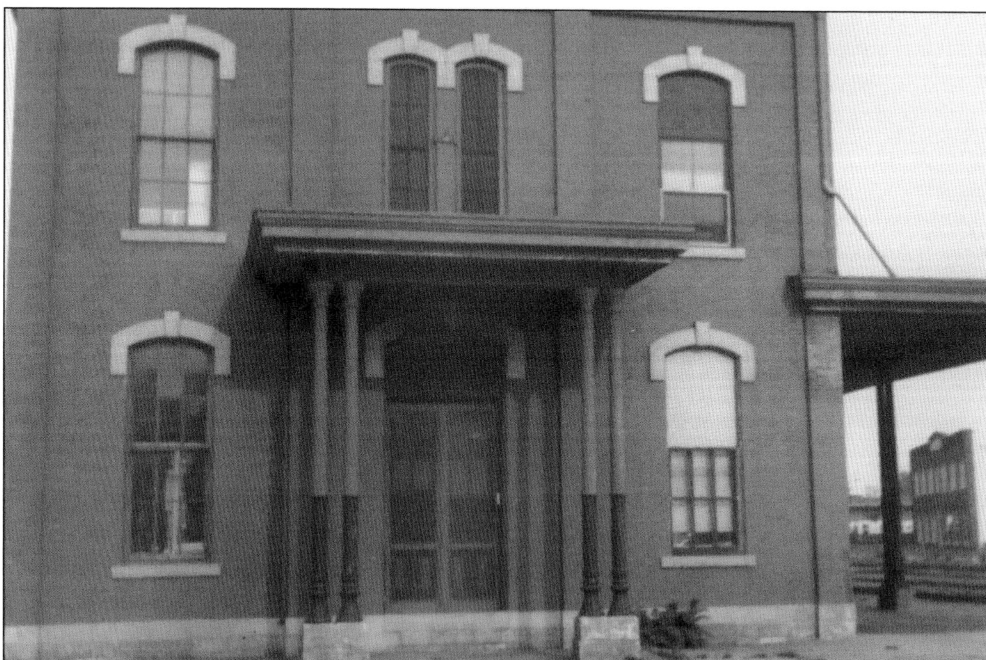

Even though passenger service ceased in 1941, this 1950s photograph shows the PRR station to be in relatively good condition. The building was demolished in the late 1960s, while the freight tracks on the right of the photograph were removed in the early 1970s. (Author's collection.)

By the early 1900s, NYC&HR continued to grow, changing its name to the NYC Lines and then to NYC System. With its growth came a new and larger passenger station in Rochester. Shown in this c. 1910 photograph is the Clinton, Central, and Joseph Avenues area that was cleared for the new station that would replace the one built in 1883. Note the train shed of the 1883 station can be seen in the background. (Courtesy of Rochester Museum & Science Center, Albert R. Stone Collection.)

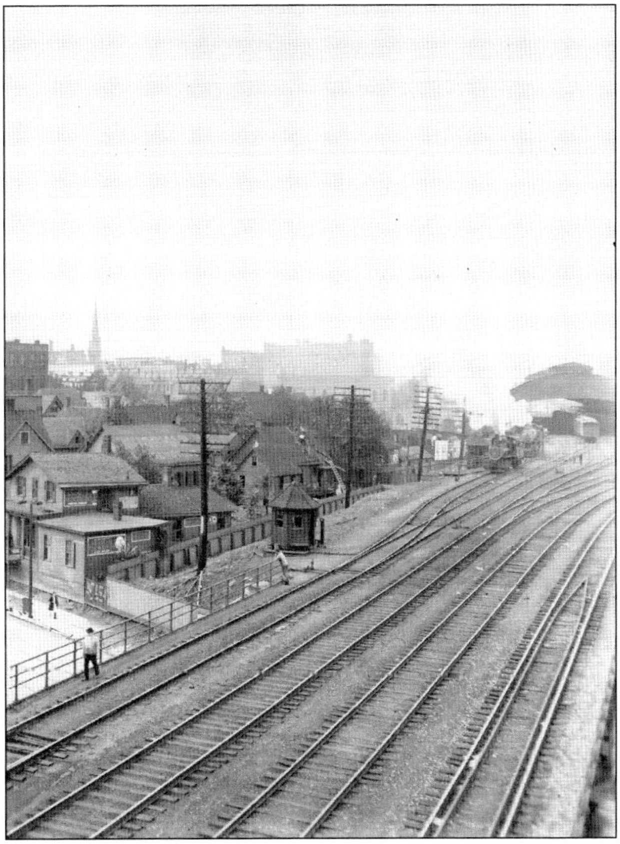

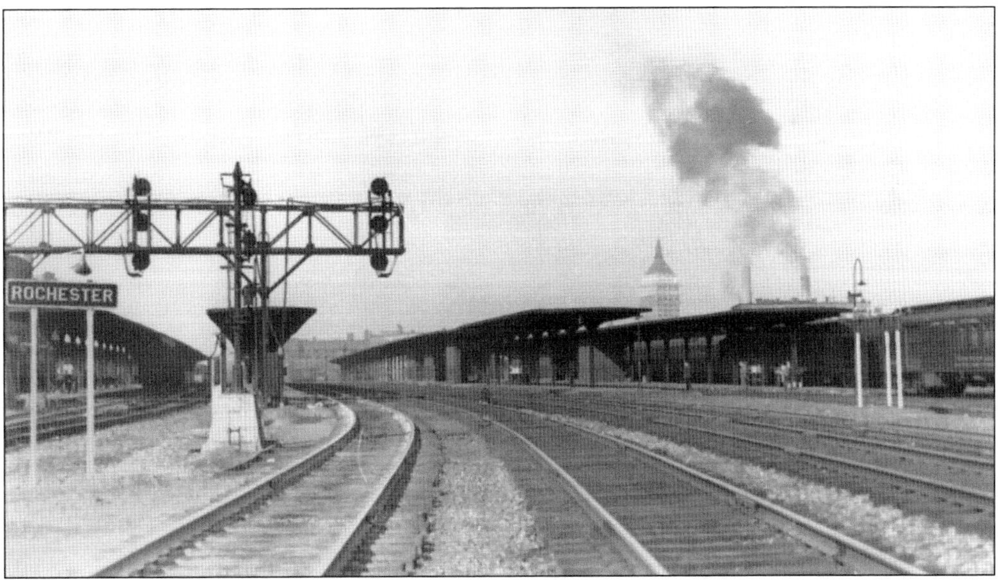

Built in 1914, the new passenger station was NYC's third and largest in Rochester. It provided the space for additional tracks, about 15 in all. Kodak Tower, headquarters of the Eastman Kodak Company, appears in the background of this mid-1900s photograph. The smokestacks are probably those of the Beebee power plant. (Courtesy of Robert Pastorkey.)

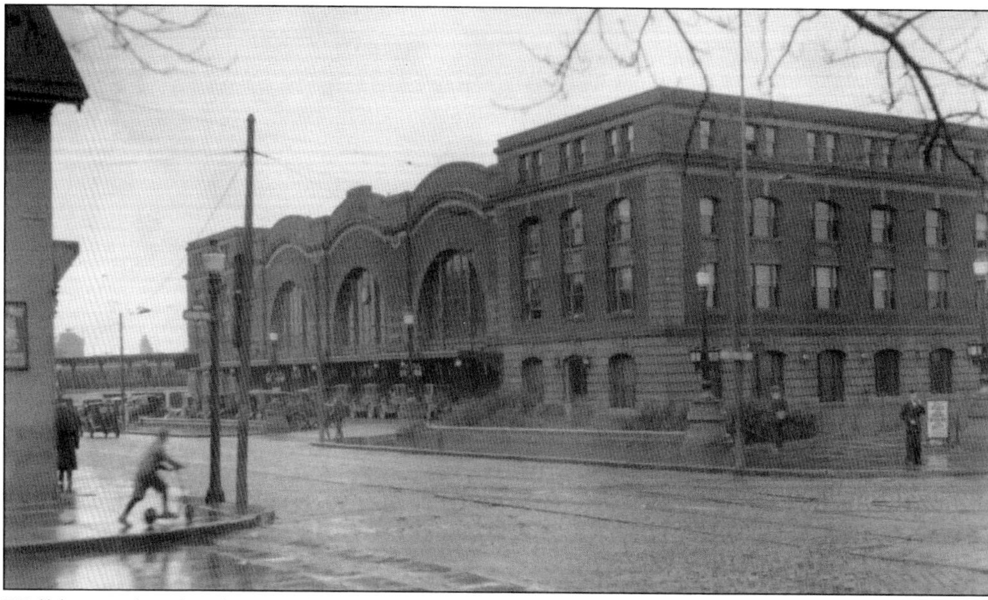

Well-known local architect Claude Bragdon designed the new NYC passenger station. The result was one of NYC's most beautiful stations. Known as Bragdon Station, it was a major stop for the many trains on the NYC main line, advertised as the "Water Level Route." Passengers would board from one of several canopied platforms. Today, an Amtrak station occupies the site, with one platform adjacent to the station available for boarding. (Courtesy of Rochester Museum & Science Center, Albert R. Stone Collection.)

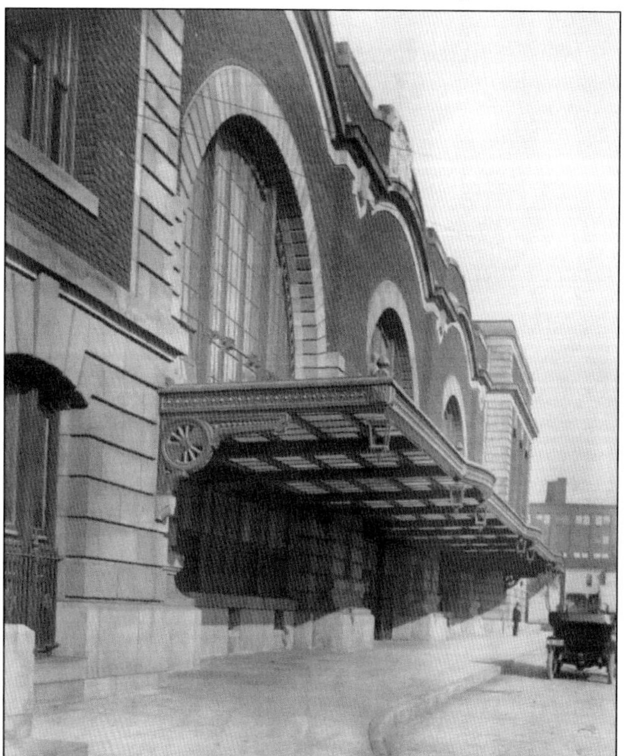

A close look at the Central Avenue entrance to the new NYC station reveals the architectural talent of its designer. The entrance had three large, semicircular windows, reminders of large steam engine driving wheels. The sandstone around the perimeter of each window blended perfectly with the reddish brick that extended upward toward the attractive masonry along the top of station. (Courtesy of *Rochester Images*: Rochester Public Library Local History Division.)

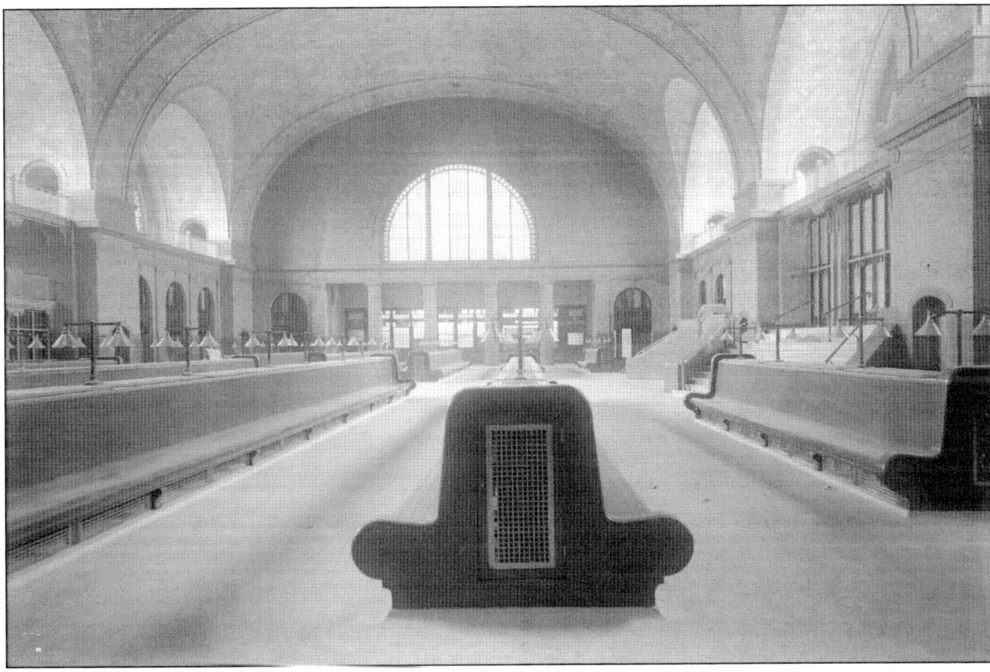

Claude Bragdon also used his talents designing the interior of the new NYC station. It received as many raves as the external design of the building. For the vaulted ceiling of the waiting room, Bragdon chose a self-supporting masonry arch of colorful Guastavino tile. It was said that because of the curvature of the ceiling, the acoustics in the waiting room were such that one could stand at a specific location and hear conversations that were taking place some distance away. (Courtesy of Rochester Museum & Science Center, Albert R. Stone Collection.)

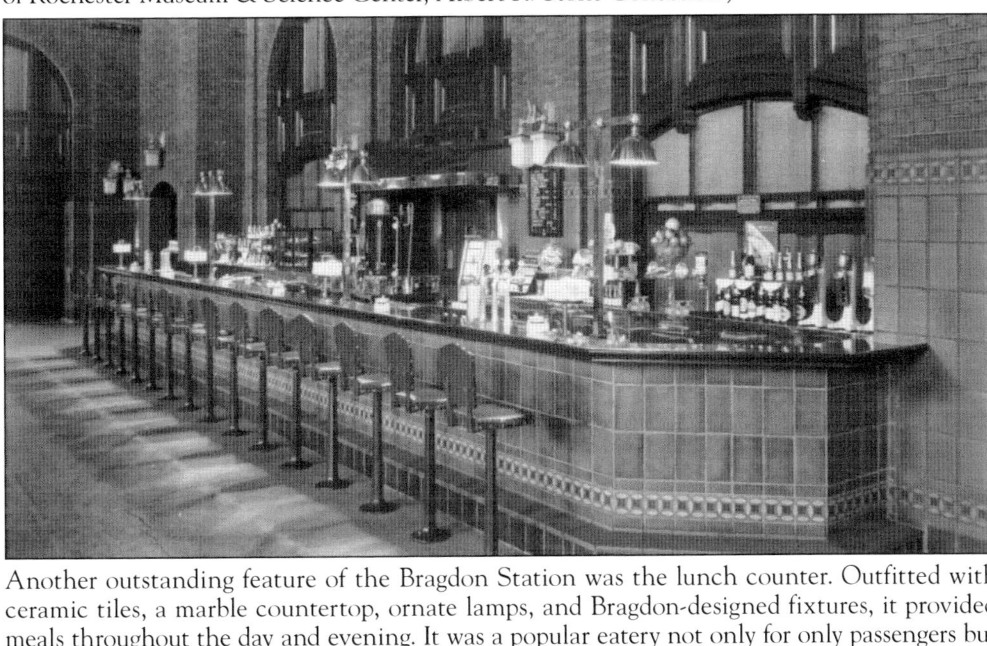

Another outstanding feature of the Bragdon Station was the lunch counter. Outfitted with ceramic tiles, a marble countertop, ornate lamps, and Bragdon-designed fixtures, it provided meals throughout the day and evening. It was a popular eatery not only for only passengers but also for taxi drivers and station workers as well. (Courtesy of *Rochester Images*: Rochester Public Library Local History Division.)

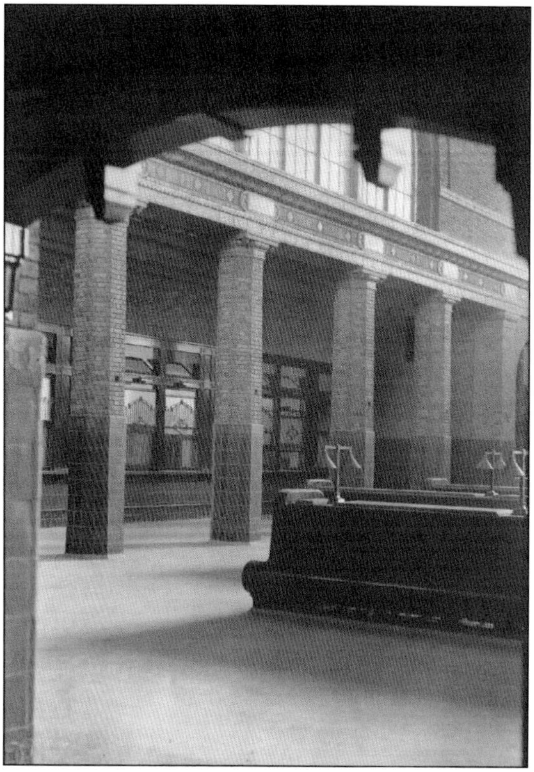

This photograph of the east end of the Bragdon Station waiting room shows how the design of the ticket counter area blended with the station columns. The many benches throughout the waiting room were popular with passengers, as they were equipped with Bragdon-designed reading lamps, as seen in the photograph. (Courtesy of *Rochester Images*: Rochester Public Library Local History Division.)

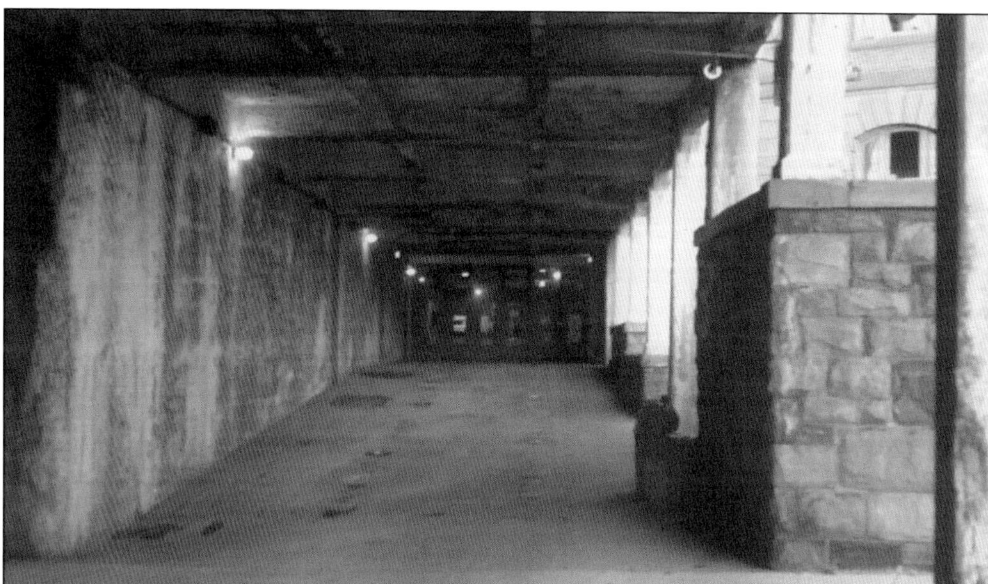

By the mid-1960s, most of the Bragdon Station was demolished. Only the west end of the original structure along Clinton Avenue remained. The 1977 photograph of what remained shows the walkway to the ticketing and waiting area. This entrance was used by NYC, then by Penn Central after the 1968 merger of NYC and PRR, and then by Amtrak after its formation in 1971. It was a far cry from the ornate Bragdon Station entrance. In the late 1970s, to make room for a new Amtrak station, what was left of the Bragdon Station was demolished. (Courtesy of Duncan Richards.)

Two

Rails and River Meet in Charlotte

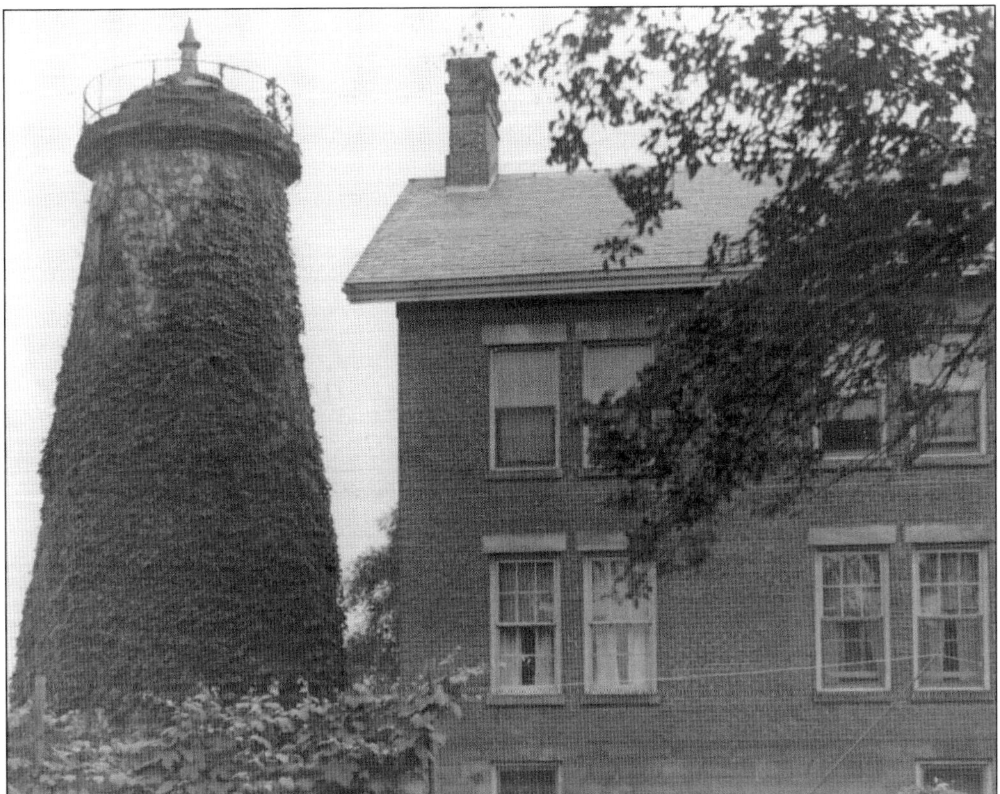

North of downtown is a section of Rochester known as Charlotte, where the Genesee River flowing north empties into Lake Ontario. One of the most significant landmarks in Charlotte is the 1822 Genesee River Lighthouse, shown in this photograph. Standing about 40 feet high and located on a hill just west of the river, it is one of the oldest existing lighthouses on Lake Ontario. (Courtesy of *Rochester Images*: Rochester Public Library Local history Division.)

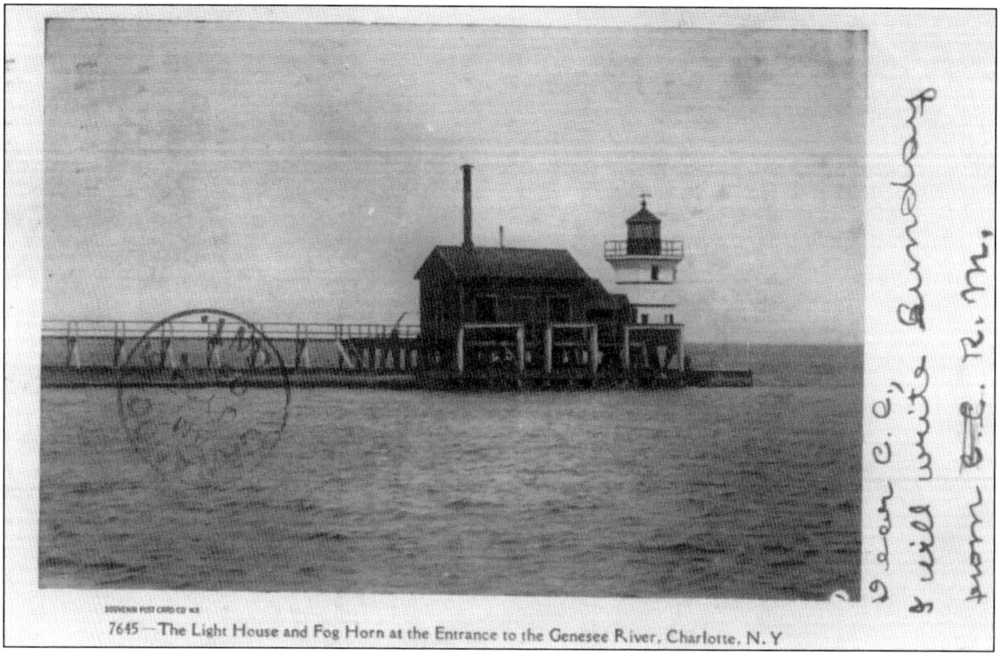

Charlotte's Genesee River Lighthouse ceased operation in the 1880s when piers extending into the mouth of the river were constructed. The piers shown in this postcard provided a better entry to the Genesee River for lake freighters and steamers as well as pleasure craft. (Courtesy of *Rochester Images*: Rochester Public Library Local history Division.)

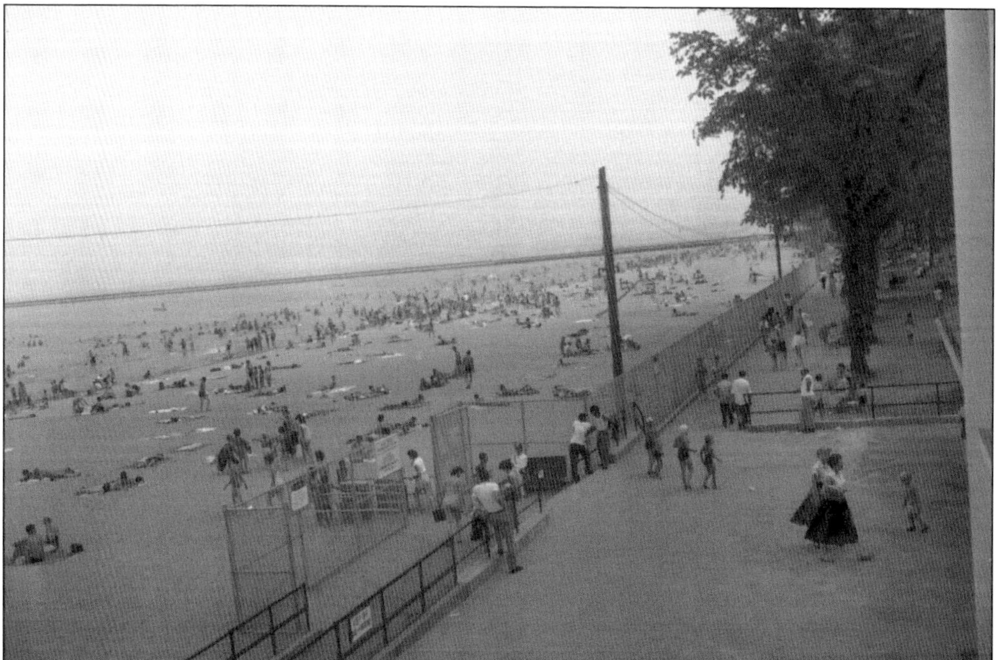

The Charlotte piers on the Genesee River can be seen in the background of this 1955 photograph of the beach and boardwalk at Ontario Beach Park. (Courtesy of the City of Rochester, New York.)

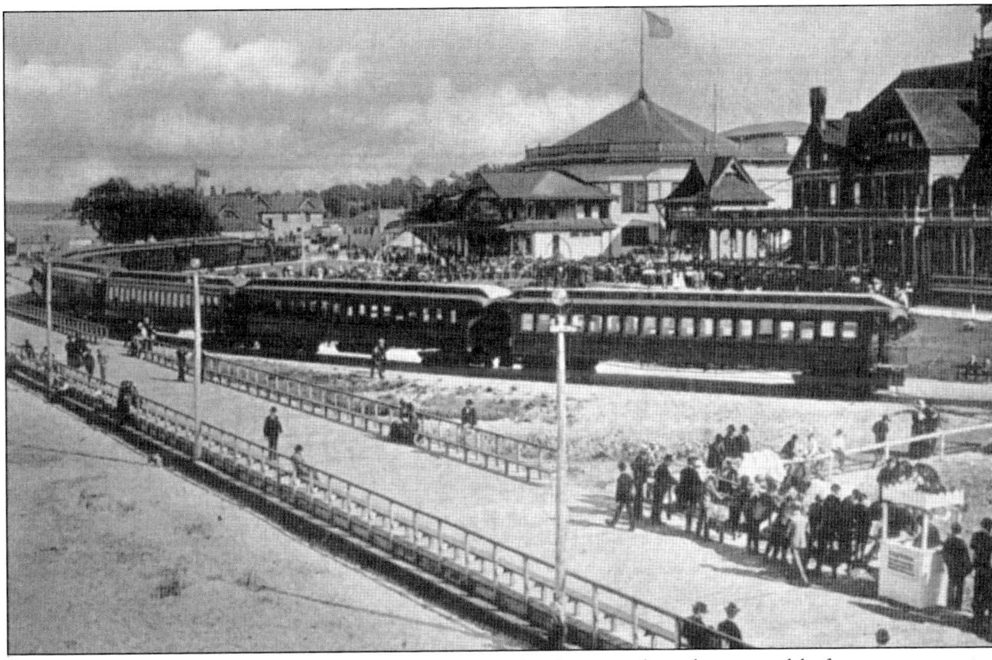

In the 1850s, NYC constructed a branch line to Charlotte and made it possible for many to enjoy Charlotte's Ontario Beach Park. The park, which opened 1884, is still popular today. (Courtesy of the City of Rochester, New York.)

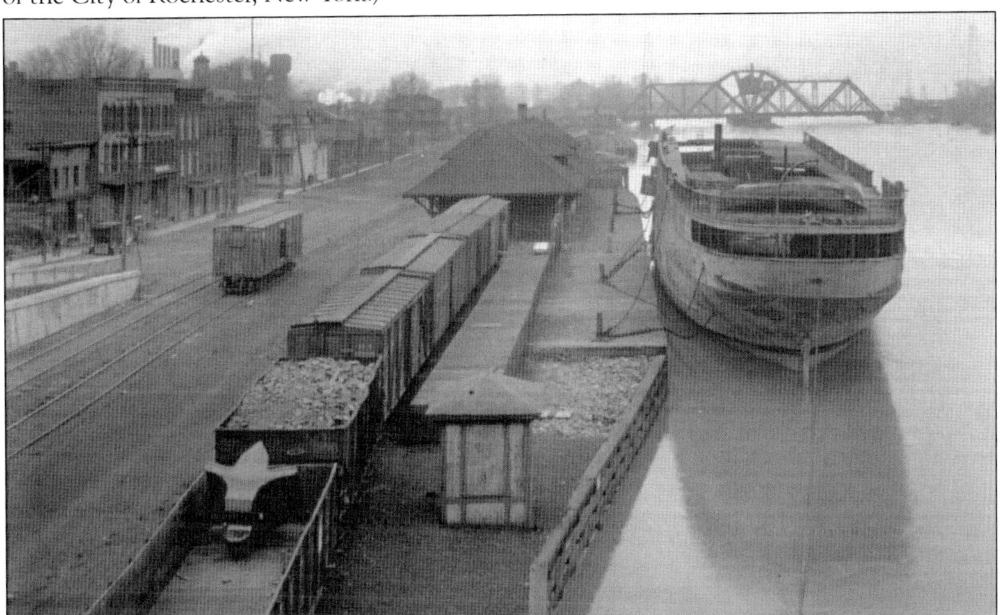

The Charlotte depot on NYC's branch line was built in the late 1800s and has been a fixture along the Genesee River ever since. This c. 1920 photograph with a view looking north shows the NYC tracks along River Street as well as the Charlotte Swing Bridge in the background. Also seen in the background, toward the upper left, is the top of the Genesee River Lighthouse. The smoke seen in that area most likely emanated from a blast furnace located north of the depot. (Courtesy of the City of Rochester, New York.)

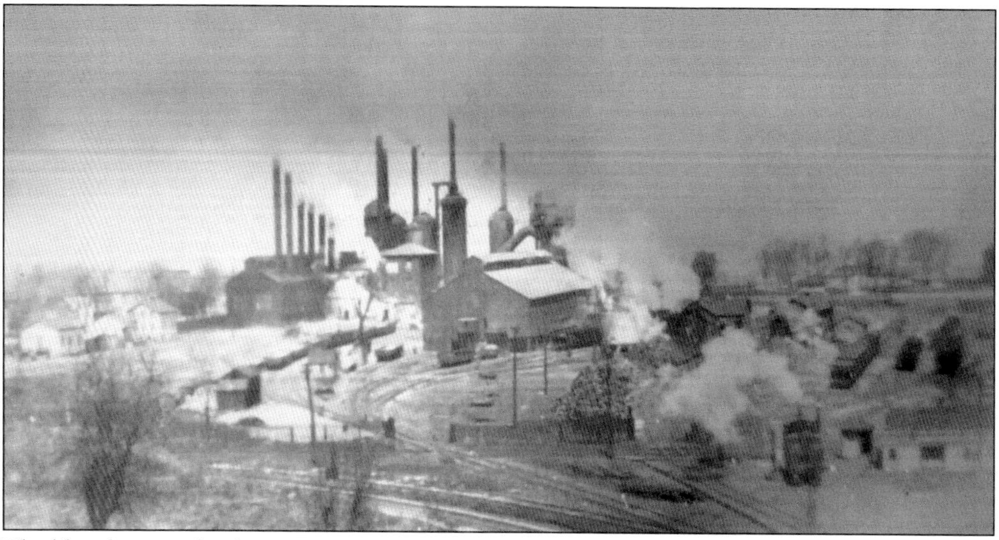

The blast furnace that began its operation in 1868 is shown in this photograph. Because of NYC's branch line to Charlotte, it was possible to bring the raw materials necessary to convert the iron ore to pig iron. The plant was razed in 1927. (Courtesy of *Rochester Images*: Greece Municipal Historian Collection.)

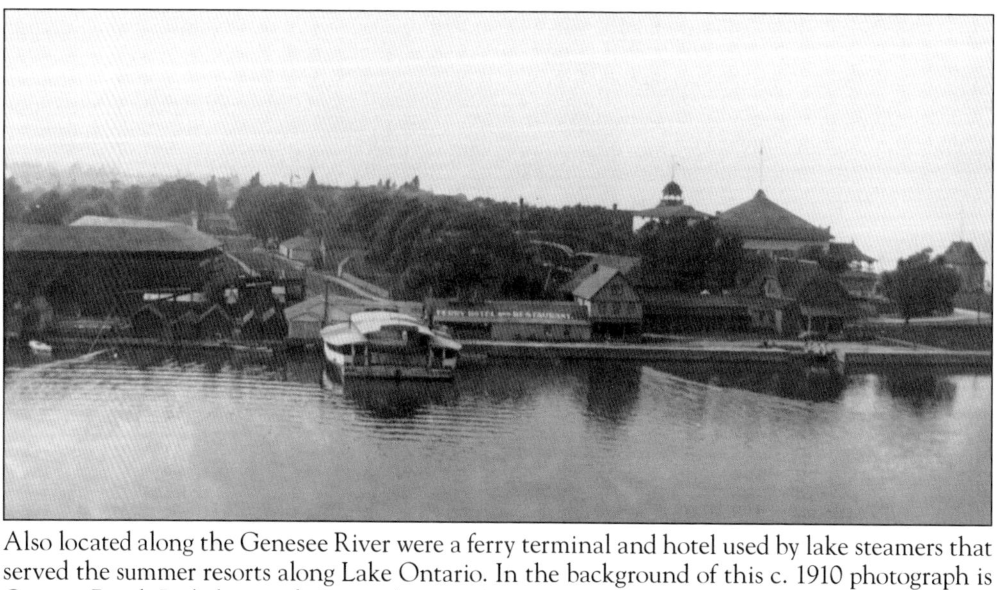

Also located along the Genesee River were a ferry terminal and hotel used by lake steamers that served the summer resorts along Lake Ontario. In the background of this c. 1910 photograph is Ontario Beach Park, home of a Dentzel carousel. This popular carousel was manufactured around 1905 in Philadelphia by the Dentzel Carousel Company and can still be enjoyed today. (Courtesy of *Rochester Images*: Rochester Public Library Local History Division.)

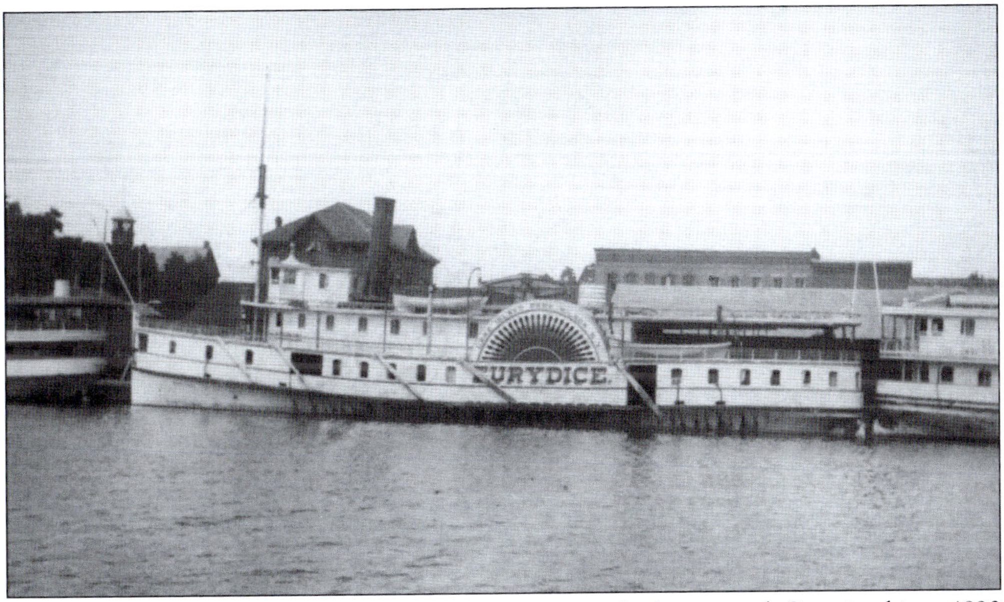

The *Eurydice*, a wooden side-wheeler, was an interesting-looking vessel. Seen in this c. 1890 photograph docked on the Genesee River, it was used as a lake steamer for excursions between Charlotte and various Lake Ontario ports. (Courtesy of *Rochester Images*: Rochester Public Library Local History Division.)

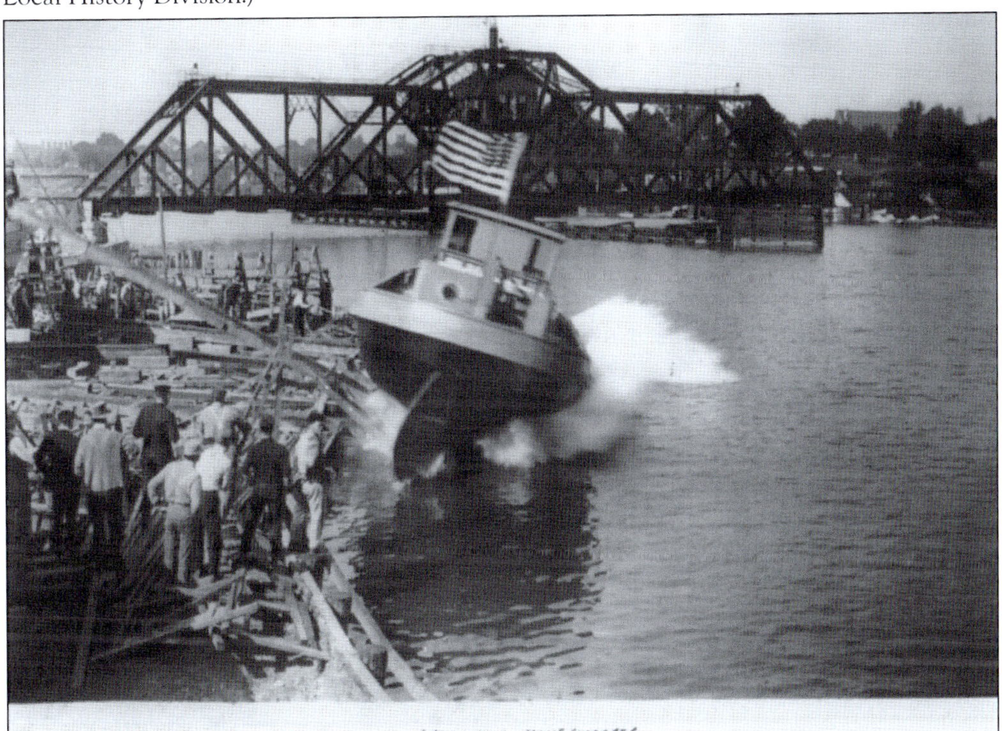

Also interesting on the Genesee was this 1918 launching of a minesweeper built at the Rochester Boat Works. The Charlotte Swing Bridge that carried the rail traffic across the Genesee River is again seen in the background. (Photograph by Gail Bauch, courtesy of Richard Margolis.)

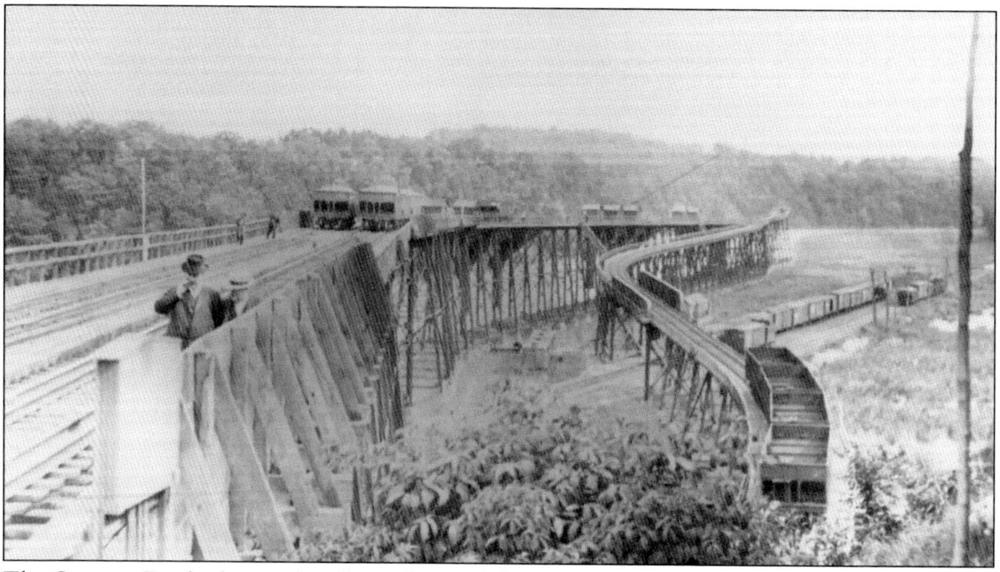

The Genesee Docks, known locally as the "coal docks" and located south of the Charlotte depot, began receiving coal transported by the BR&P (later part of the B&O) around 1900. The trestle shown in the photograph was used to transfer coal to vessels destined for Canada. The trestle was engineered so that empty hopper cars would return by gravity to the tracks below. (Courtesy of *Rochester Images*: Rochester Public Library Local History Division.)

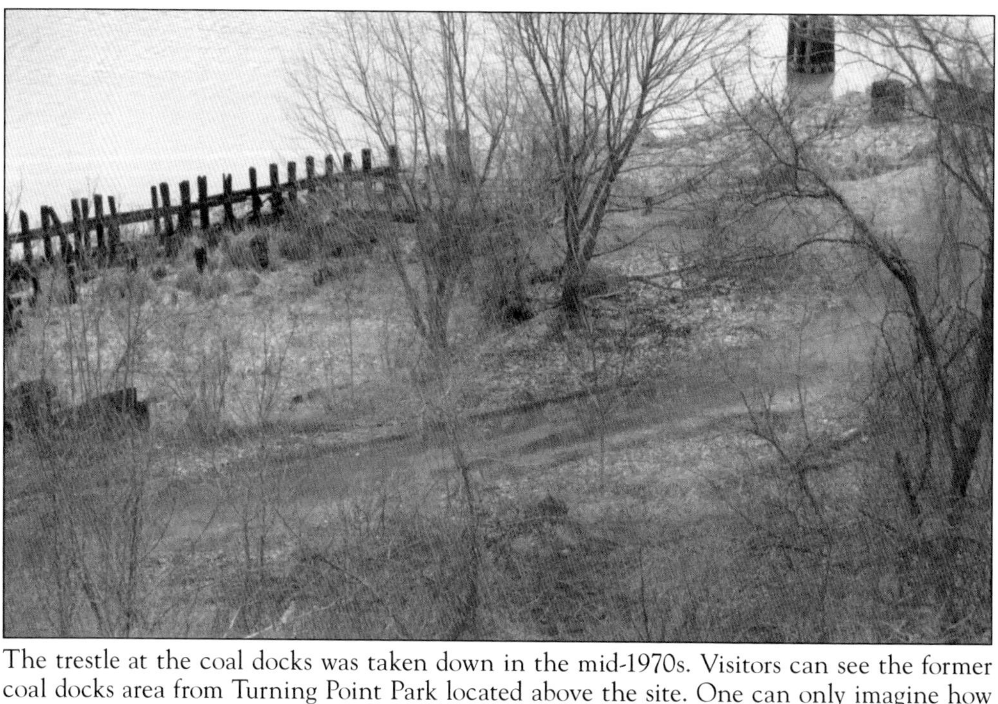

The trestle at the coal docks was taken down in the mid-1970s. Visitors can see the former coal docks area from Turning Point Park located above the site. One can only imagine how busy this area was with hopper cars moving along the trestle and boats awaiting their cargoes. (Author's collection.)

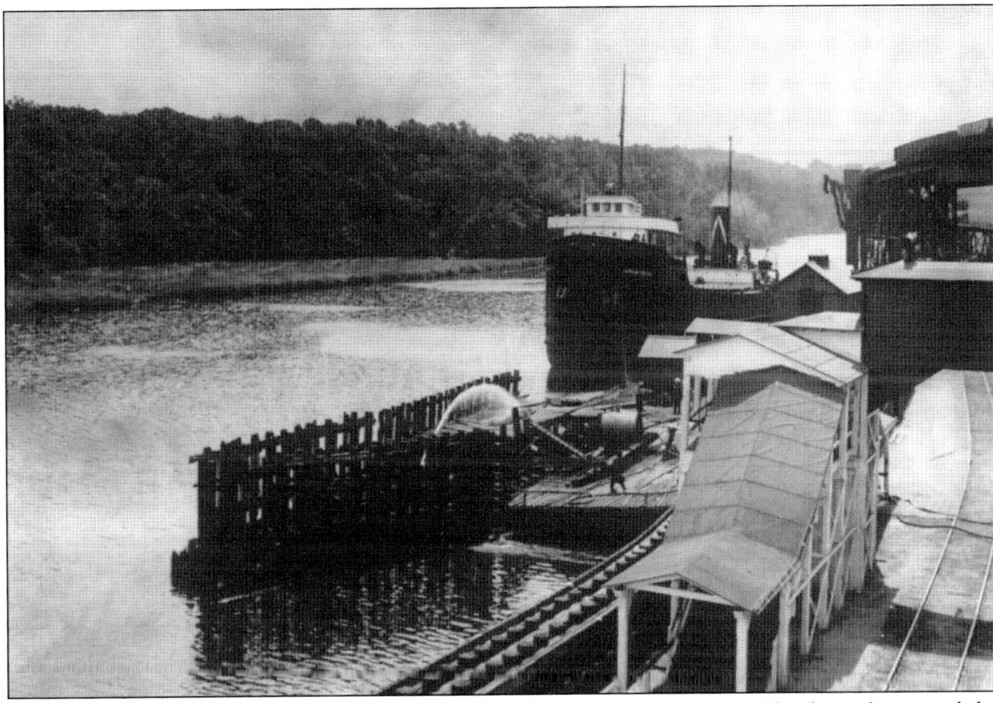

After the lake freighters had their cargo, they would steam north past the Charlotte depot and the swing bridge toward the piers leading to Lake Ontario. (Courtesy of *Rochester Images*: Rochester Public Library Local History Division.)

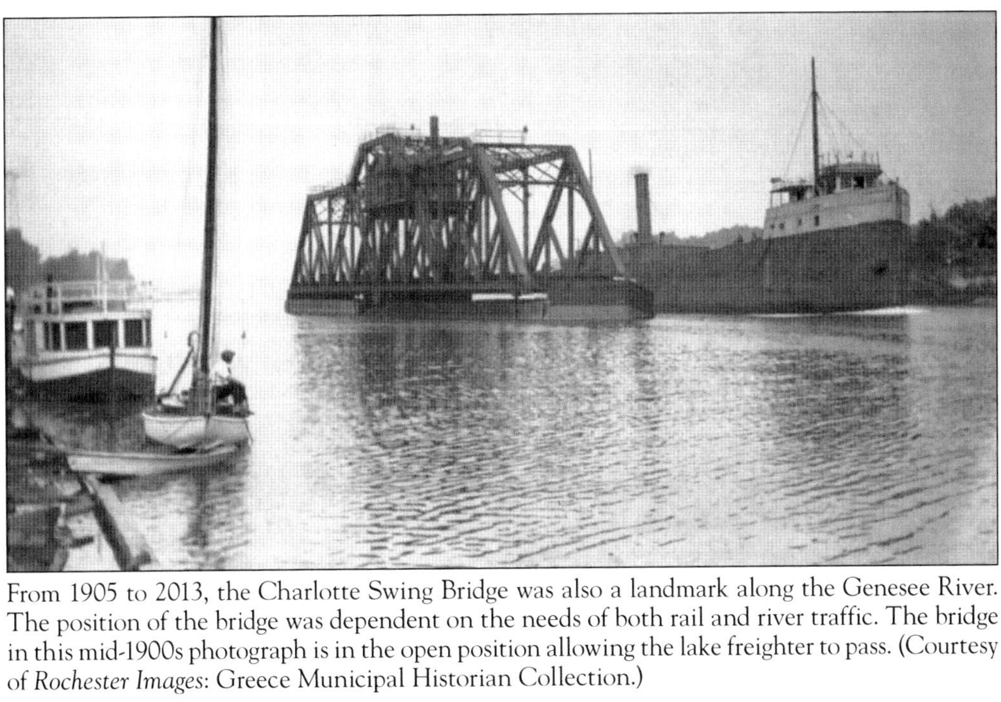

From 1905 to 2013, the Charlotte Swing Bridge was also a landmark along the Genesee River. The position of the bridge was dependent on the needs of both rail and river traffic. The bridge in this mid-1900s photograph is in the open position allowing the lake freighter to pass. (Courtesy of *Rochester Images*: Greece Municipal Historian Collection.)

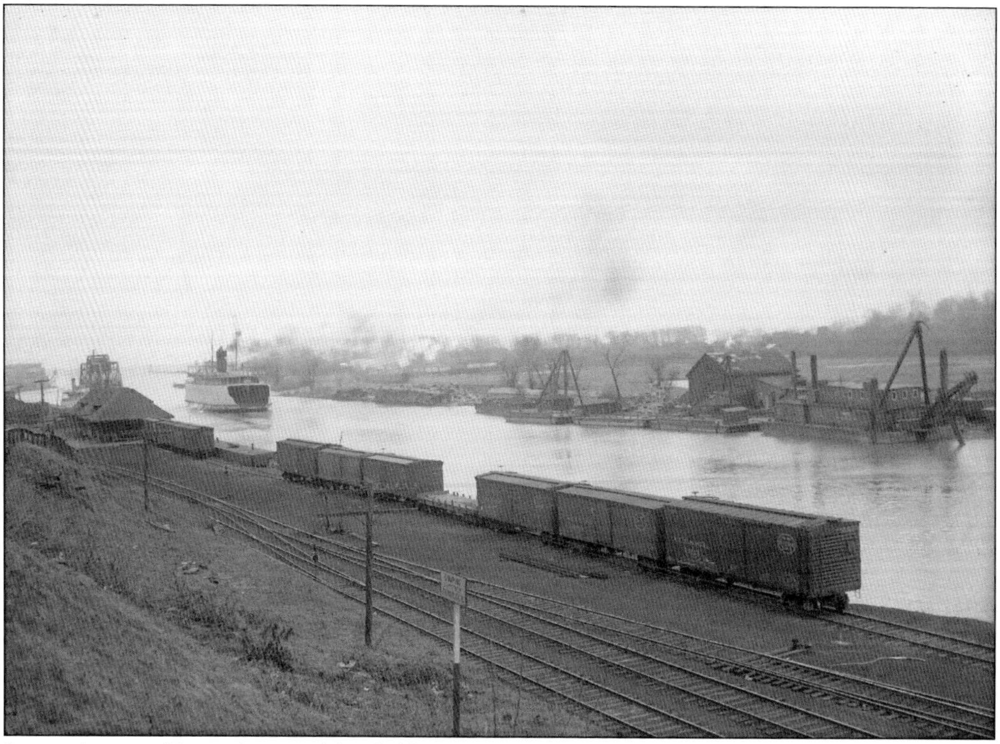

It was also possible to place coal-loaded hopper cars on one of two ferries, *Ontario I* or *Ontario II*. The coal was shipped from Charlotte to Cobourg, Ontario, to be used by Canada's Grand Trunk Railroad. In this c. 1915 photograph, one of the ferries is seen heading north past the Charlotte depot and the swing bridge. Note the CCC&StL boxcar. It belonged to the Cleveland, Cincinnati, Chicago & St. Louis Railway, also known as the Big Four, which was part of the New York Central Lines. At the time of the photograph, NYC&HR, along with its affiliated railroads such as the Big Four, became the NYC Lines. In the 1930s, the railroad changed its name to NYC System. (Courtesy of Rochester Museum & Science Center, Albert R. Stone Collection.)

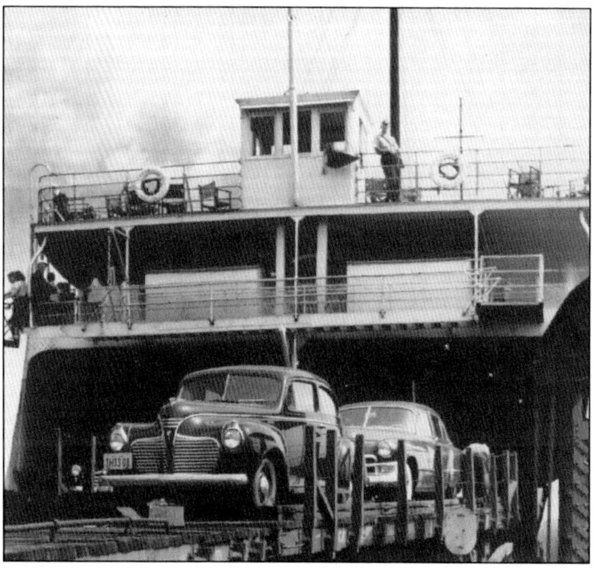

In addition to carrying hopper cars, the ferries to Cobourg carried passengers and automobiles. Shown in this 1940s photograph are automobiles that were carried on the ferry. (Courtesy of *Rochester Images*: Greece Municipal Historian Collection.)

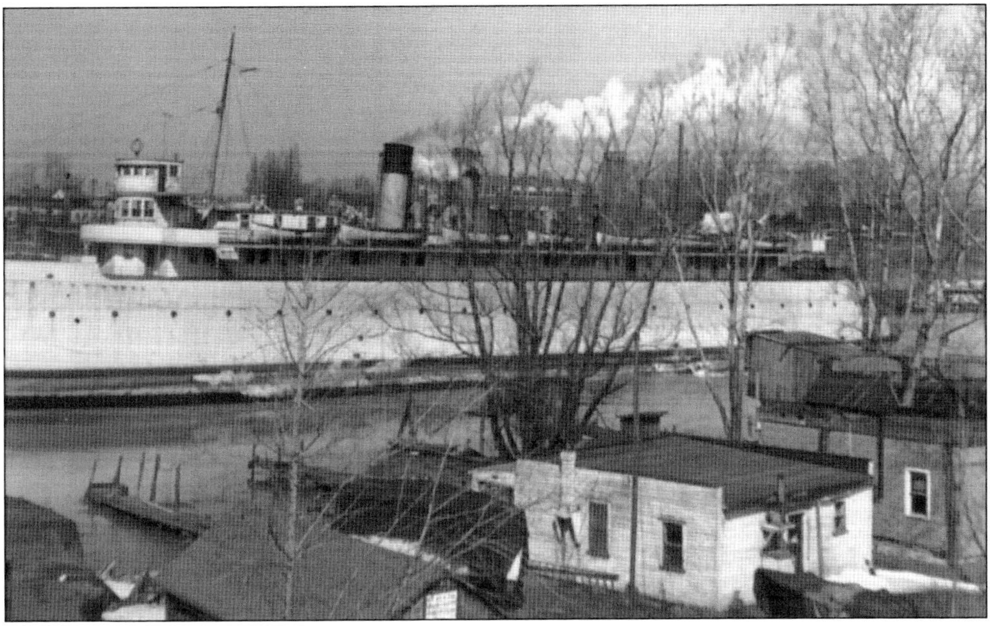

The *Ontario I* and *II* were both built in Canada in the early 1900s. They were quite a sight to those onlookers on the Charlotte piers as they steamed their way along the Genesee River. In this 1947 photograph, *Ontario II* is seen at the mouth of Genesee River heading south to its dock to unload and pickup passengers and cargo and head back to Canada. Both ferryboats ceased operating in 1949. (Courtesy of *Rochester Images*: Greece Municipal Historian Collection.)

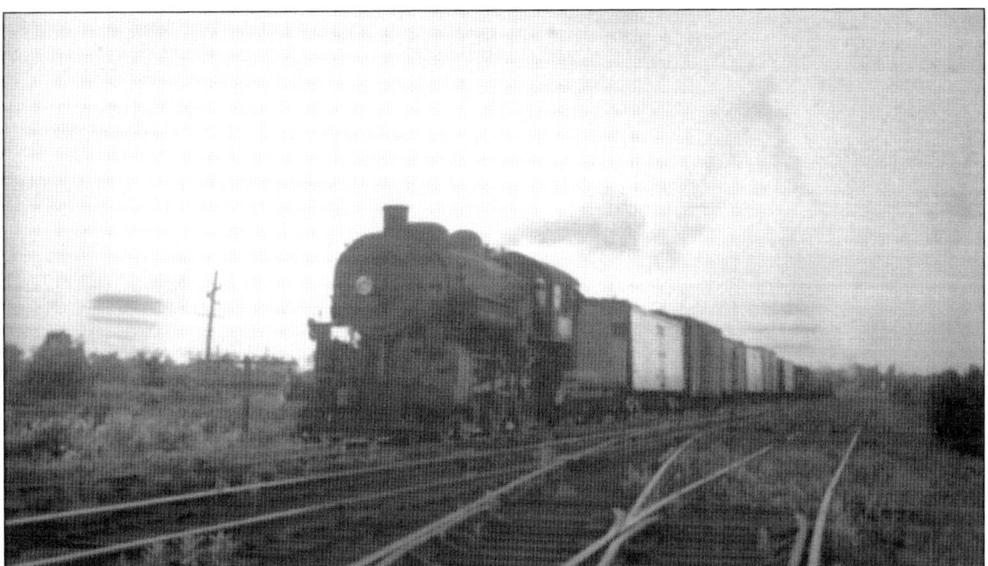

The Charlotte depot was the last stop on the NYC branch line. Before reaching the Charlotte depot, the "Charlotte Runner" (the eventual nickname for the branch line) had to cross Rochester streets. The 1940s photograph shows a 4-6-0 class F-12 10-wheeler at Ridge Road (Route 104), about five miles south of Charlotte. (Photograph by Ed Van Leer, courtesy of Jeff Hands.)

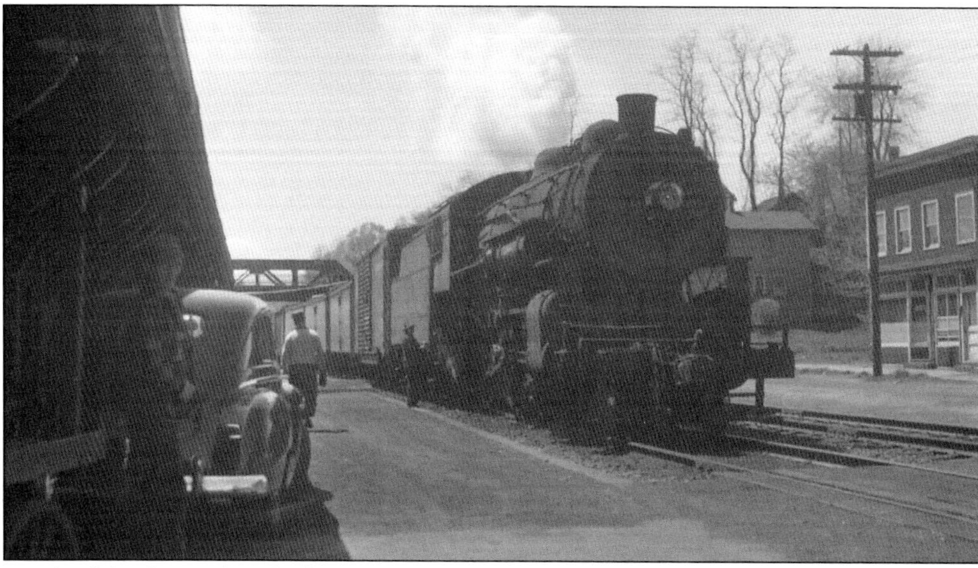

North of the depot, the Charlotte Runner connected to NYC's Ontario Division, better known as the Hojack, or to some the West Hojack or the East Hojack depending on which direction the line was headed. The West Hojack turned west from Charlotte entering the town of Greece past the Rochester Gas and Electric Corporation's (RG&E) Russell coal-fired power plant, while the East Hojack headed east across the Charlotte Swing Bridge and entered the town of Irondequoit. The freight at the Charlotte depot in this 1940s photograph is powered by a 4-6-0 class F-12g 10-wheeler. (Photograph by Ed Van Leer, courtesy of Jeff Hands.)

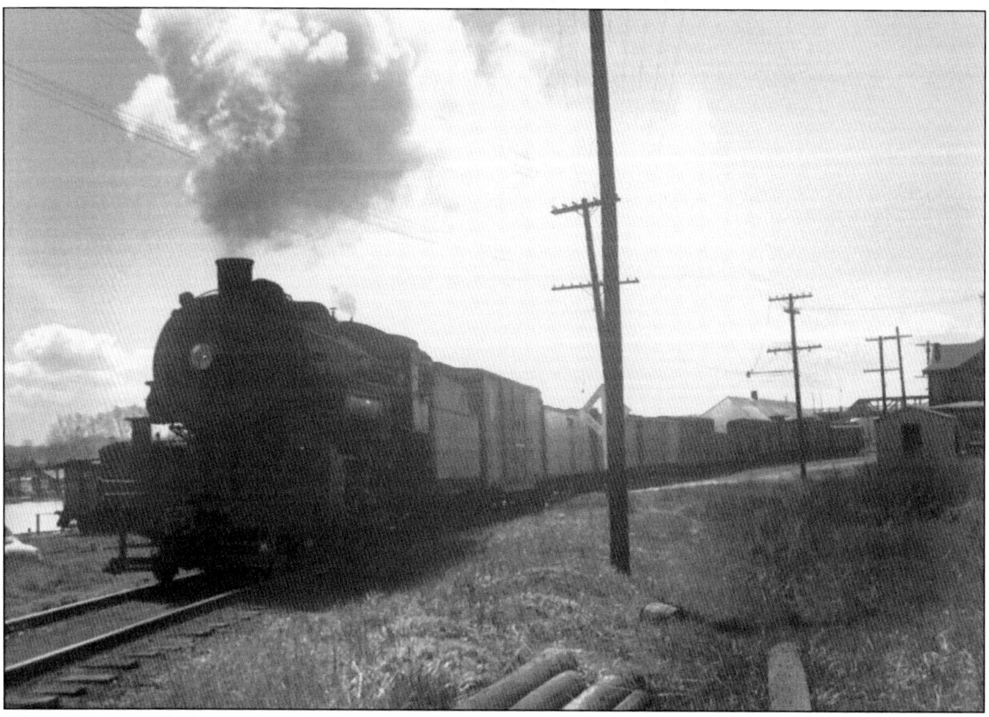

This photograph shows the same 10-wheeler after it has left the Charlotte depot and is about to head west toward the town of Greece. (Photograph by Ed Van Leer, courtesy of Jeff Hands.)

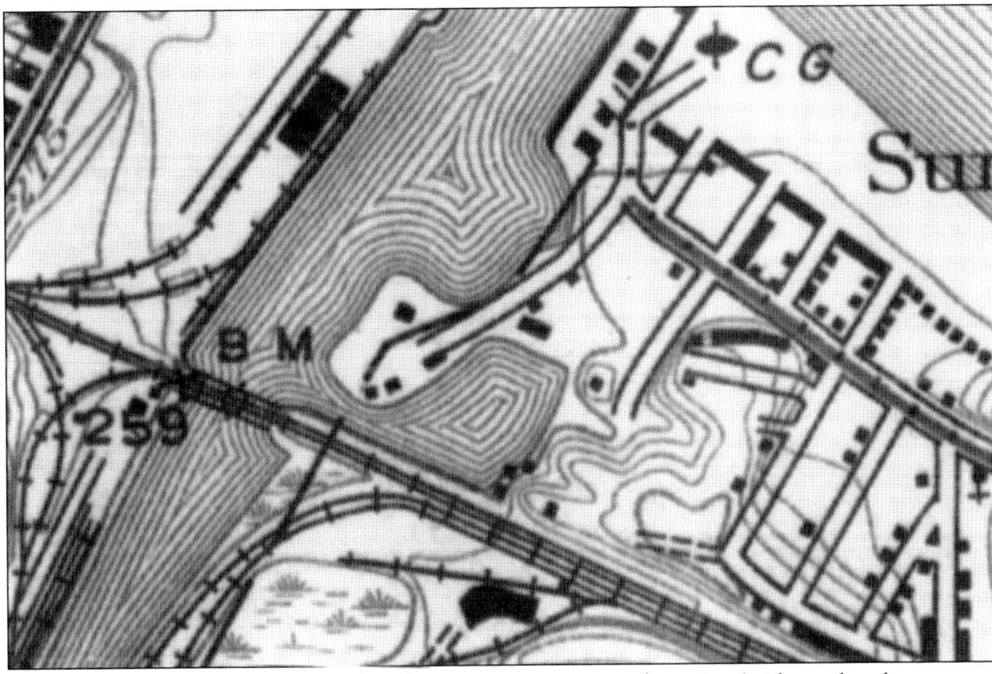

From the Charlotte depot, the rather sharp turn to get onto the swing bridge to head east across the Genesee River necessitated a turnout to the west and then a swing back over a crossing, or "diamond," to get onto the swing bridge. Positioning of the turnout and crossing are shown in the lower-left portion of the US Geological Survey map. (Courtesy of Allen Hilborn.)

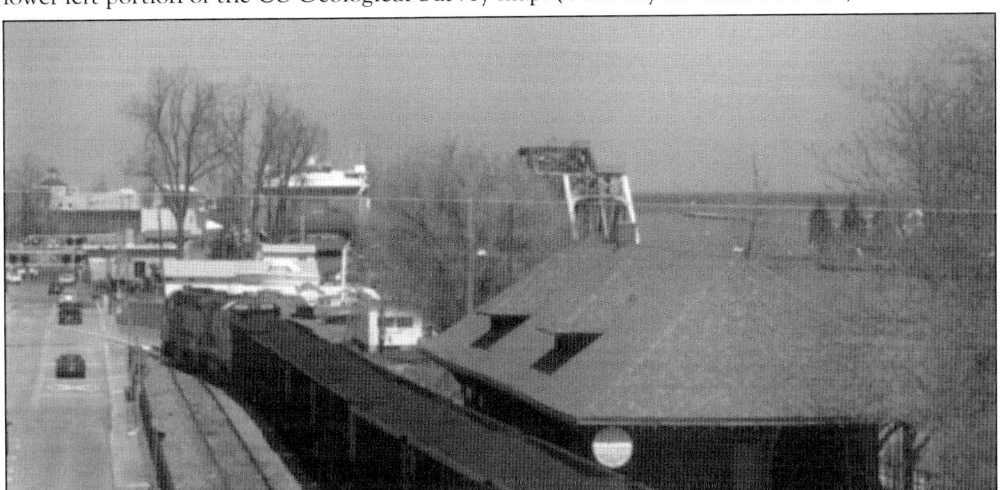

In this 2004 photograph, a Conrail coal train on the Charlotte Runner is seen passing the Charlotte depot and is about to switch onto the West Hojack heading to RG&E's Russell power station. In 1998, several loaded hopper cars were derailed, spilling coal and blocking River Street in front of the depot. (Courtesy of Scot Lawrence.)

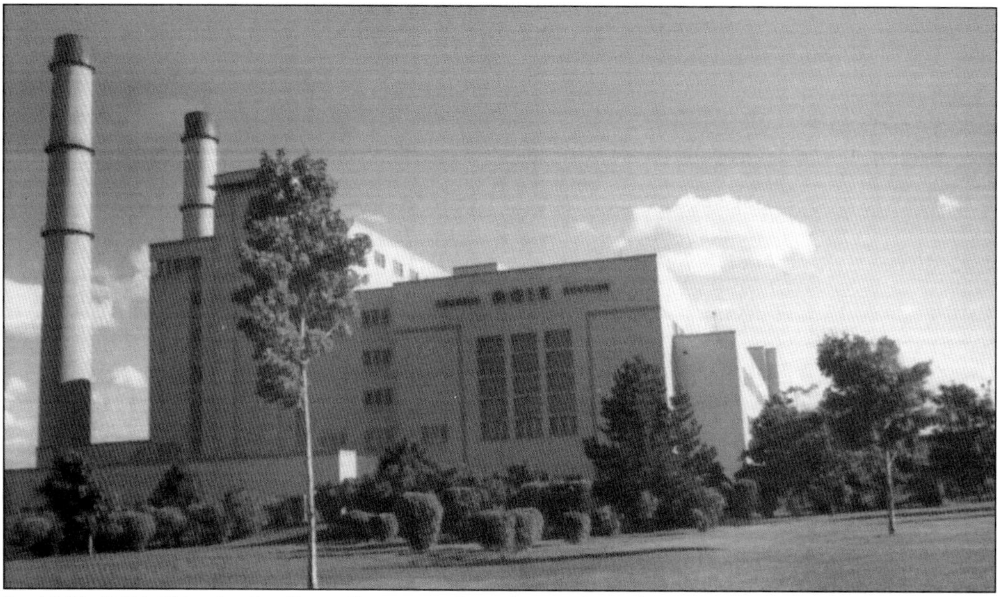

In 1948, RG&E built the Russell power plant located in the town of Greece, northwest of Rochester. It was one of two RG&E coal-fired power plants. The other plant, the Beebee power station, located in the city of Rochester, will be presented as part of the next chapter. (Courtesy of *Rochester Images*: Greece Municipal Historian Collection.)

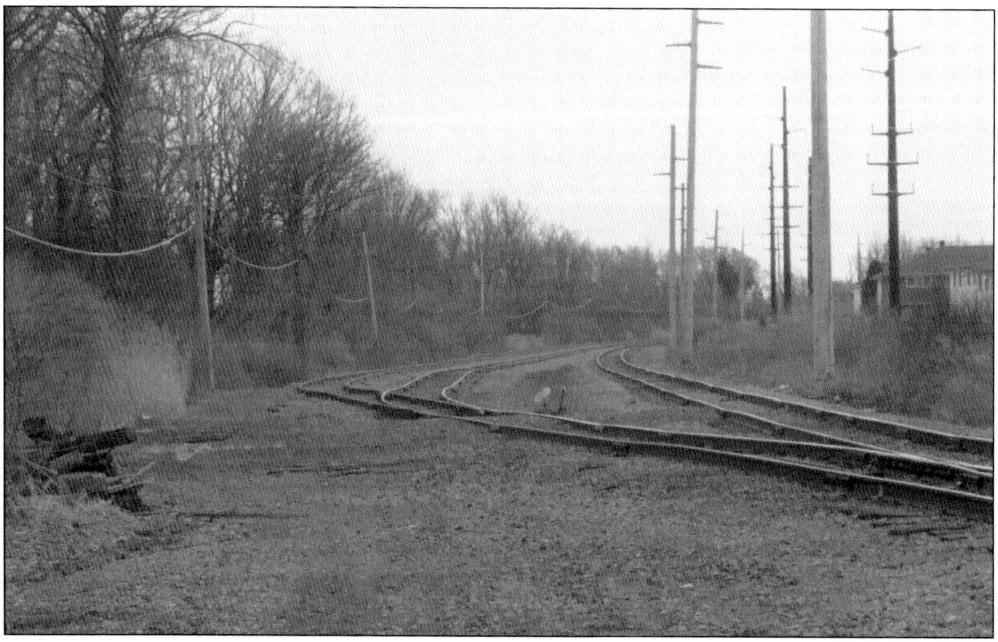

With the closing of the Russell Station power plant in 2008, the once active West Hojack rail yard in the back of the plant lies dormant, as shown in this 2014 photograph. In 2015, the remediation and demolition of the facility was initiated. (Author's collection.)

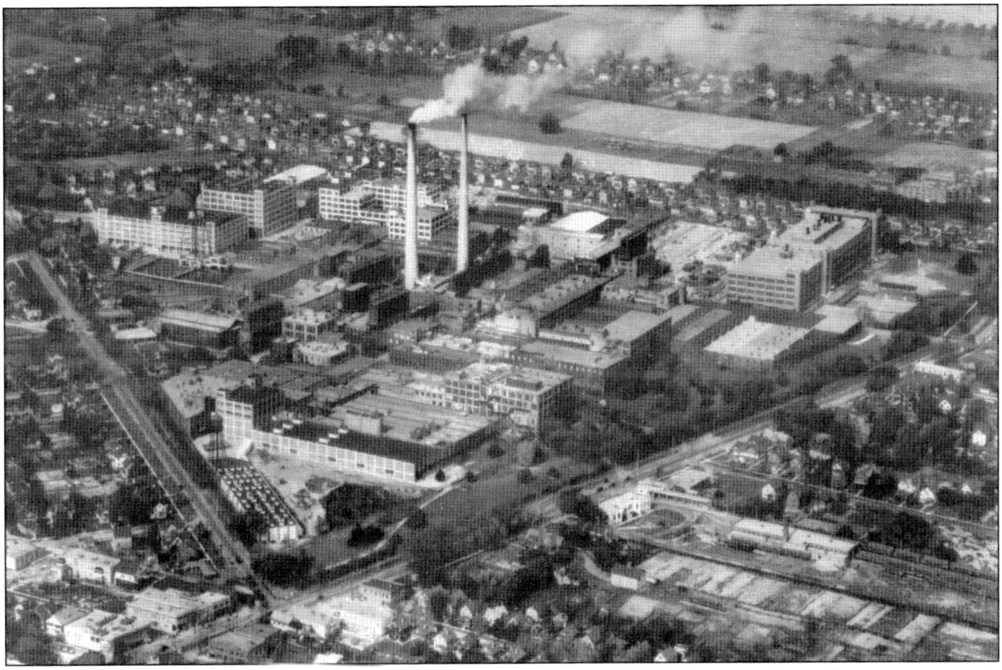

In addition to bringing coal to the Russell Station, the Charlotte Runner brought raw materials to the Eastman Kodak Company's manufacturing plant known as "Kodak Park." This 1990s photograph shows the vastness of the plant that was at one time the largest photographic products manufacturing facility in the world. (Courtesy of *Rochester Images*: Rochester Public Library Local History Division.)

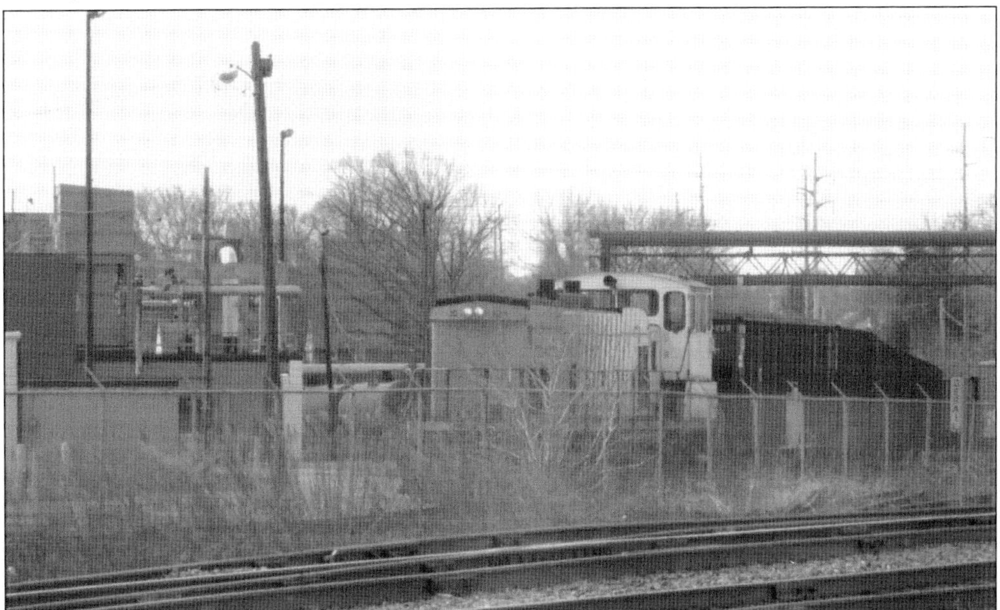

Today, Kodak Park has been downsized but still maintains the intraplant railroad that it started in the early 1900s to handle rail deliveries. Shown in action in this recent photograph is Kodak switcher No. 10, an EMD MP15AC diesel switch engine. (Author's collection.)

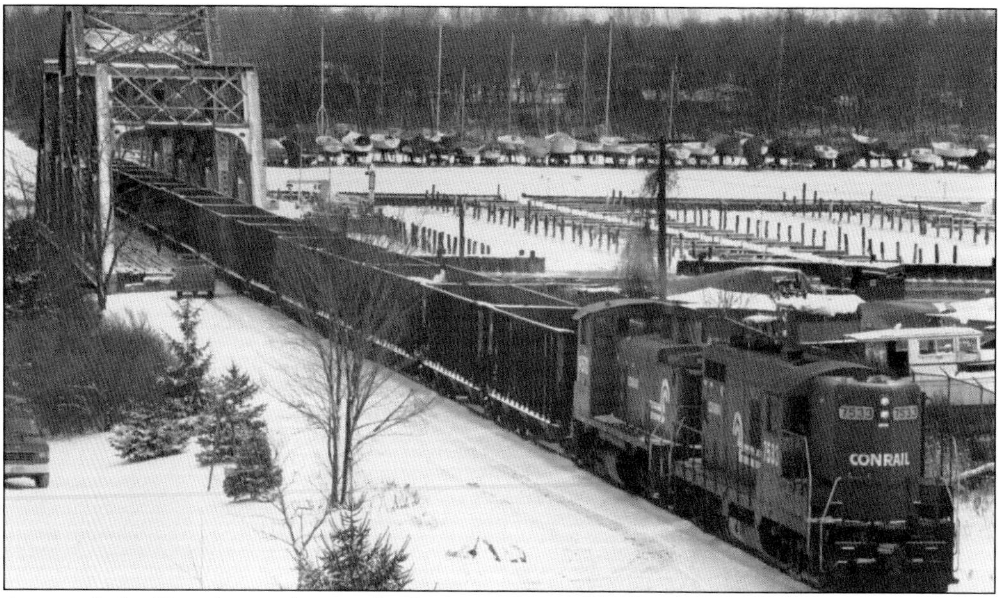

As noted, the Hojack was also involved in carrying coal to the Beebee plant, located on State Street in downtown Rochester. By the 1990s, Conrail was in charge of freight service throughout the Northeast. This photograph shows a Conrail EMD GP10 diesel road-switcher (a rebuilt former NYC GP9) hauling empty hoppers from the Beebee plant west across the Charlotte Swing Bridge. (Courtesy of Duncan Richards.)

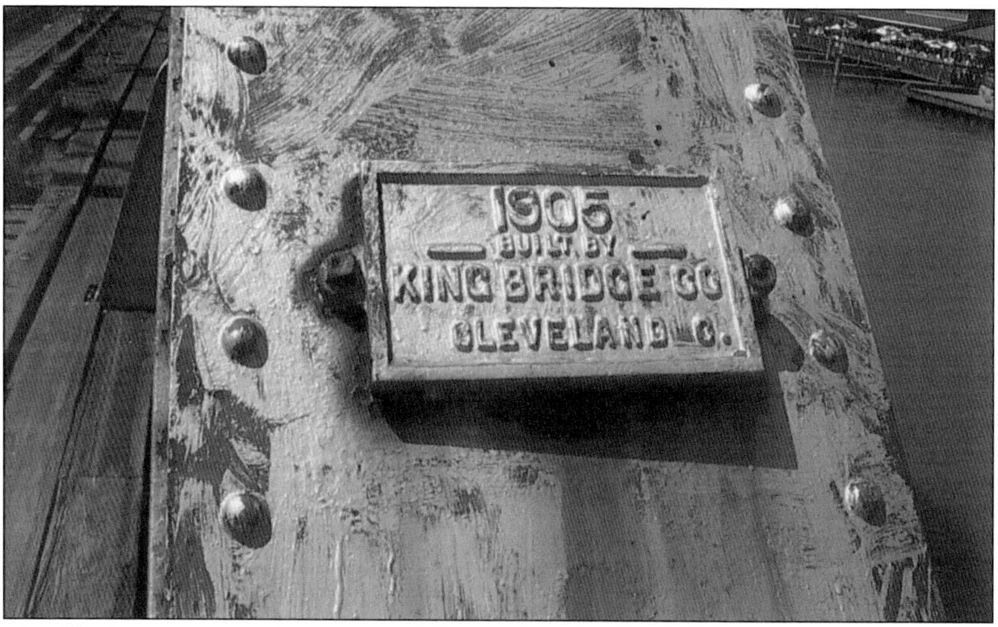

The Charlotte Swing Bridge was built by the King Bridge Company and installed in 1905, as shown by this nameplate on the bridge. The King Bridge Company of Cleveland, Ohio, was a leader in moveable bridge design and manufacture. Its moveable bridges were seen in many large cities throughout the Northeast and Midwest. (Photograph by Edmund Finucane, courtesy of Richard Margolis.)

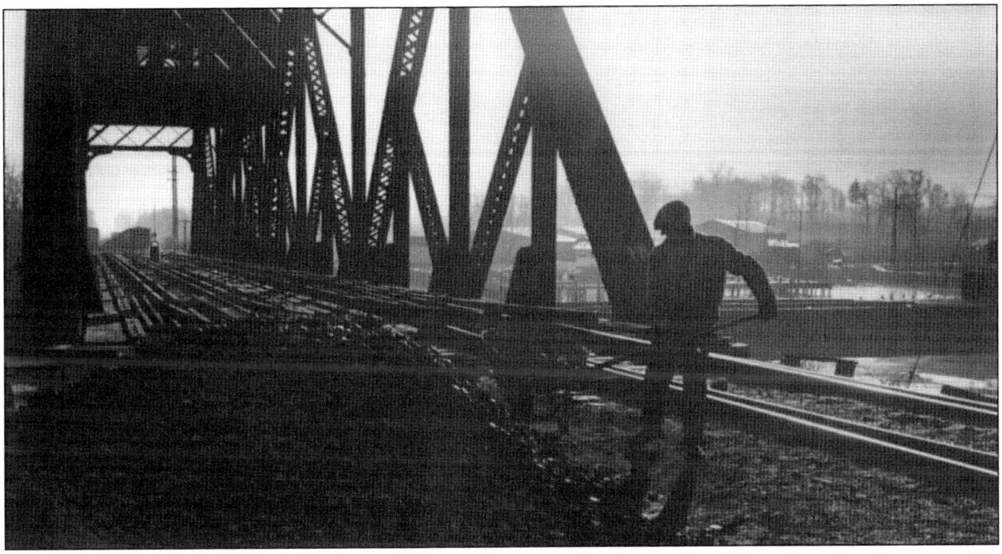

This interesting backlighted photograph shows the swing bridge tender filling the wheelbarrow with the coal for transfer to the control cabin where the small Lidgerwood steam engine that powered the movement of the swing bridge was located. The transfer bucket that carried the coal to the cabin can be seen in the background of the photograph. Today, the Lidgerwood engine is part of the Charlotte Swing Bridge exhibit at the New York Museum of Transportation, located in nearby Rush, south of Rochester. (Photograph by Whitey Roemer, courtesy of Richard Margolis.)

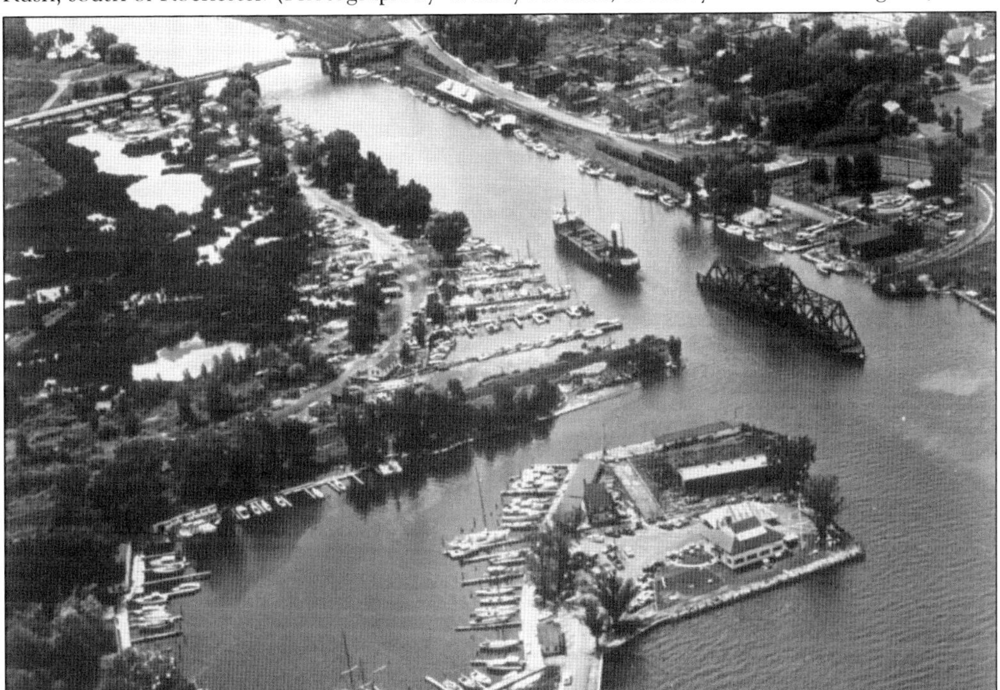

This aerial view looking south shows the Charlotte Swing Bridge and NYC's Charlotte depot as well as the 1918 Stutson Street automobile and pedestrian bridge. Note that the Stutson Street Bridge is opening to let the lake freighter pass. (Photograph by Henry Dewolf, courtesy of Richard Margolis.)

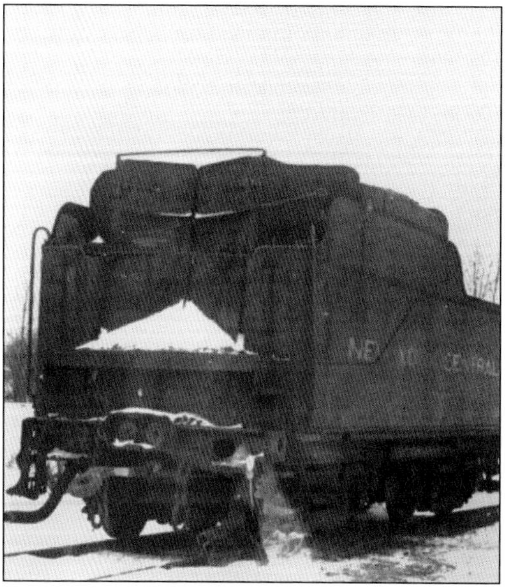

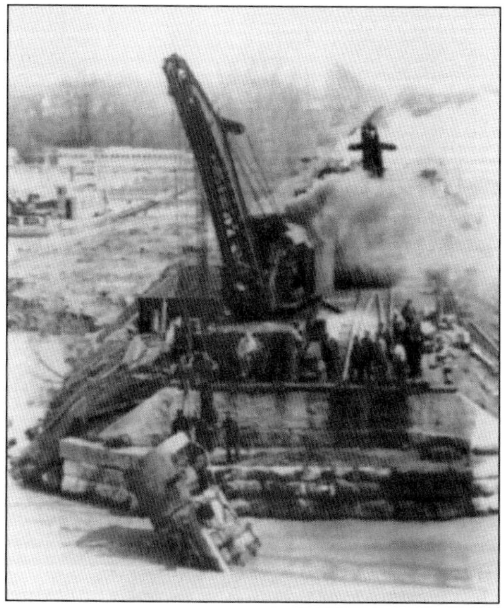

During the approximately 100 years of service, rail traffic on the Charlotte Swing Bridge had an excellent safety record. However, people do remember one incident in 1947 when an engineer approaching the east end of the bridge in the early morning hours missed a stop signal, causing the engine to plummet into the Genesee River. The fireman survived, but the engineer did not. Shown in the left photograph is the tender that separated from the engine and remained on land. The NYC engine that went into the Genesee River was a 2-8-2 class H-5La Mikado. Shown in the right photograph is the engine as it was lifted from the river bottom. (Left, courtesy of Jeff Hands; right, courtesy of Greece Municipal Historian Collection.)

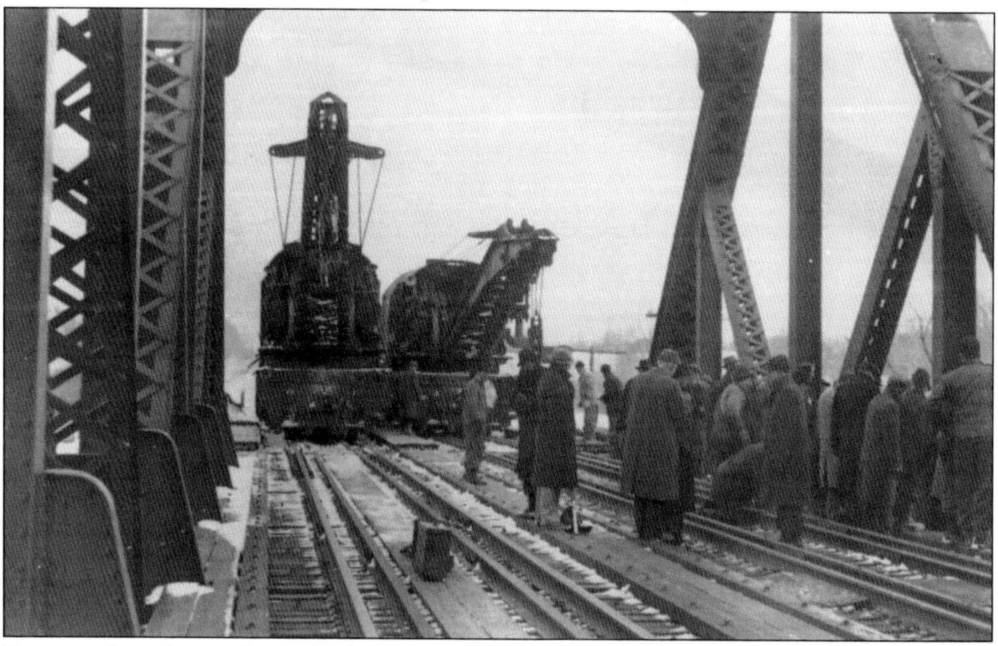

Because of weather and a muddy bottom of the Genesee River, recovery of the engine was not an easy task. Shown in this photograph on the swing bridge are two of the large NYC cranes, or "hooks" as they were called, that had to be used. (Courtesy of Jeff Hands.)

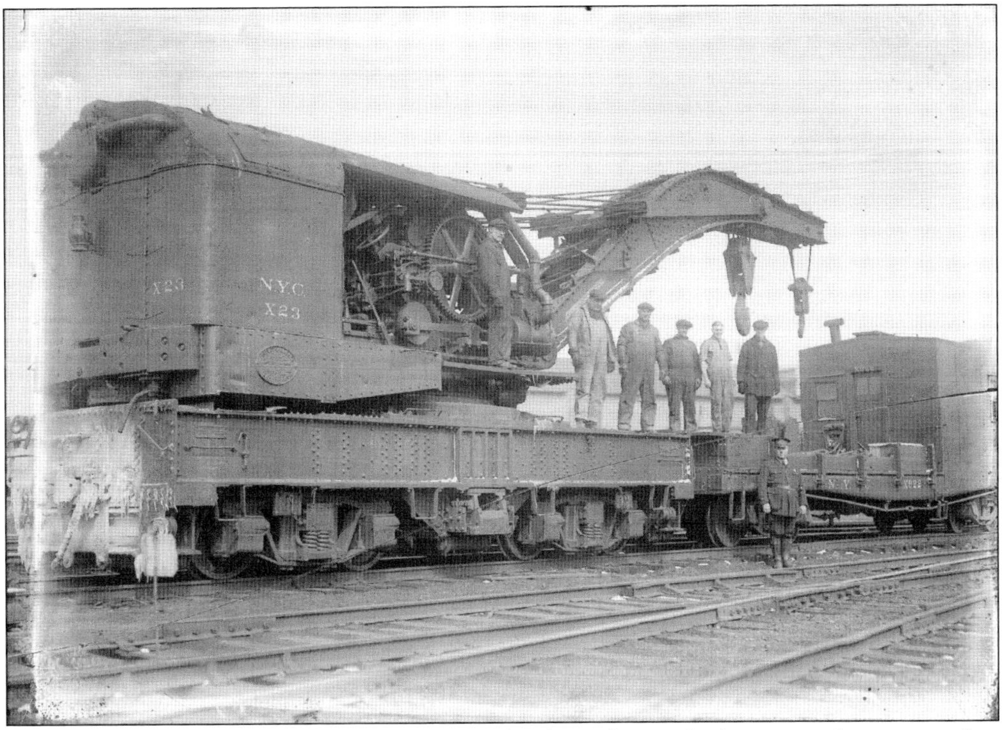

It is interesting to peer inside these heavy-duty hooks and view the large complex gearing that is required to provide the lift necessary when dealing with derailments such as happened at the Charlotte Swing Bridge in 1947. (Courtesy of Rochester Museum & Science Center, Albert R. Stone Collection.)

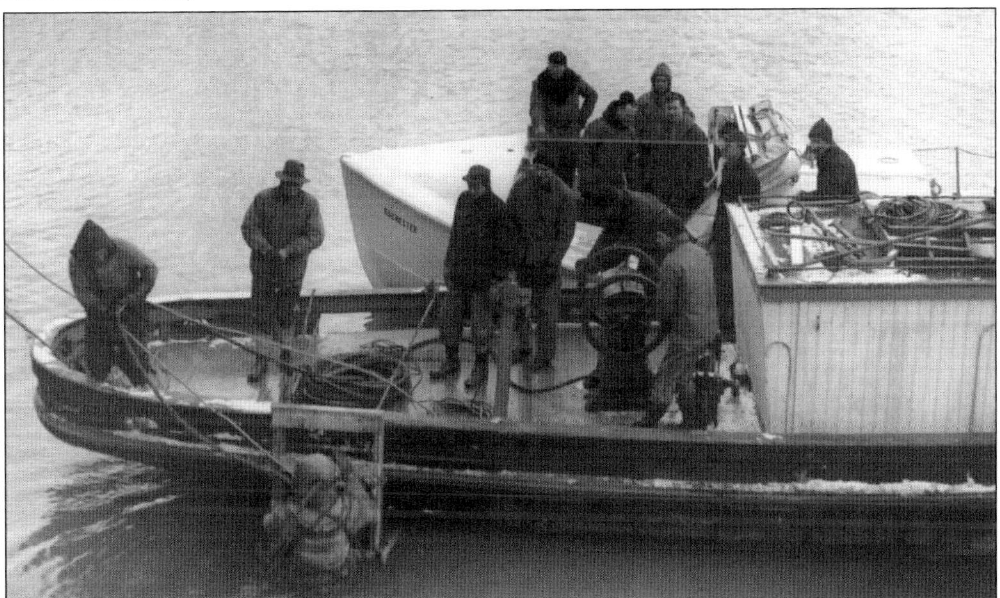

The divers shown in the photograph played an important role in the engine recovery. It was their job to locate the engine and to fasten the necessary chains required for the lifting operation. (Courtesy of *Rochester Images*: Rochester Public Library Local History Division.)

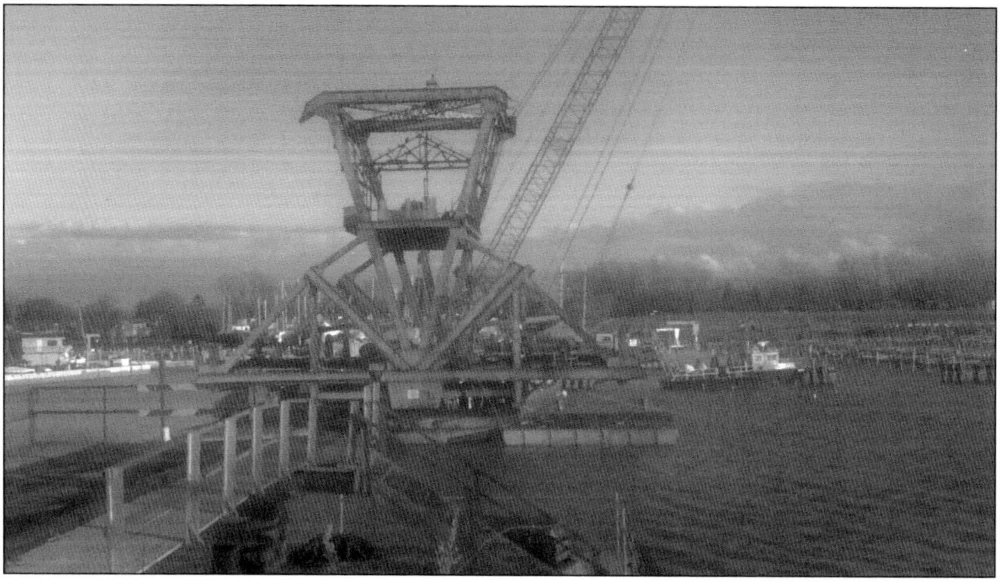

Rail traffic on the Charlotte Swing Bridge declined steadily through the 1980s and 1990s. In the late 1990s, CSX was ordered to make plans for its removal. After a long legal battle with preservationists, the demolition of the Charlotte Swing Bridge was underway in the spring of 2013, as shown in the photograph. (Photograph by Manuel Melendez.)

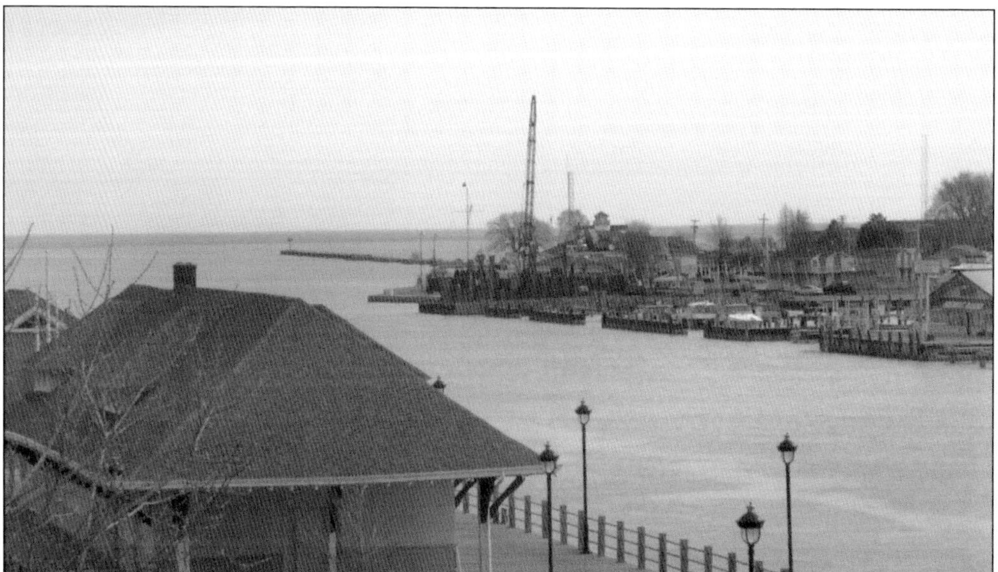

A recent photograph shows the Charlotte harbor without the swing bridge. To some, things do not look quite the same. (Author's collection.)

Three

The Historic Hojack Line

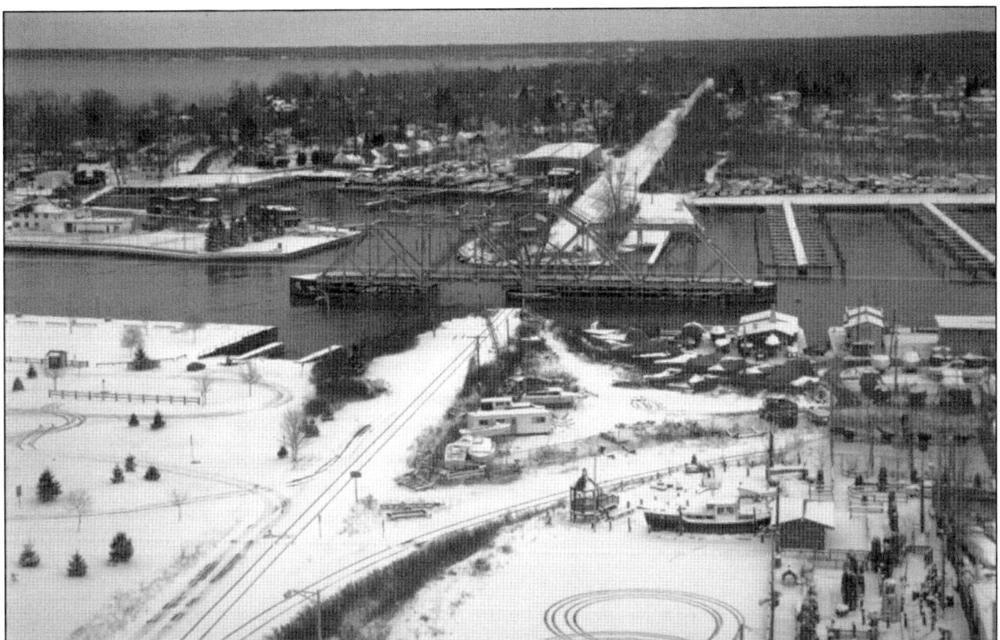

This 1961 aerial view looking east from Charlotte across the Genesee River toward the town of Irondequoit and the neighborhood communities of Summerville and Windsor Beach shows the Charlotte Swing Bridge and the Hojack line. Also in the photograph is the Charlotte Runner and its intersection with the Hojack line. Note that Lake Ontario appears in the upper-left portion of the photograph. (Courtesy of the City of Rochester.)

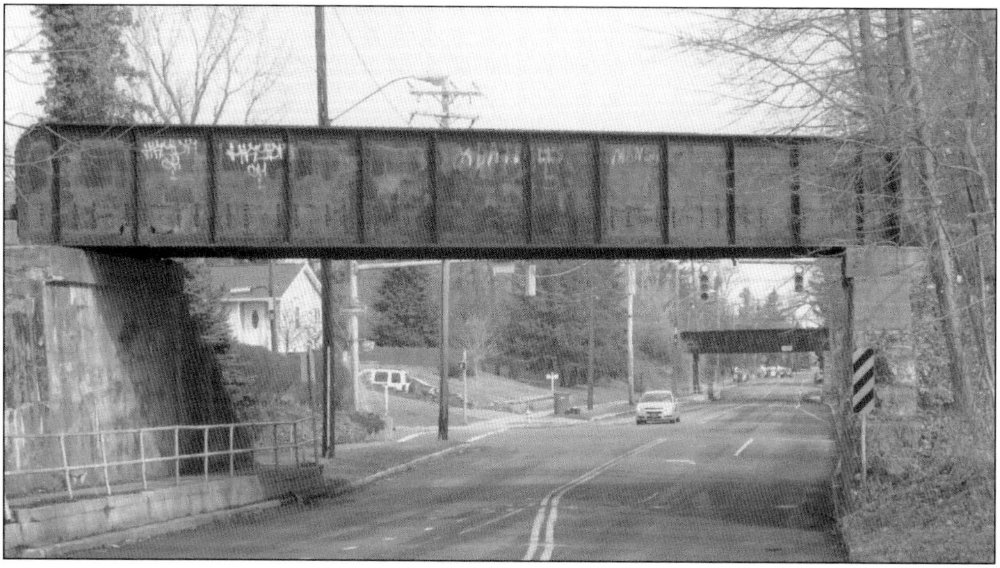

Near Summerville and Windsor Beach, there are the two important former NYC railroad bridges shown in this recent photograph. The bridge in the background carried the East Hojack over St. Paul Boulevard, while the bridge in the foreground did likewise for NYC's State Street branch line. The latter, which intersected the East Hojack at Windsor Beach, was used to bring coal south to the RG&E's Beebee power station on State Street in Rochester. Conrail abandoned the State Street branch line in 1997, and because of the deteriorating condition of the bridge, the Town of Irondequoit removed the bridge from the roadway in 2014. (Author's collection.)

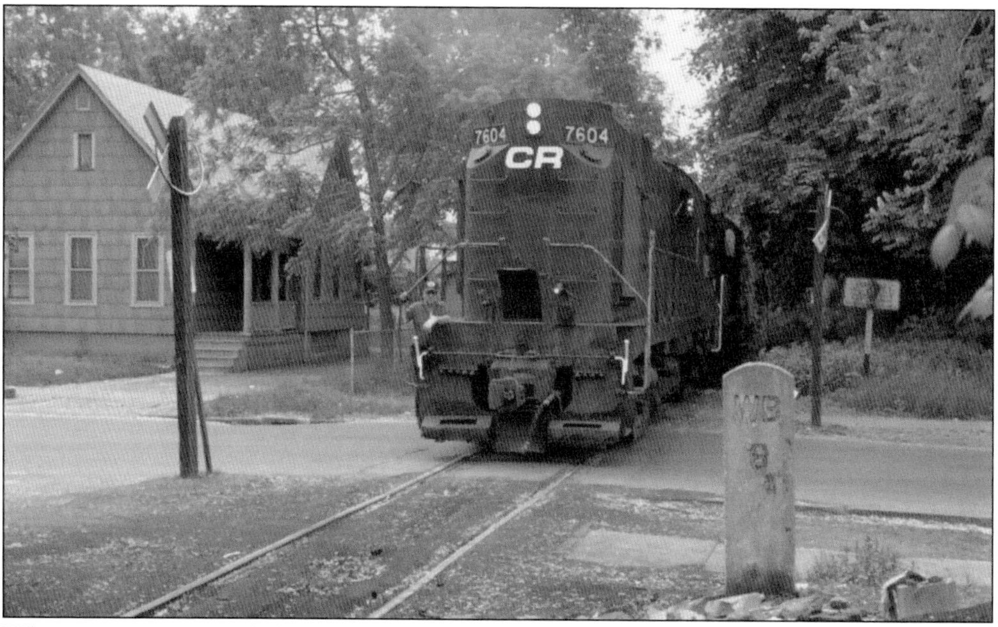

When it was operational, the State Street branch line, after making its way through the town of Irondequoit, entered the city of Rochester on its way to the trestle bridge that carried coal trains back across the Genesee River to the Beebee power station. Shown in this c. 1990 photograph is a Conrail Alco RS-11 diesel road-switcher on the headend as it crosses Avenue A in Rochester, six miles south of Windsor Beach on the East Hojack. (Courtesy of Duncan Richards.)

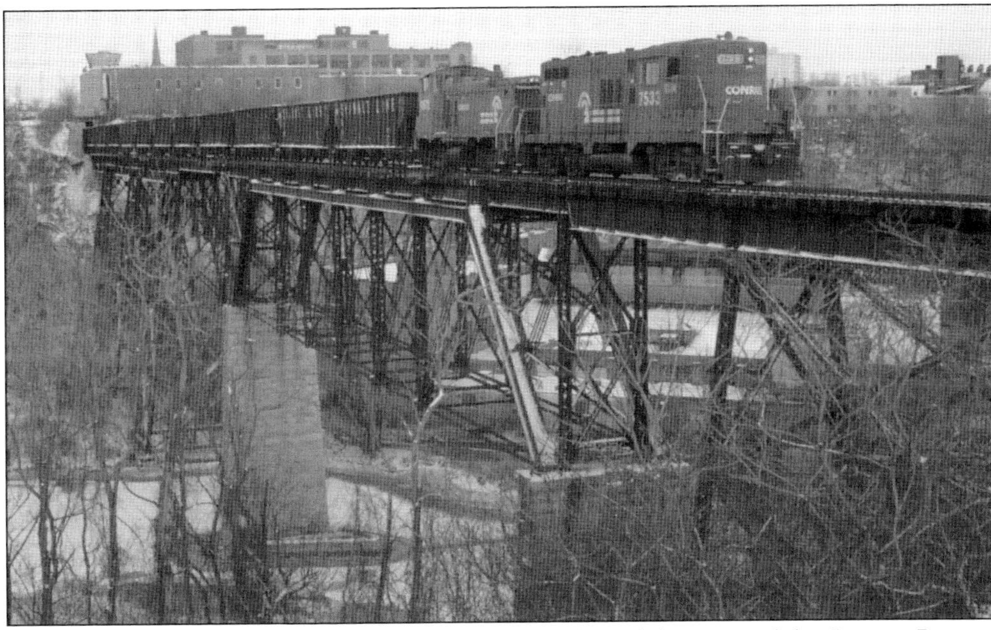

Approximately a mile from Avenue A, the State Street branch line crossed the Genesee River to reach the Beebee power plant on State Street. Shown in this c. 1990 photograph is a Conrail GP10 (a rebuilt former NYC GP9 diesel road-switcher) followed by a Conrail SW1500 switcher on the front end of the coal train as it crosses the trestle. Built in the 1880s, this trestle is no longer in use and is today part of Rochester's scenic Genesee River gorge. (Courtesy of Duncan Richards.)

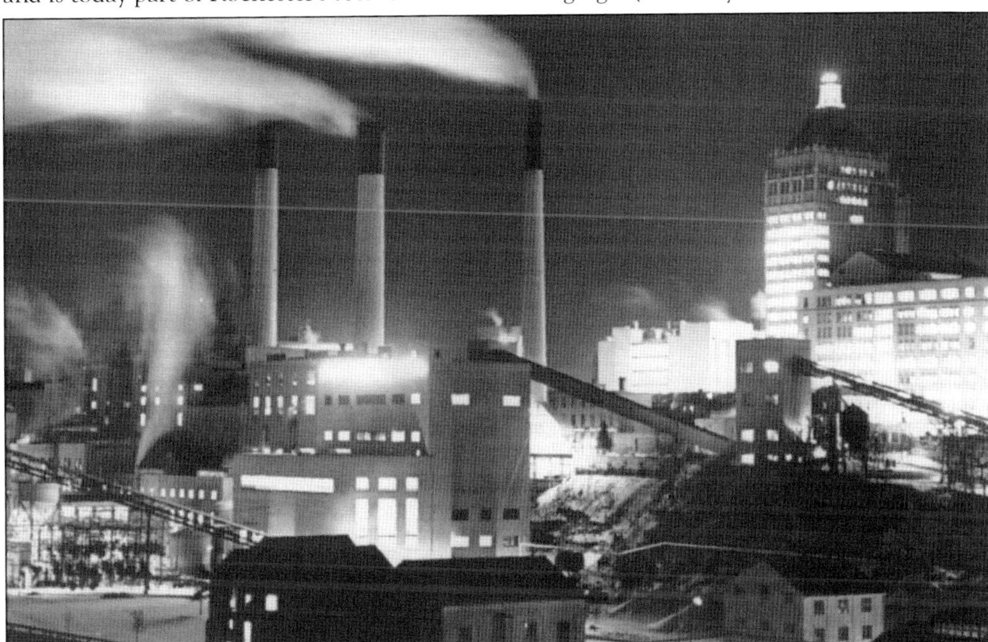

Shut down in 1999, the coal-fired Beebee power plant was used to produce power for Rochester's industries since the early 1900s. The plant was located near downtown Rochester, as evidenced by the Kodak Tower in the background of this nighttime photograph. (Courtesy of *Rochester Images*: Rochester Library Local History Division.)

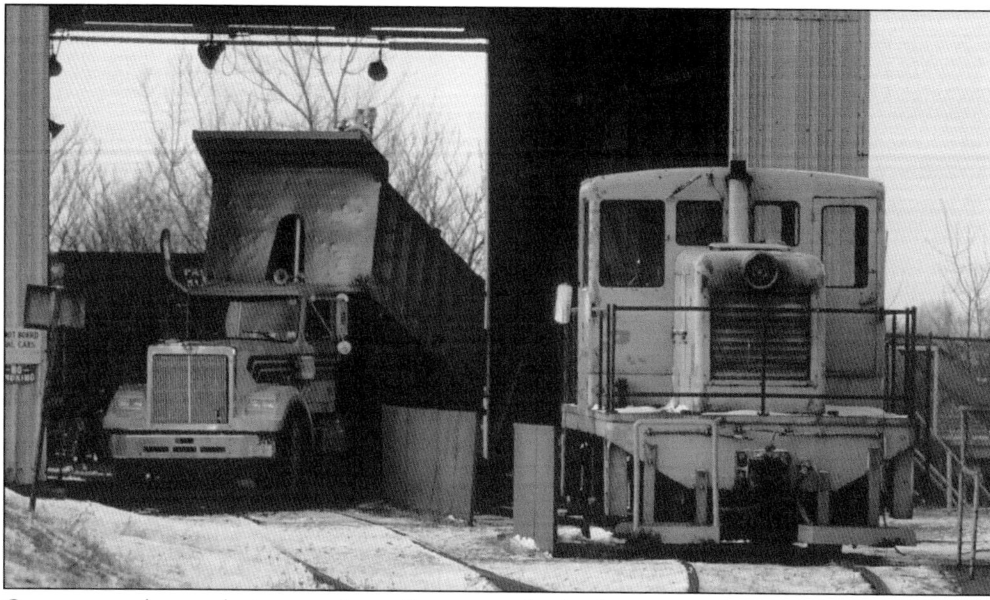

Once across the trestle, it was a short distance to the Beebee power plant. At the Beebee plant, a General Electric (GE) 45-ton, center-cab switcher took over and brought the loaded hopper cars to this transfer station. The coal was bottom-dropped to a conveyor belt for transport to the main plant. The appearance of the coal truck in this early-1990s photograph does not bode well for the future of coal delivery by rail. As noted previously, the rail line to the Beebee plant was abandoned in 1997. For railfans, the switcher can be seen at the Rochester and Genesee Valley Railroad Museum in nearby Rush, south of Rochester. (Courtesy of Duncan Richards.)

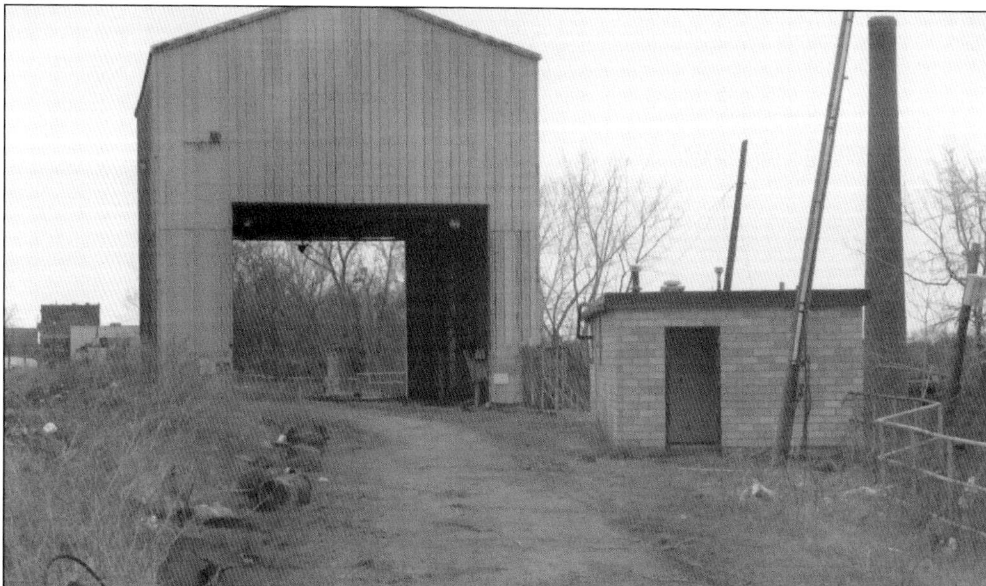

When the Beebee plant shut down in 1999, the transfer station was no longer needed and is dormant today, as shown in this recent photograph. Because the transfer station area is located near the Genesee River, it would not be surprising after cleanup to see the area become a scenic overlook much like Turning Point Park in Charlotte. (Author's collection.)

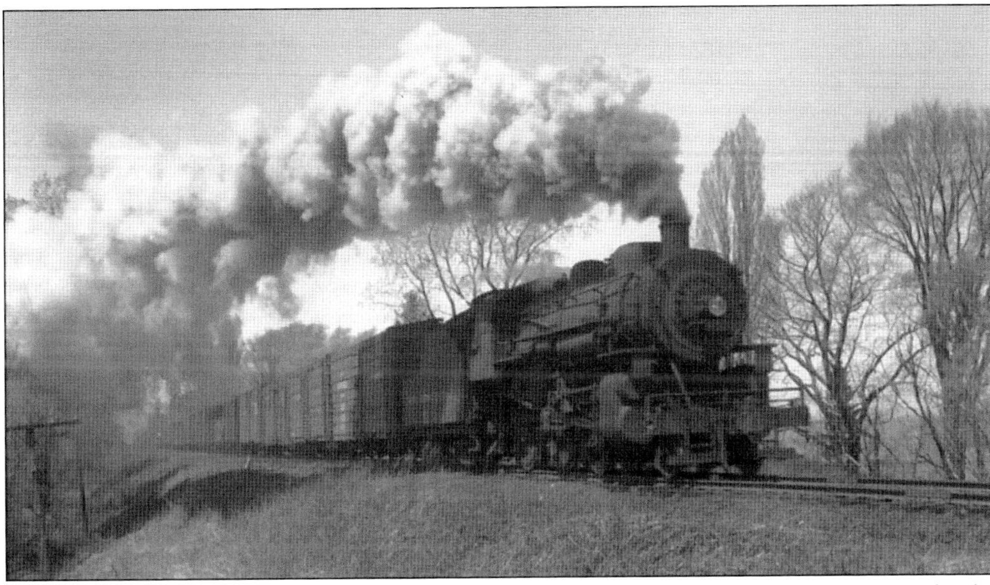

Returning to the East Hojack, this 1940s photograph shows a 4-6-0 class F-12g 10-wheeler chugging its way along the Lake Ontario's shore in the vicinity of the Durand-Eastman Park, just east of Windsor Beach. With the tracks abandoned by Conrail in the late 1970s, the former Hojack track bed has been converted into a running trail. (Photograph by Ed Van Leer, courtesy of Jeff Hands.)

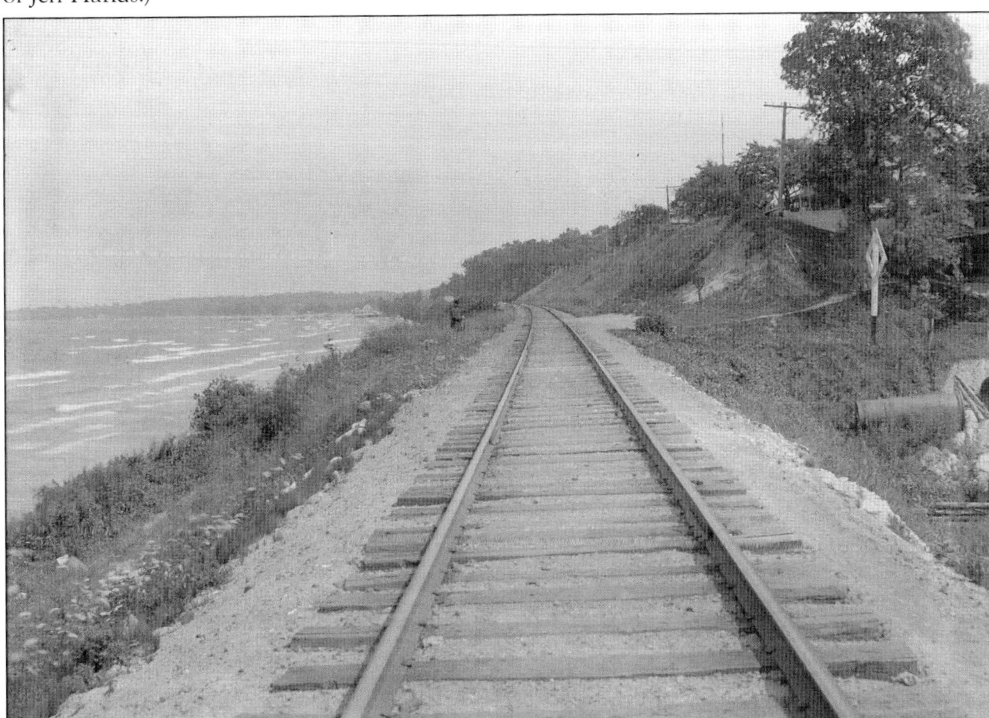

This early-1900s photograph, taken near the newly completed Durand-Eastman Park, shows just how close the East Hojack track was to Lake Ontario's shore. (Courtesy of Rochester Museum & Science Center, Albert R. Stone Collection.)

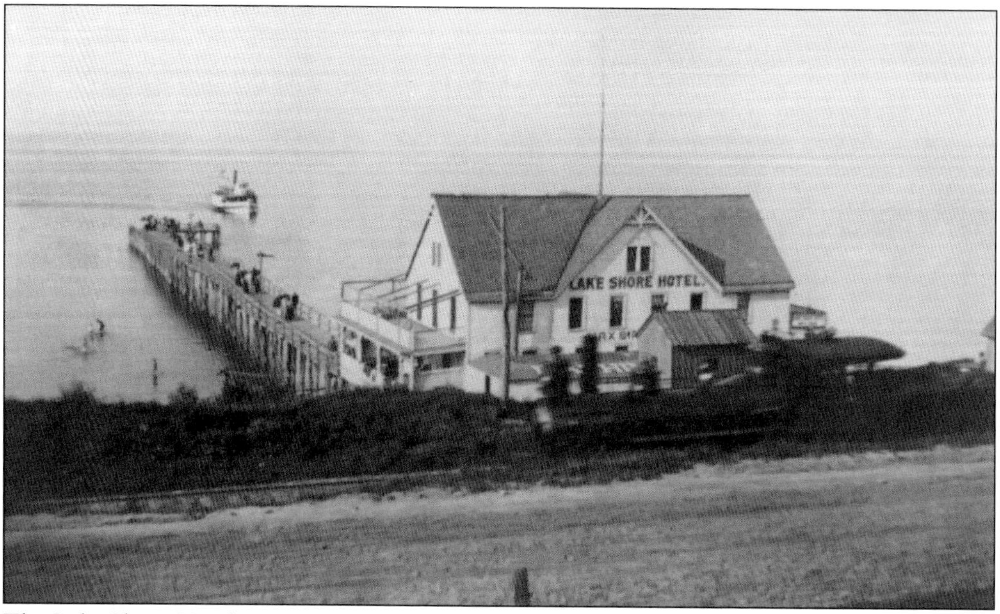

The Lake Shore Hotel once stood on the shore of Lake Ontario near Durand-Eastman Park. In this 1890s photograph, people are visible on the dock of the hotel awaiting the lake steamer that most likely came from Charlotte. About the time of the photograph, NYC leased the Rome, Watertown and Ogdensburg Railroad, whose track and engine are seen on the ridge above the hotel. (Courtesy of *Rochester Images*: Rochester Library Local History Division.)

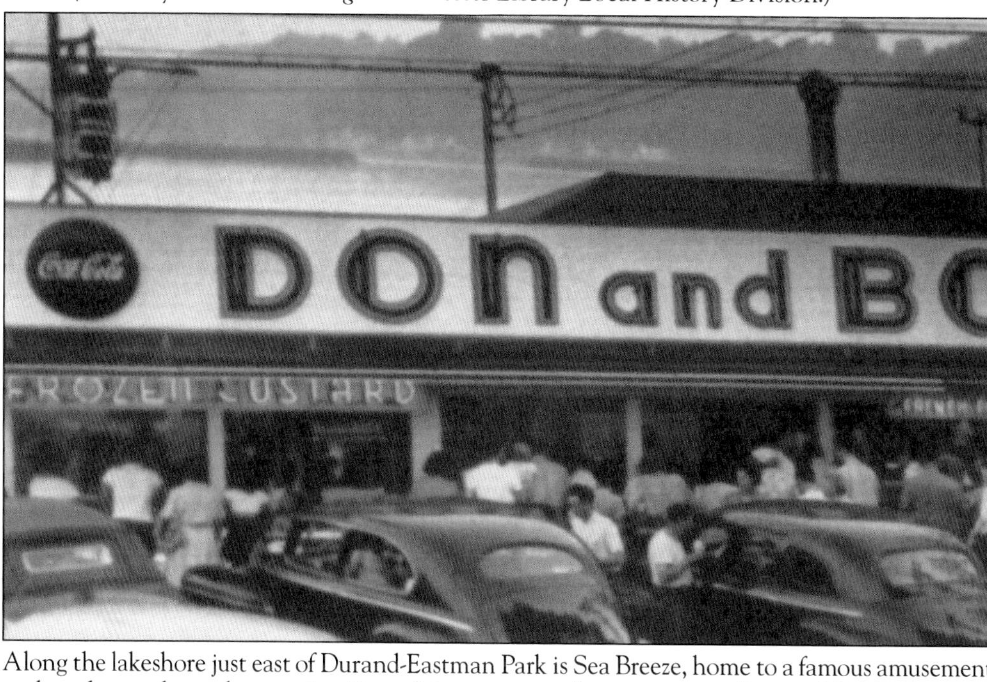

Along the lakeshore just east of Durand-Eastman Park is Sea Breeze, home to a famous amusement park and several popular eateries. One of the more popular eateries was Don and Bob's, shown in this 1940s photograph. On an embankment directly across from Don and Bob's on Culver Road was the East Hojack track. The restaurant, in business today as Don's Original, is as popular as ever. (Courtesy of Terry Klee.)

Just east of Sea Breeze is Irondequoit Bay. In this 1918 view from Lake Ontario, the bridge that carried the East Hojack across the Irondequoit Bay inlet is seen. (Courtesy of Rochester Museum & Science Center, Albert R. Stone Collection.)

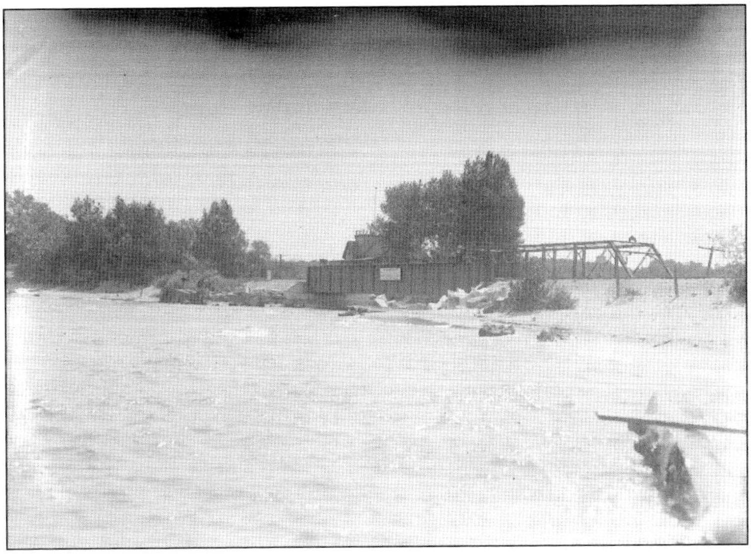

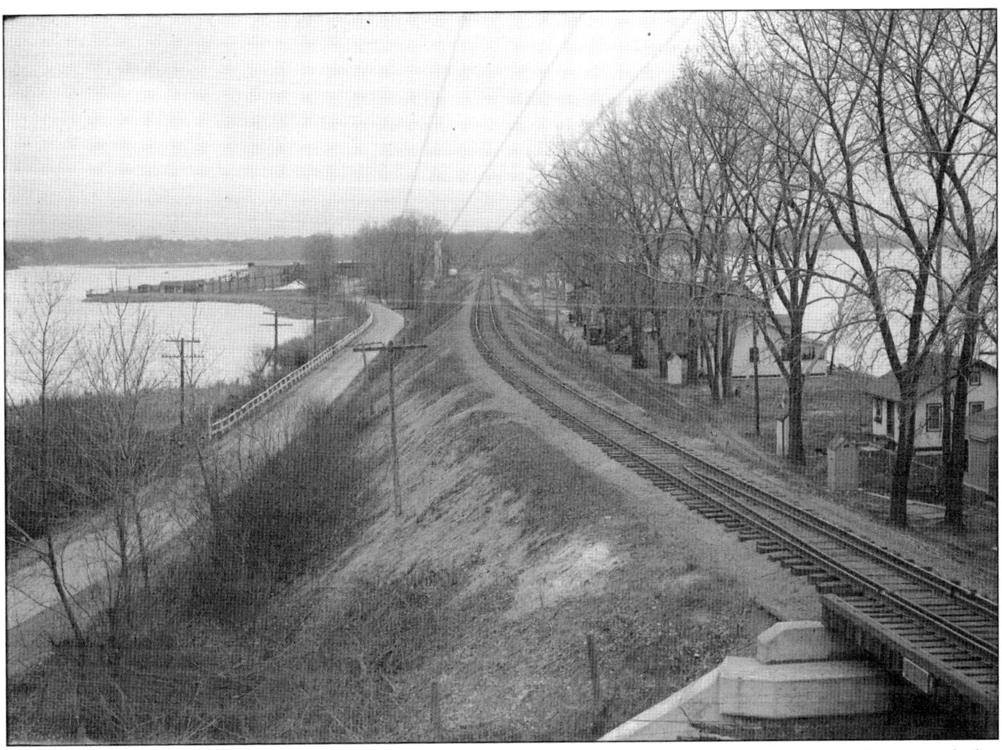

Once across the Irondequoit Bay Bridge, the East Hojack entered the town of Webster and the small isthmus community known as Oklahoma Beach. In this 1924 photograph of Oklahoma Beach, Irondequoit Bay is to the left of the East Hojack track and Lake Ontario is to the right. (Courtesy of Rochester Museum & Science Center, Albert R. Stone Collection.)

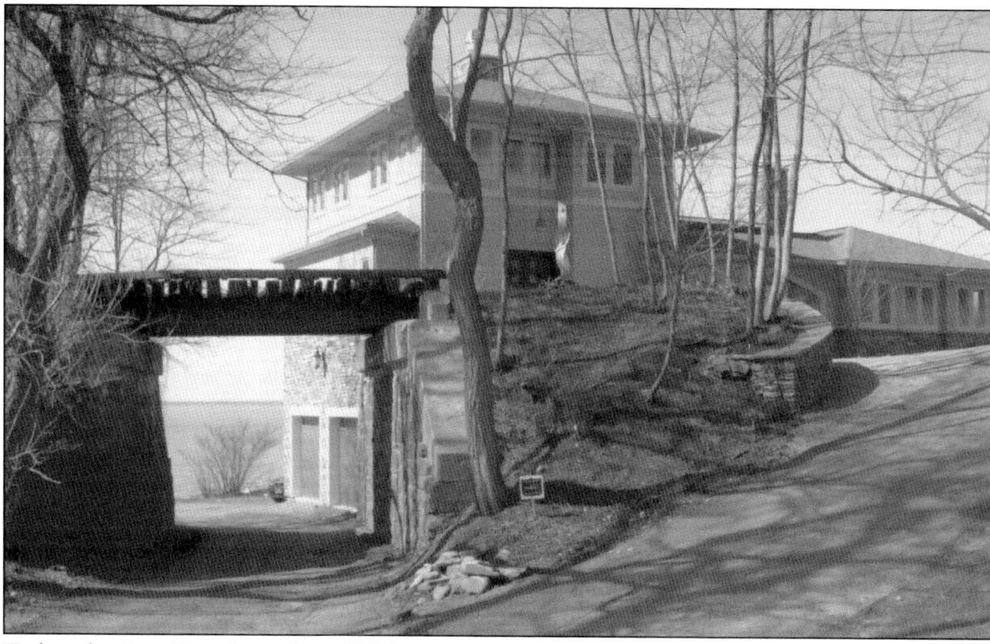

Today, the East Hojack track at Oklahoma Beach is gone, but this wooden trestle remains as a reminder of where the trains once ran. In this recent photograph, note that the original embankment seems to be part of the homeowner's landscaping. (Author's collection.)

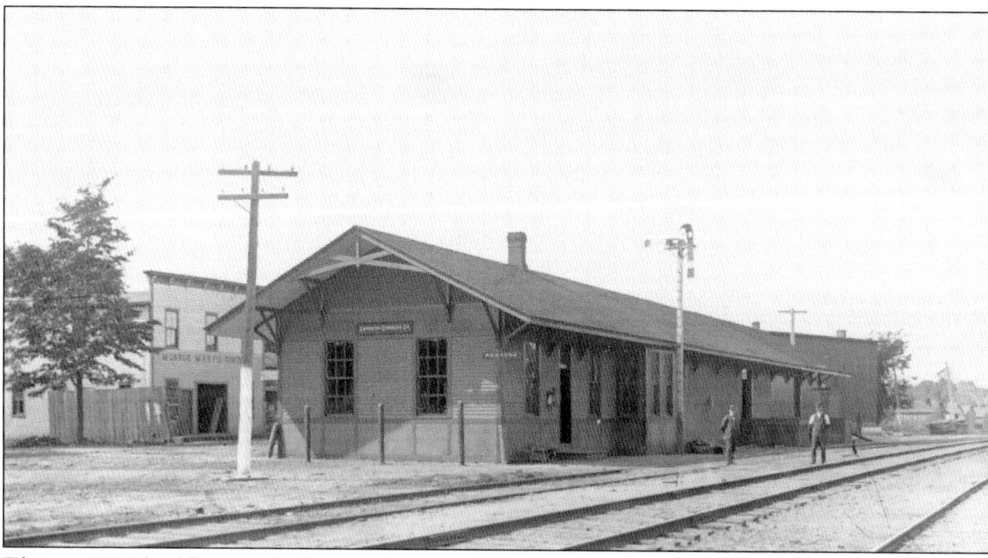

This c. 1900 building with the overhanging eaves and decorative brackets served as the East Hojack passenger depot and freight house for both the town and the village of Webster and probably the town of Penfield to the south as well. In the mid-1920s, fire destroyed the passenger depot, but the freight house portion survived with only partial damage. Shortly after the fire, funding was received to build a new depot and repair the freight house. By the 1940s, the depot had been moved to a location just east of the original site. With the Hojack no longer offering passenger service, the depot closed its doors in the mid-1960s, and in the mid-1970s it was home to the Hojack Restaurant. Today, the former depot serves as a day care center. (Courtesy of Town of Webster historian.)

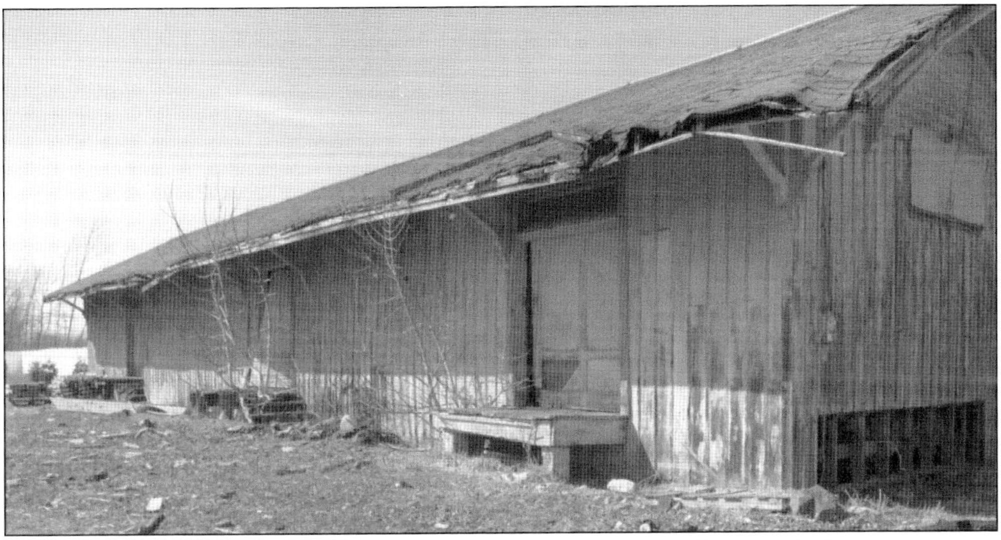

The East Hojack freight house in Webster was not moved. It was badly in need of repair, as seen in this recent photograph, and there were plans to take it down and build an apartment complex on the site. As with the Charlotte Swing Bridge, saving a historic structure like the Webster freight house was important to some residents. A local construction group has agreed to dismantle and store the structure until it can be rebuilt at a different site. (Author's collection.)

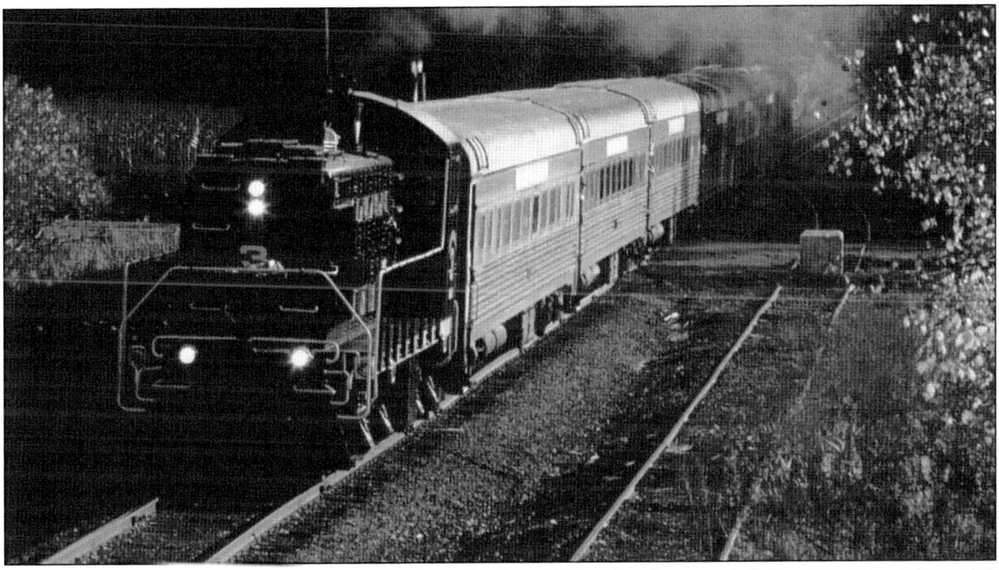

With Conrail abandoning the East Hojack in the late 1970s, the Ontario Midland Railroad (OMID) took over the line from Webster east to Wallington and Wolcott in Wayne County, providing service to well-known companies such as Xerox Corporation and the former Duffy-Mott facility. OMID also took possession of the former PRR line from Wallington to Newark where it joins the CSX (former NYC) main line. OMID took advantage of the beautiful countryside along its tracks and ran popular fall foliage excursions. The photograph shows one such trip in 2001 with a former Pittsburgh & Lake Erie Alco S-4 diesel powering the train near Quarry Road south of Wallington. As an aside, NYC had a controlling interest in the P&LE, and it was thus considered part of the New York Central System. It provided NYC with access to one of the richest steel-producing areas in the world. (Courtesy of Duncan Richards.)

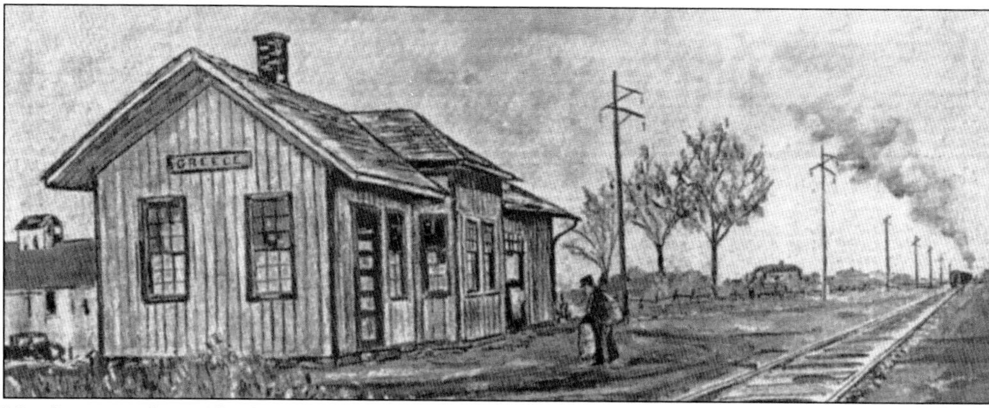

Heading west from Charlotte rather than crossing the Genesee River on the swing bridge brought the Hojack to the town of Greece. Shown in this sketch is the West Hojack's North Greece depot as it appeared in the early 1900s. Note the stationmaster carrying the mail from the train that has just departed. (Sketch by William Aeberli, courtesy of Alan Mueller.)

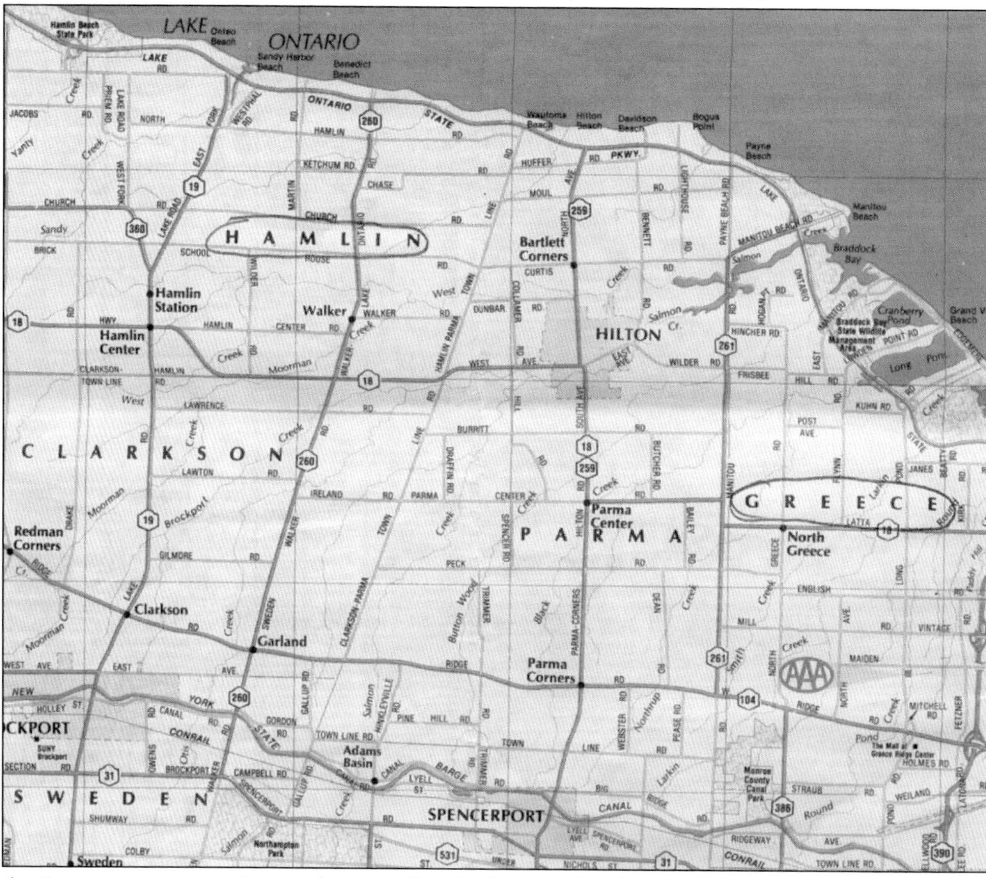

An important perspective can be gained by looking at this Automobile Association of America (AAA) map of the area. The town of Greece as well as the towns of Parma and Hamlin is highlighted. Also, it should be noted that beaches of Lake Ontario, shown in the upper portion of the map, were accessible by electric streetcar lines (discussed in chapter 6). (Map provided by AAA.)

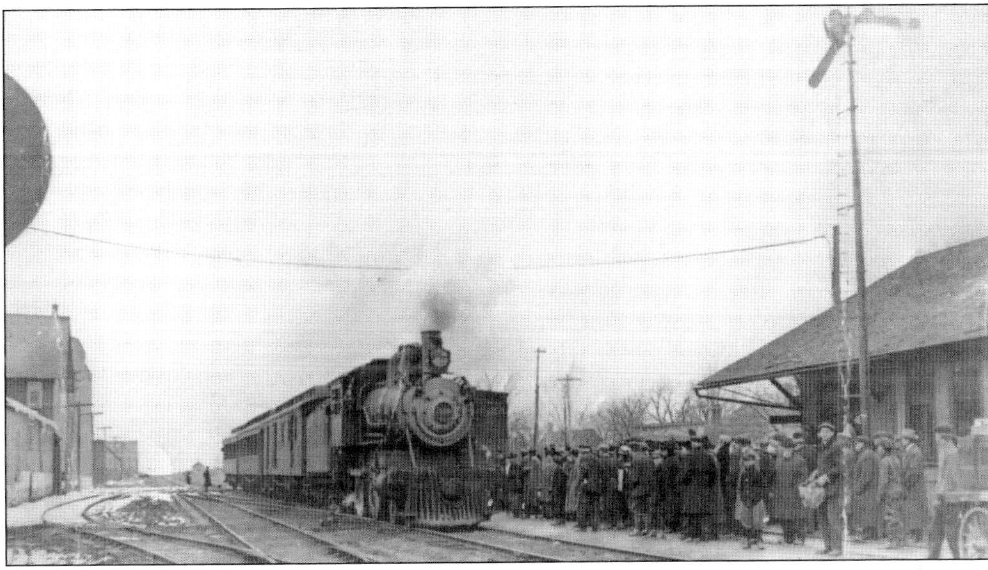

In 1914, the West Hojack brought Ernest Crabill, a well-known evangelist, to the town of Parma. In this photograph, the crowd at the depot in the village of Hilton has gathered to bid farewell to the evangelist and his wife after a successful stay in the area. (Courtesy of *Rochester Images*: Village of Hilton, New York.)

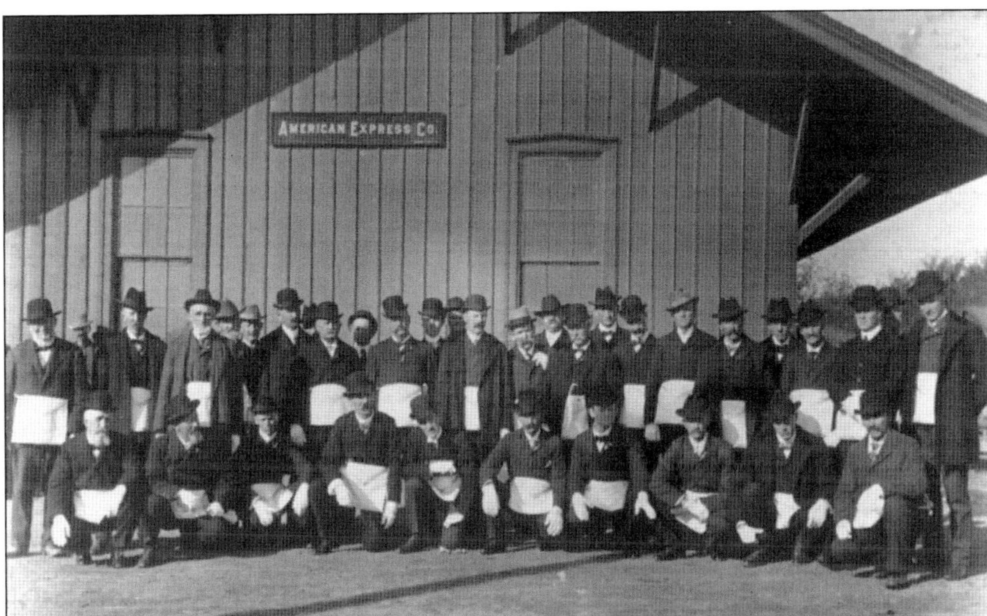

The West Hojack also enabled travel outside the area. In 1901, this group of Freemasons poses in front of the Hilton depot before boarding a train to view the new Masonic temple in Rochester. Increased popularity of the automobile, however, led to the end of passenger service on the West Hojack in 1933. (Courtesy of *Rochester Images*: Village of Hilton, New York.)

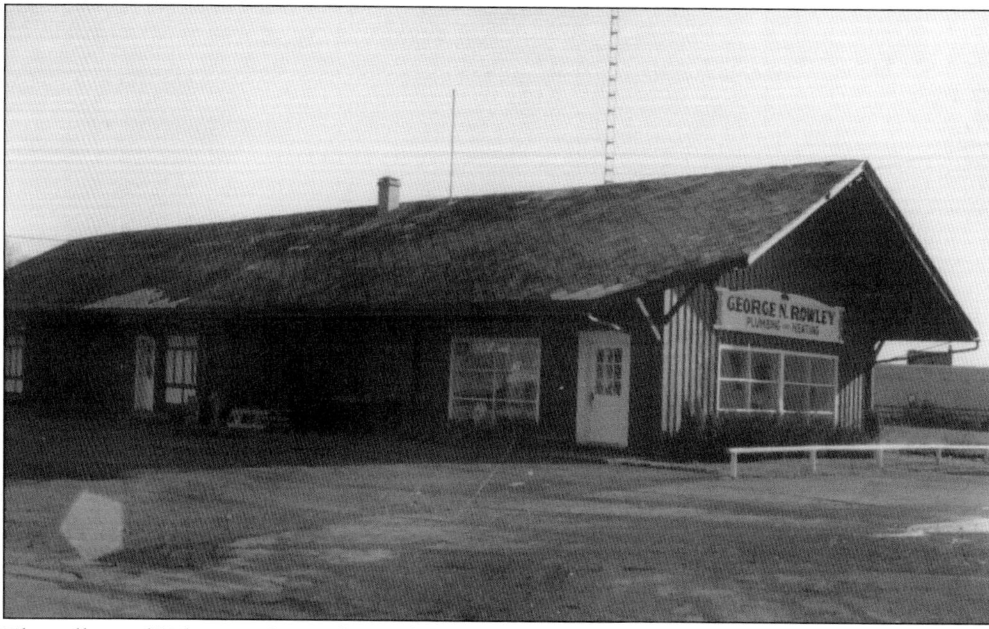

The village of Hilton made good use of the former West Hojack depot. The photograph shows Rowley's Hardware and Heating Store, which operated in the depot building from 1962 to 1973. (Courtesy of *Rochester Images*: Village of Hilton, New York.)

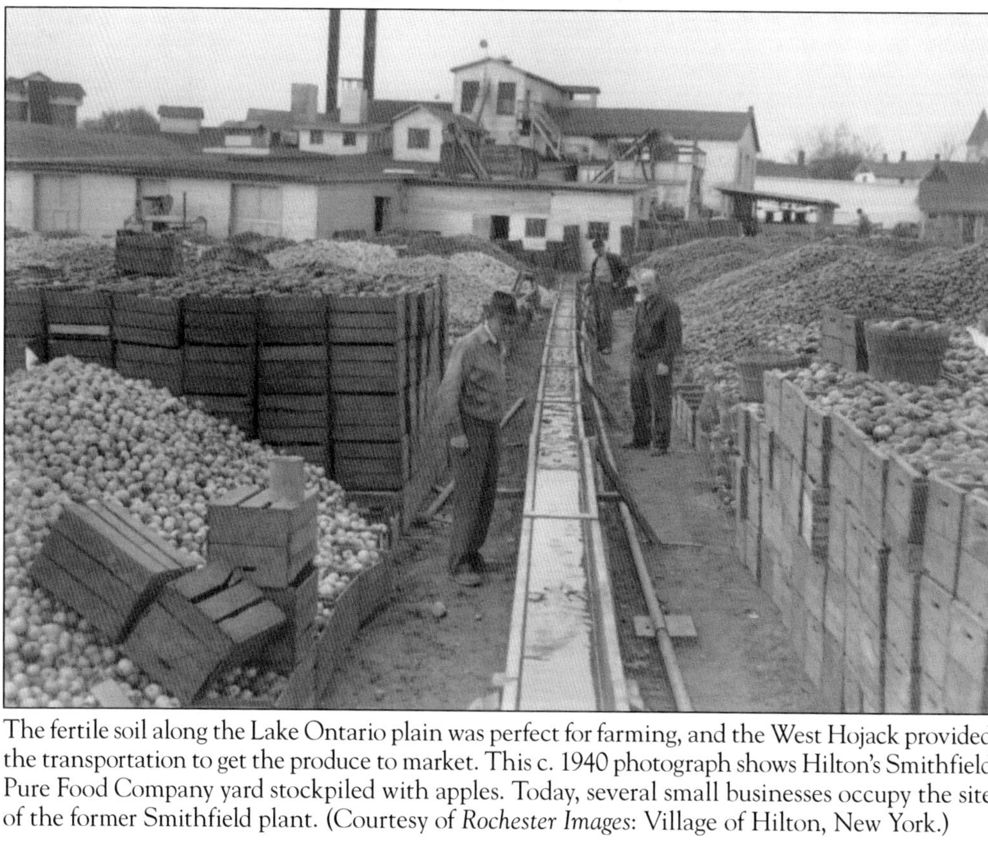

The fertile soil along the Lake Ontario plain was perfect for farming, and the West Hojack provided the transportation to get the produce to market. This c. 1940 photograph shows Hilton's Smithfield Pure Food Company yard stockpiled with apples. Today, several small businesses occupy the site of the former Smithfield plant. (Courtesy of *Rochester Images*: Village of Hilton, New York.)

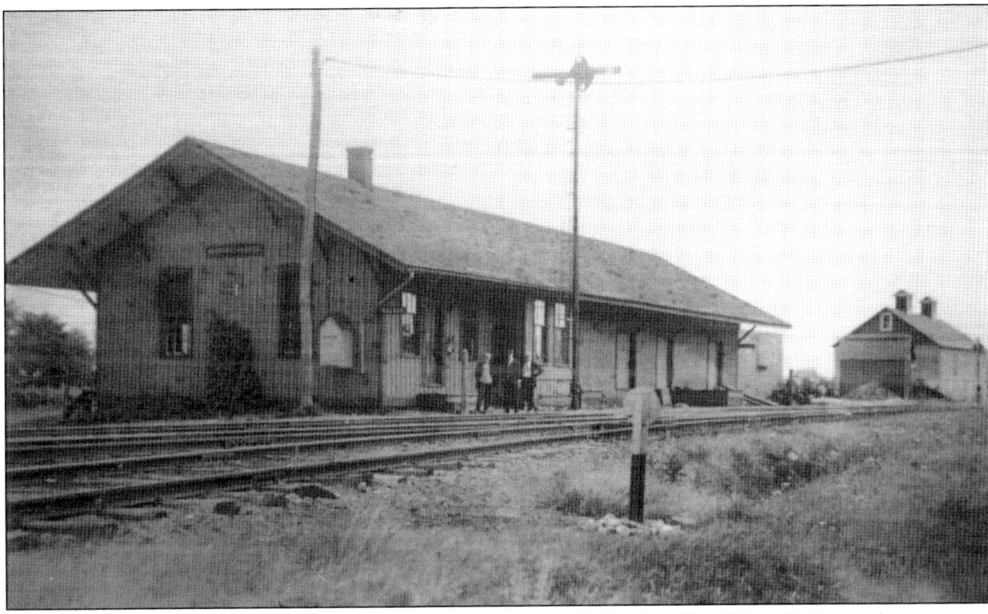

Just west of Hilton is the hamlet of Walker (town of Hamlin). The West Hojack depot that serviced Walker was built around 1875 and is shown in this c. 1900 photograph. (Courtesy of *Rochester Images*: Hamlin Municipal Historian Collection.)

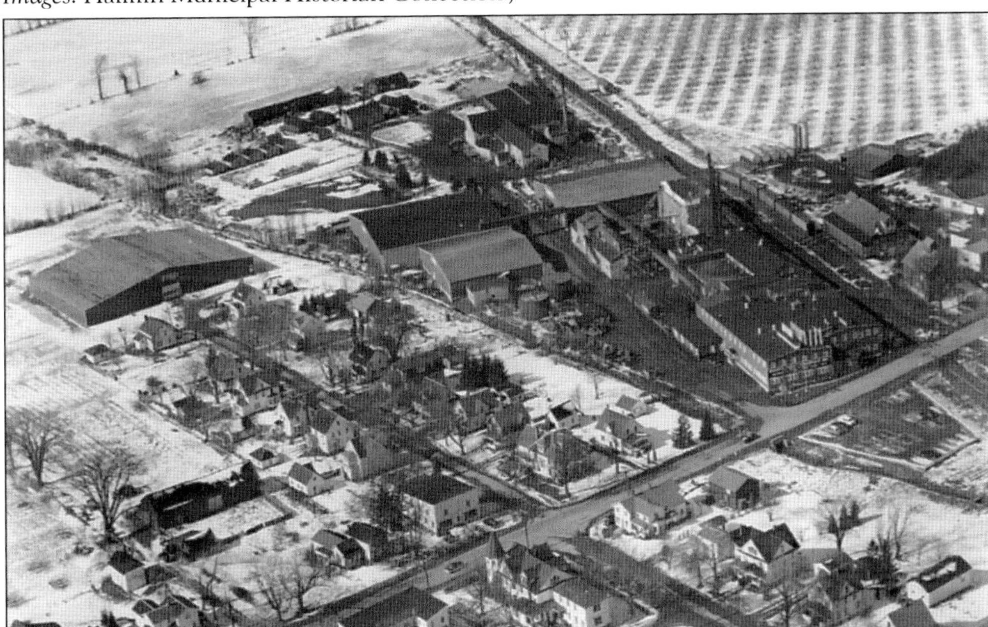

The hamlet of Hamlin Station (town of Hamlin) is a few miles west of Walker. Like Hilton, it was home to apple growers and fruit processors. The Duffy-Mott Company facility opened here in 1900 and is shown in this 1950s aerial photograph. Note the West Hojack tracks that serviced Duffy-Mott next to the plant. The Duffy-Mott plant closed in the mid-1970s. (Courtesy of *Rochester Images*: Hamlin Municipal Historian Collection.)

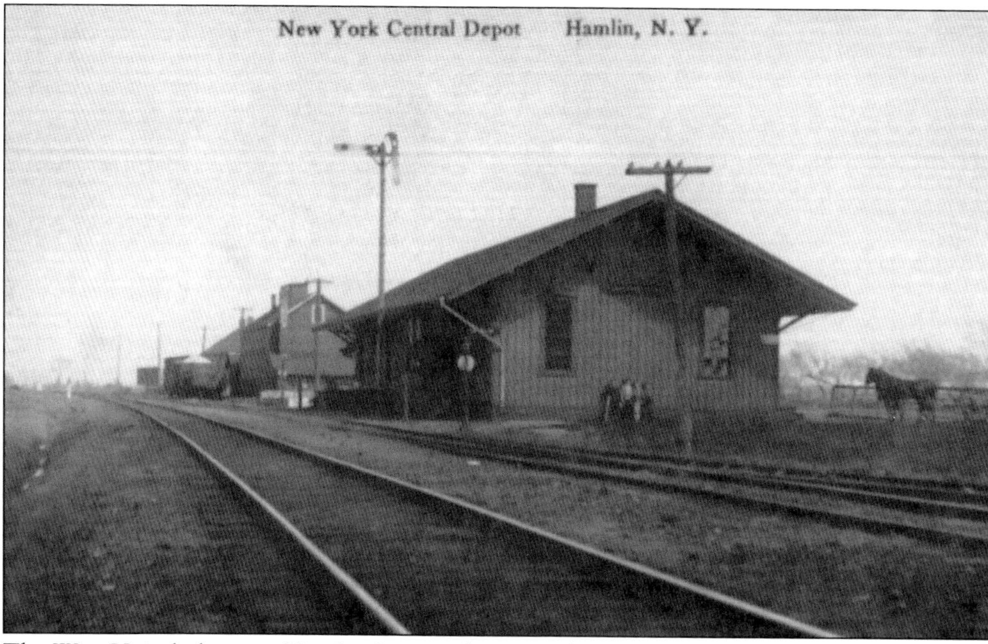

The West Hojack depot in Hamlin Station shown in this c. 1906 photograph was built in 1875. After passenger service on the West Hojack ended in 1933, the building was used as a courthouse, antique store, church, and then a day care center. (Courtesy of *Rochester Images*: Hamlin Municipal Historian Collection.)

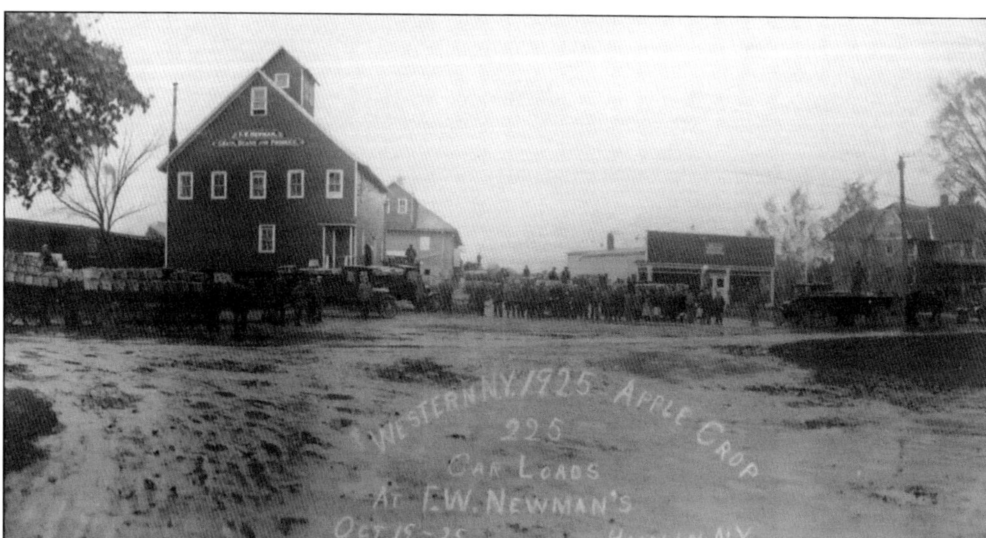

Near the West Hojack tracks in Hamlin Station, the F.W. Newman Produce Company operated the apple shipping facility shown in this 1925 photograph. Note both the horse-drawn carts and flatbed trucks filled with apples as well as the NYC boxcars on the siding ready to take the produce to market. (Courtesy of *Rochester Images*: Hamlin Municipal Historian Collection.)

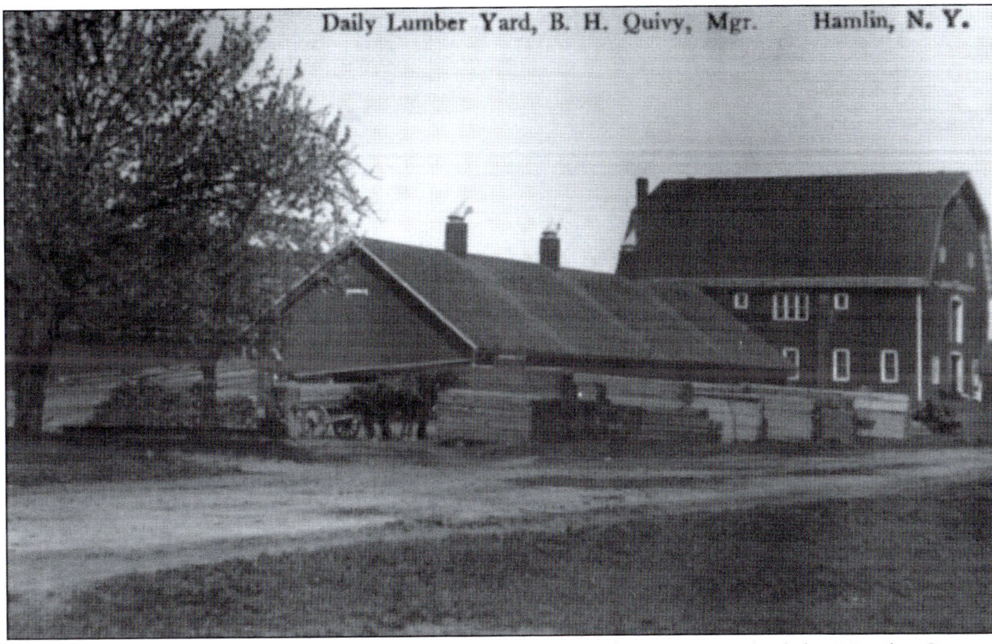

The Daily Lumber Yard, shown in this c. 1910 photograph, was typical of the Hamlin Station businesses that sprang up along the West Hojack. (Courtesy of *Rochester Images*: Hamlin Municipal Historian Collection.)

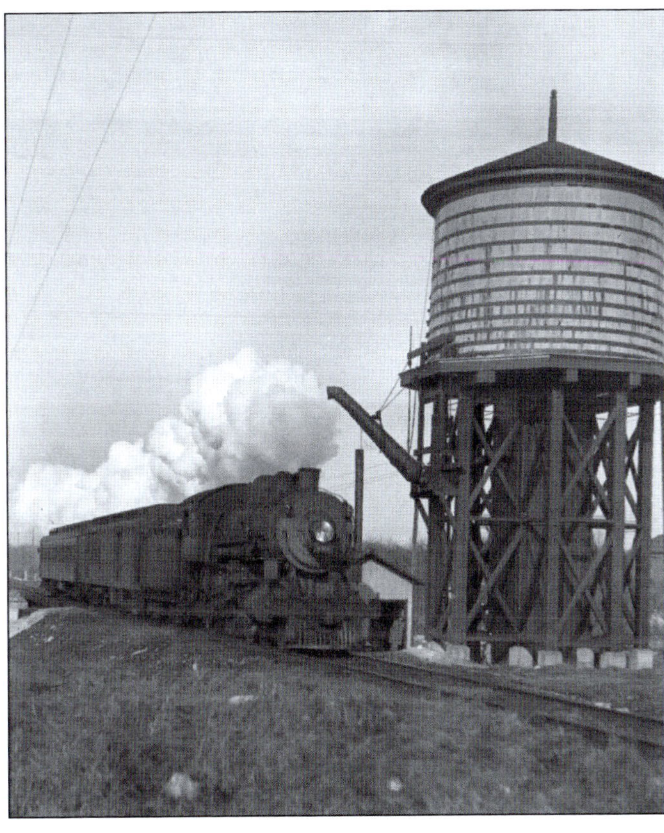

In this 1925 photograph, a two-car West Hojack passenger train, with a class F-12g 10-wheeler on the headend, stopped for water at the Sandy Creek water tower west of Hamlin Station. Note the pumping station for the tower in the background. (Courtesy of *Rochester Images*: Hamlin Municipal Historian Collection.)

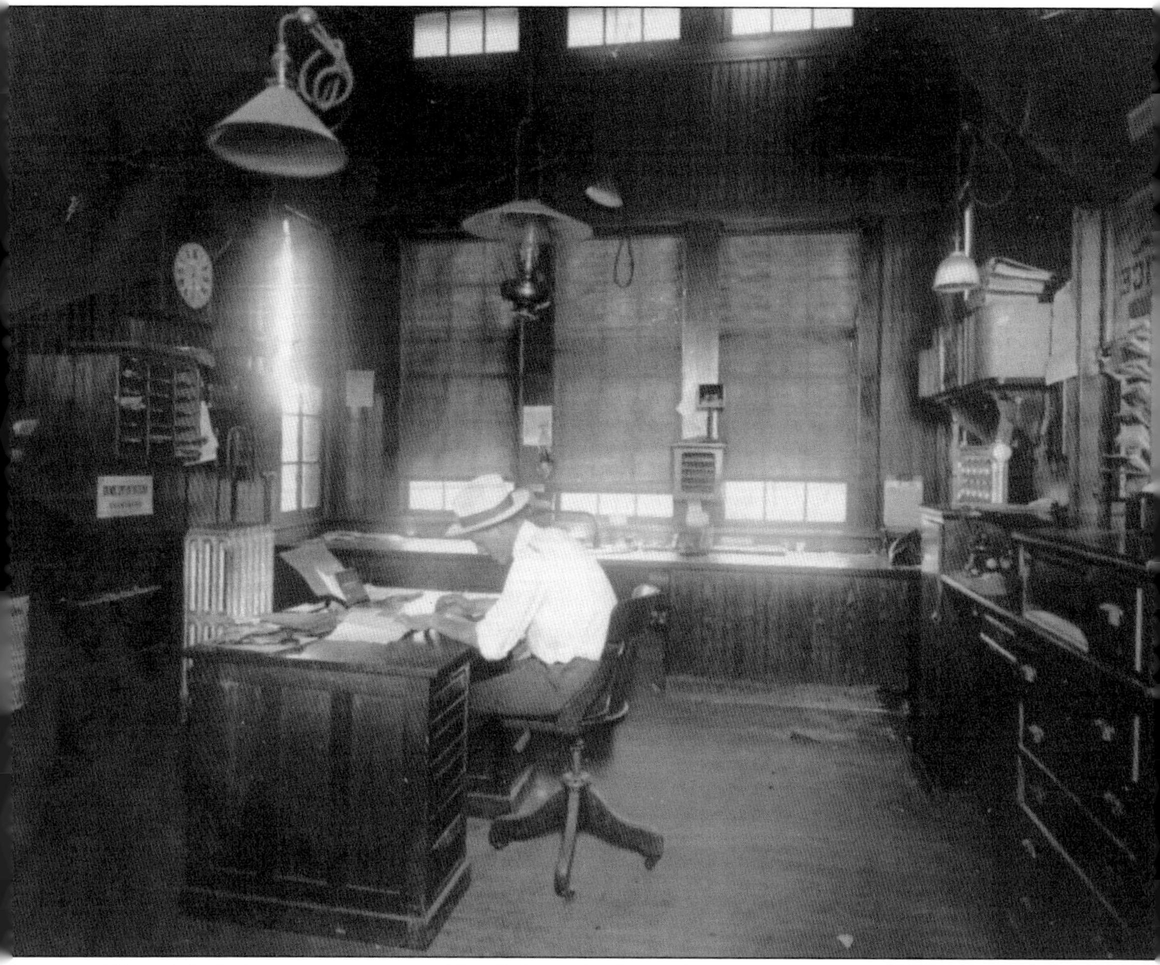

The Hojack depots were manned by dedicated telegraph operators such as William Burchfield, shown in this c. 1917 photograph inside the Morton depot. Morton is a hamlet just west of Hamlin Station on the Monroe County–Orleans County line. This depot was built around 1911, replacing the 1897 depot that serviced Morton until it was destroyed by fire. Note the signs hanging on the wall. One details the office rules, while the other warns of spitting on the floor. (Courtesy of *Rochester Images*: Hamlin Municipal Historian Collection.)

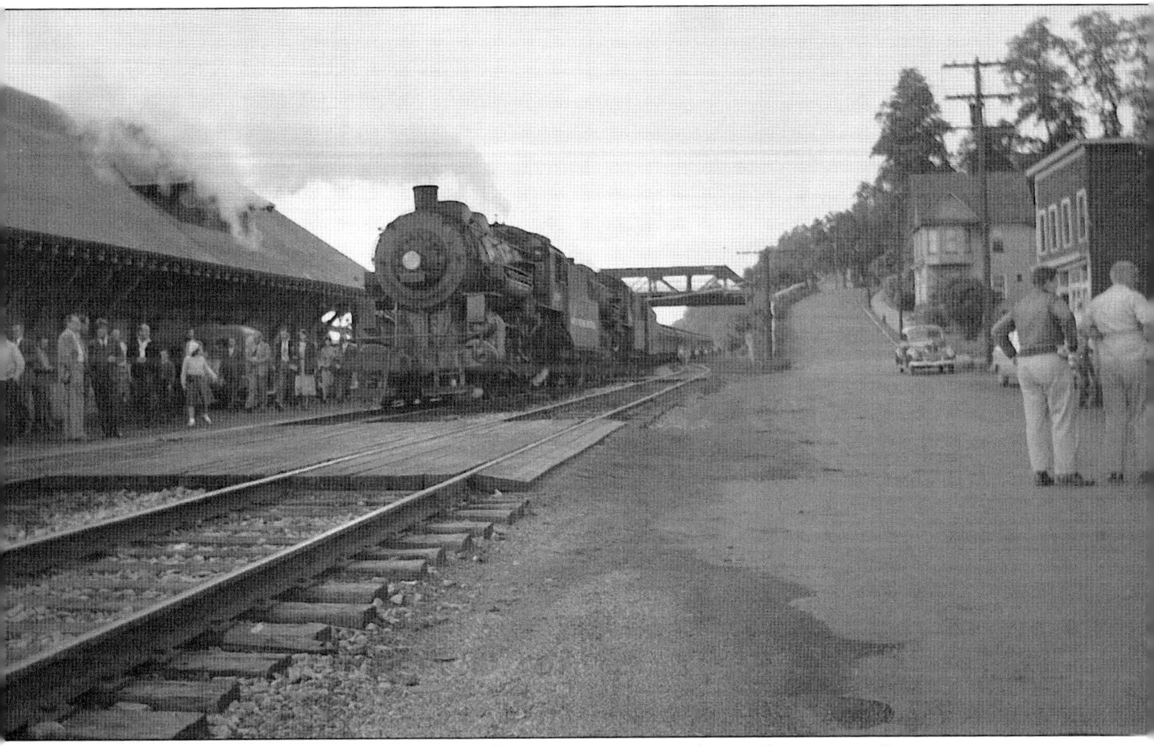

With passenger service ending in 1933, fan trips were popular with train enthusiasts as a way to view the West Hojack. This photograph shows a 1950 excursion powered by two class F-12g 10-wheelers. Railfans are gathered at the Charlotte depot looking well dressed and pleased about the trip that will take them into northwest Monroe County and then west into Orleans County and then into Niagara County. (Photograph by Robert Gerling, courtesy of Jeff Hands.)

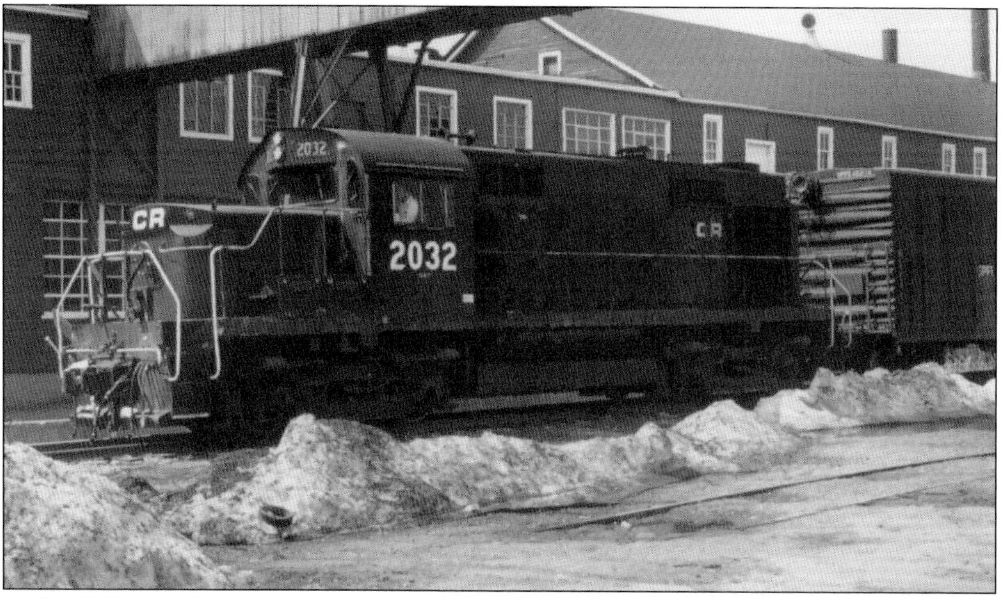

In the 1950s, diesel power replaced steam power for freight service on the West Hojack. There were other changes. With larger trucks and improved roadways, demand for service on the West Hojack declined. By this time, Conrail was in charge of freight service throughout the Northeast. Powered by a former NYC Alco RS-32 diesel road-switcher, the last freight train ran on the West Hojack in 1978. The train is shown here at the Duffy-Mott plant in Hamlin Station that was no longer in operation. (Courtesy of *Rochester Images*: Hamlin Municipal Historian Collection.)

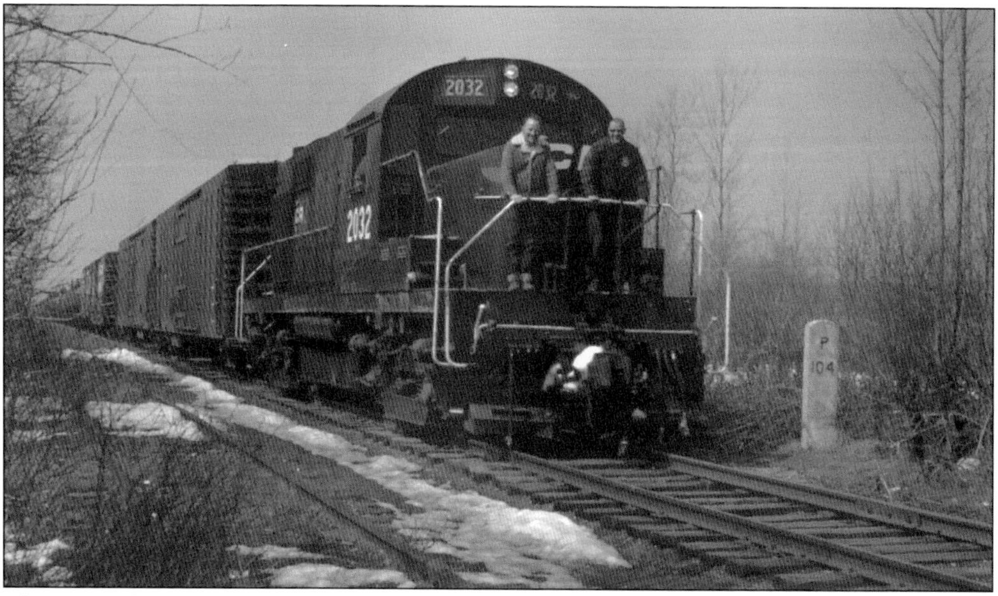

This 1978 photograph again shows the last freight train on the West Hojack. The Conrail engine is the same former NYC Alco RS-32, but now the location is the village of Hilton, and as the milepost says, some 100 miles west of Pulaski in Oswego County. The trainmen appear willing to cooperate with the photographer, but their feelings must be bittersweet. The track bed in the photograph is now the Old Hojack Lane, with the milepost still in place. (Courtesy of Duncan Richards.)

Four

Railroads of the Genesee River Valley

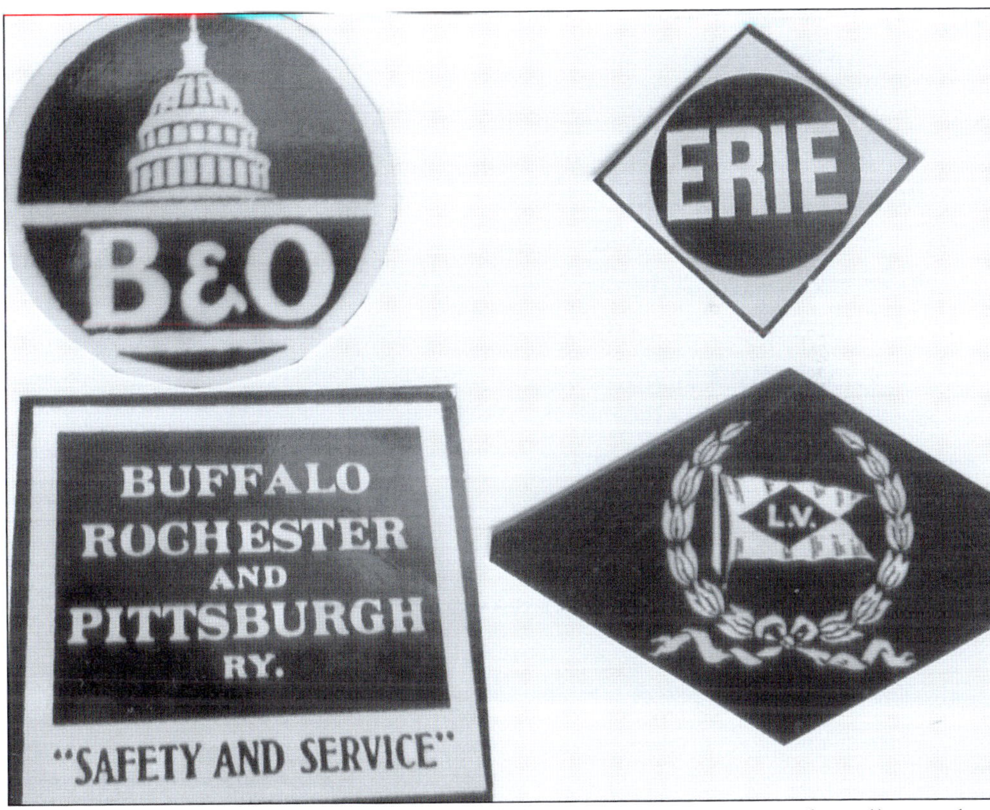

Branch lines of several major railroads served the many communities in the valley south of Rochester where the Genesee River flows northward from Pennsylvania. The recognizable logos of the railroads are shown here. (Author's collection.)

Rochester & State Line Railway

TIME TABLE No. 6.

To take effect Monday, Oct. 8th, 1877.

	EASTWARD.				WESTWARD.			
Dist. from Rochester.	1 Ex-press.	3 Fr'ght &Pass.	5 Ex-press.	NAMES OF STATIONS AND PASSING PLACES.	2 Ex-press.	4 Fr'ght and Pass.	6 Ex-press.	Dist. btw. Stations.
Mls.	A.M.	P.M.	P.M.	*Arr. Leav.*	A.M.	A.M.	P.M.	Ms.
	9.30	3.45	6.35	..Rochester..	7.55	10.30	5.35	
1.25	*9.27	*3.40	*6.32	Lincoln Park	*7.58	*10.35	*5.38	1 25
4.81	*9.18	*3.25	*6 23	.Maplewood.	*8.08	*10.50	*5.48	3.56
7.06	*9.12	*3.15	*6.18	..Brookdale..	*8.15	*10.58	*5 55	2.25
9.44	*9.06	*3.05	*6.12	.Willowvale.	*8.21	*11.08	*6.01	2.38
11.40	9.00	2.58	†6.07	..Scottsville..	8.27	11.17	†6.07	1.96
13.60	8.53	2.48	6.00	Garbuttsville	8.33	11.25	6.14	2.20
15.31	*8.49	*2.42	*5.55	..Wheatland..	*8.38	*11.33	*6.19	1.71
17.01	†8 44	2.35	5 48	...Mumford..	†8.44	11.40	6.23	1.70
20.99	*8.33	*2.18	*5.36	..LimeRock..	*8.53	*11.57	*6.35	3.98
						P.M.		
24.10	8.28	2.07	5 28	...Junction...	9.05	12.09	6.43	3.11
24.53	8.23	2.03	5.25	....LeRoy....	9.07	12.11	6.46	0.43
30.14	8.07	1.38	5.08	Pavilion Cen.	9.22	12.37	7.03	5.61
32.37	8.00	1.30	5.03	...Pavilion...	9.28	12.45	7.09	2.23
34.84	7.53	1.20	4.54	.Pearl Creek.	9.35	12.56	7.17	2.47
37.57	7.46	†1.07	4.47	..Wyoming...	9.43	†1.07	7.25	2.73
43.08	7.30	12.45	4.30	...Warsaw...	9.58	1.30	7.40	5.51
47.55	7.17	12.27	4.18	..Rock Glen..	10.12	1.50	7.53	4.47
		P.M.						
50.35	7.10	12.15	4.10	E.Gainesville	10.20	2.00	8.00	2.80
53.59	7.00	12.00	4.00	.Gainesville..	10.3[illegible]	2.15	8.10	3.24
	A.M.	M.	P.M.		A.M.	P.M.	P.M.	

Completed in the late 1870s, the Rochester and State Line Railroad provided an efficient means of transporting farm products from the Genesee Valley to Rochester. As shown in this advertisement, the R&SL also ran passenger service south to Salamanca in Cattaraugus County with stops in Scottsville, Wheatland, Garbutt, and Mumford, all in the town of Wheatland south of Rochester. In the late 1880s, consolidations brought the R&SL into the BR&P fold, and in the 1930s, both were part of the B&O. (Courtesy of Town of Wheatland historian.)

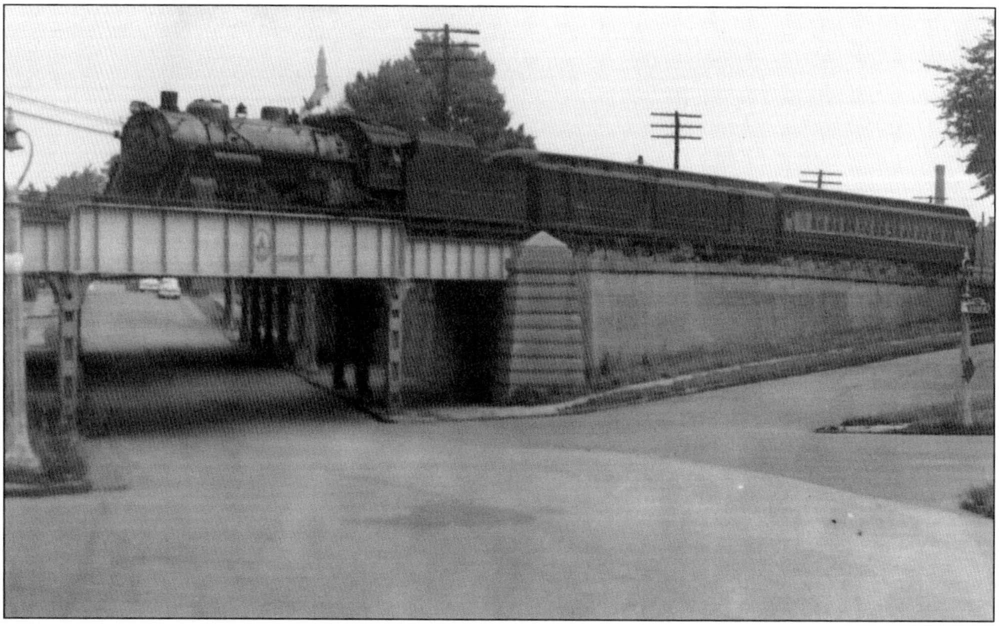

With the decline in ridership, a B&O passenger train with a 4-6-2 Class P-5a Pacific, one baggage car, and one coach is shown in this 1953 photograph at Rochester's Brown Street. It is on its way to Salamanca in Cattaraugus County and the connection south to the main line at Pittsburgh. It should be noted that B&O decided to end passenger service to Rochester a short time after this photograph was taken. (Courtesy of *Rochester Images*: Rochester Library Local History Division.)

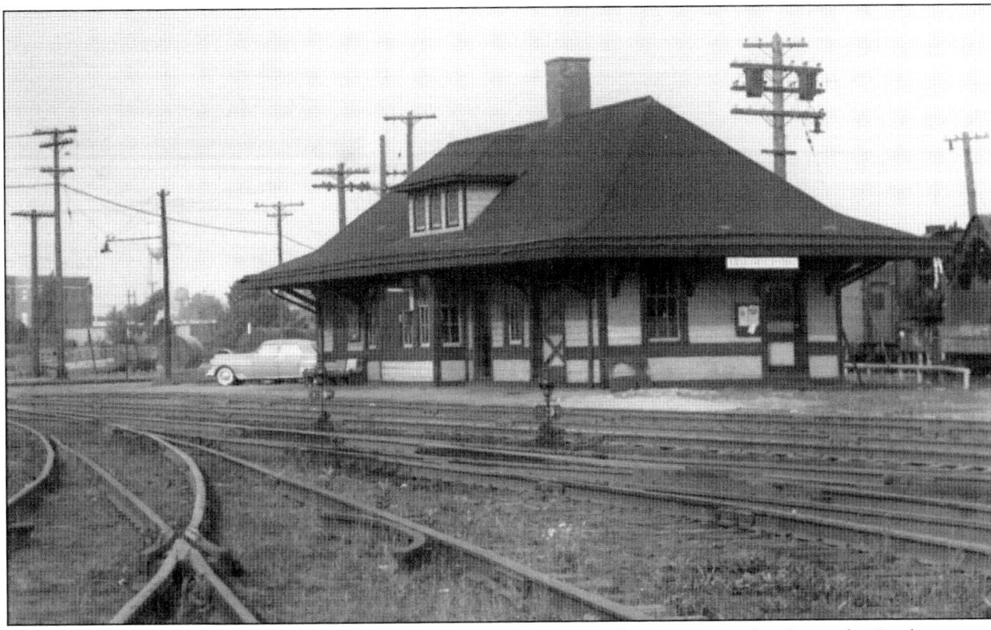

After departing the Rochester B&O depot, the train made a stop at the Lincoln Park station at West and Lincoln Avenues. The depot appears to be in fine shape in this 1940s photograph. Today, the Lincoln Park depot is gone, but the location remains a railroad interchange, this time between CSX and the Rochester & Southern Railroad (RSR). The latter uses much of the former B&O line in the Rochester/Monroe County area. (Courtesy of *Rochester Images*: Rochester Library Local History Division.)

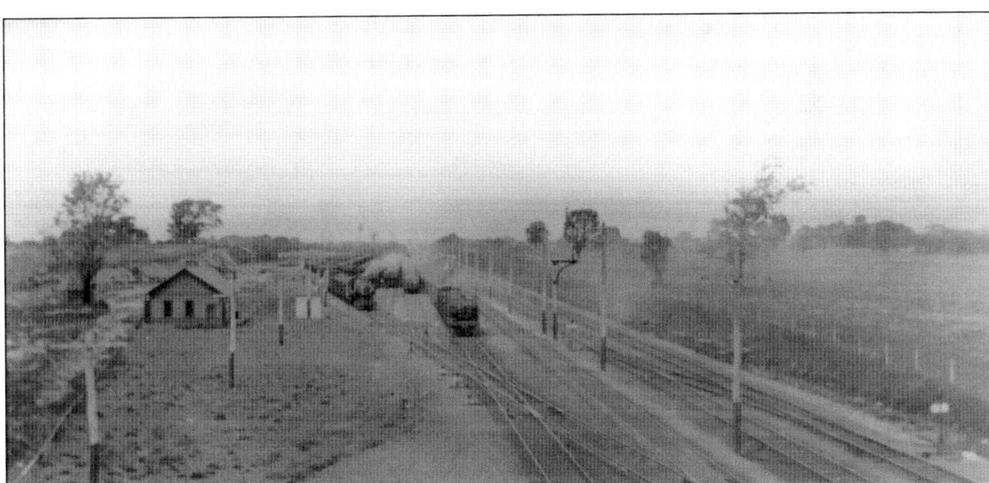

Built in 1913, the Brooks Avenue Yard, southwest of downtown Rochester in the town of Gates, was an important freight yard for the BR&P and its successor, the B&O. This c. 1916 photograph, with a view looking north, shows a busy BR&P yard. (Courtesy of *Rochester Images*: Rochester Library Local History Division.)

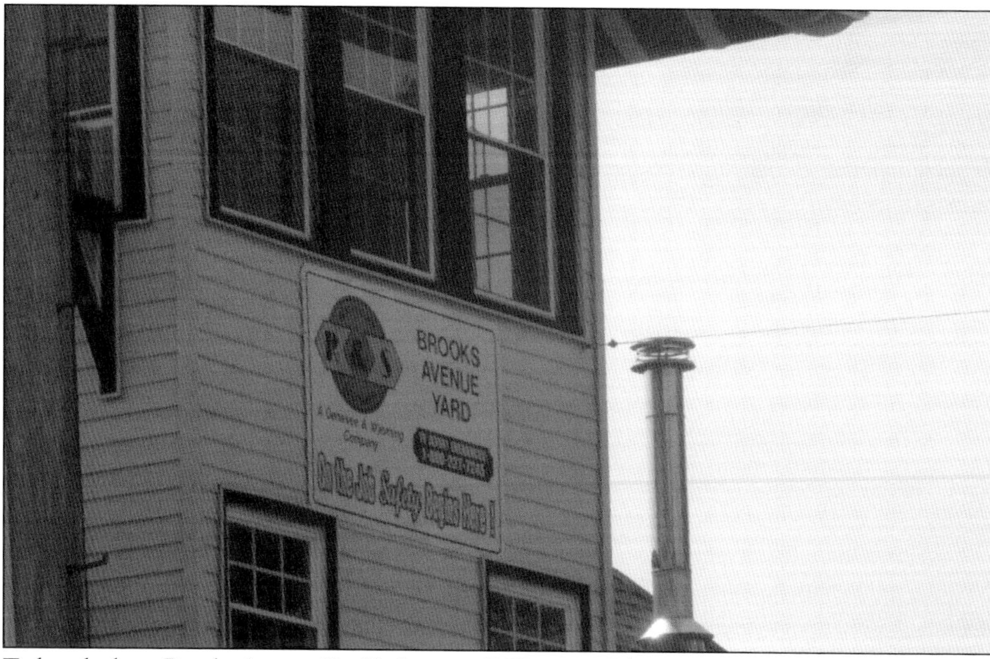

Today, the busy Brooks Avenue Yard belongs to RSR, part of the Genesee & Wyoming group. One of RSR's revenue producers has been hauling salt used for ice-melting products from the mines in Livingston County, about 25 miles southwest of Rochester. Not surprisingly, freights with covered hopper cars loaded with salt have been referred to as "saltshakers." (Author's collection.)

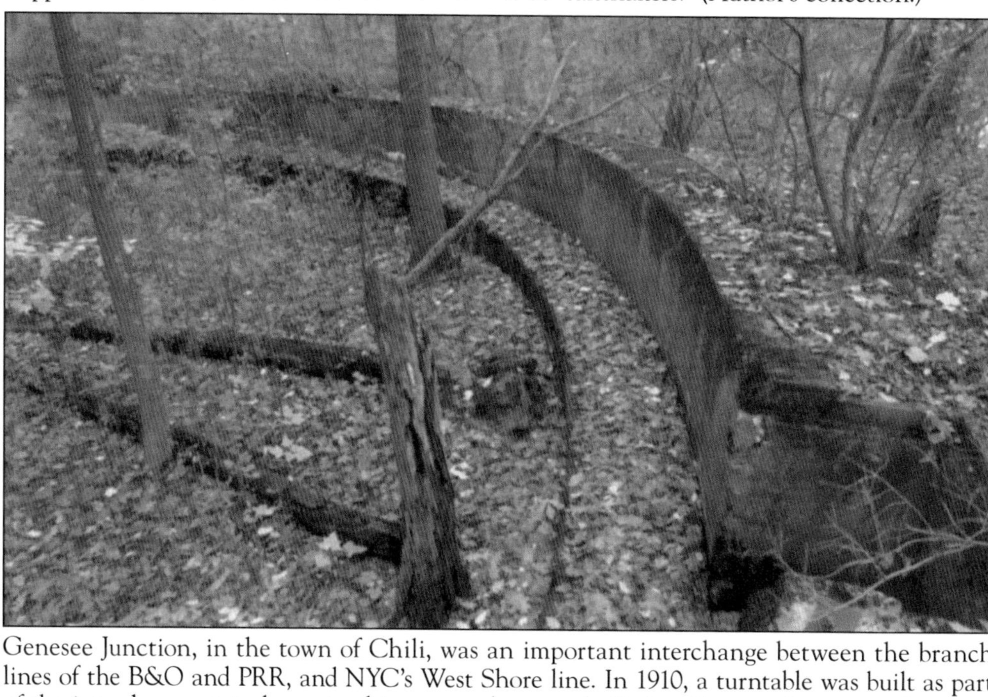

Genesee Junction, in the town of Chili, was an important interchange between the branch lines of the B&O and PRR, and NYC's West Shore line. In 1910, a turntable was built as part of the interchange; it is shown in this recent photograph. Today, Genesee Junction is home to the interchange between the RSR, CSX, and Livonia, Avon & Lakeville (LAL). (Courtesy of Scot Lawrence.)

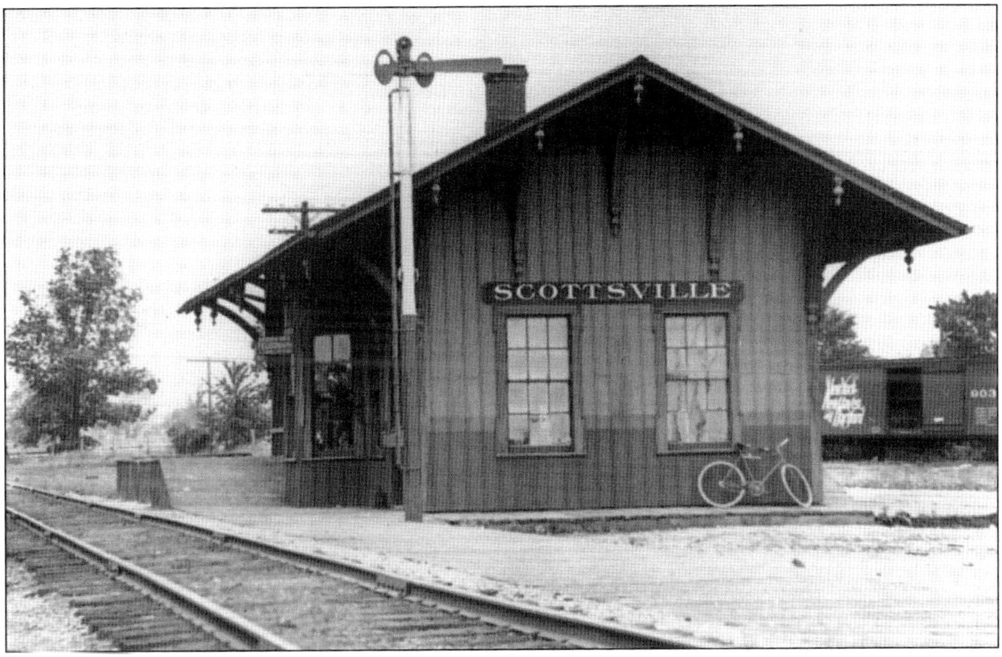

Serving the village of Scottsville in the town of Wheatland was this late-1800s frame depot. Note the boxcar sitting on the siding with the historic logo of the New York, New Haven & Hartford Railroad (NH). NH was included in the 1968 NYC/PRR merger that formed the Penn Central. (Courtesy of Town of Wheatland historian.)

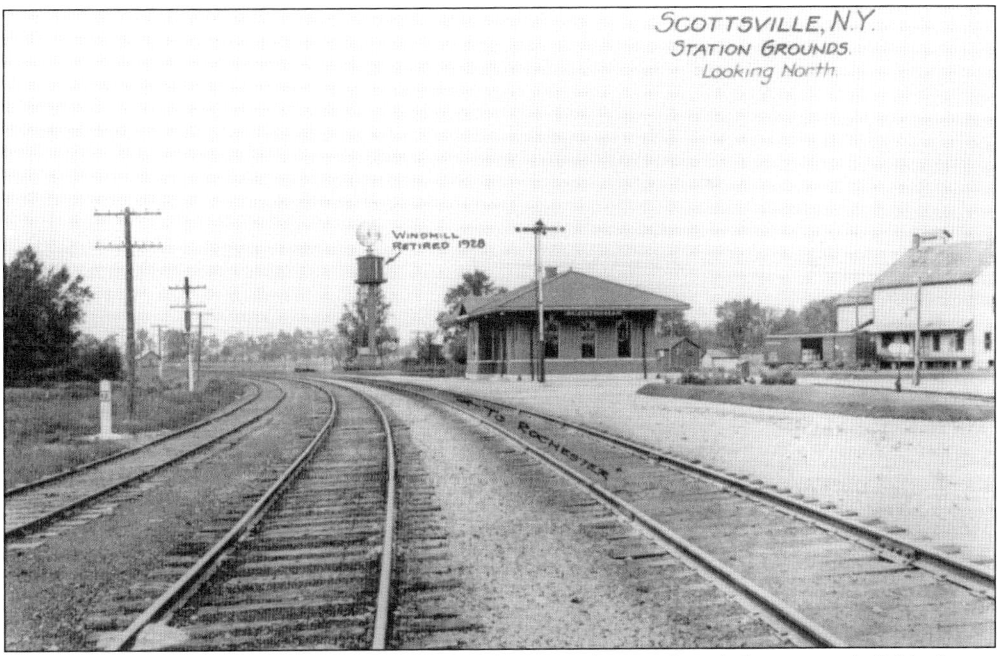

This 1920s photograph shows the BR&P brick depot that replaced the original 1800s frame structure in Scottsville. Many coal trains headed for the coal docks at Charlotte passed by this depot. The building remains, but it is no longer used as a depot. (Courtesy of Town of Wheatland historian.)

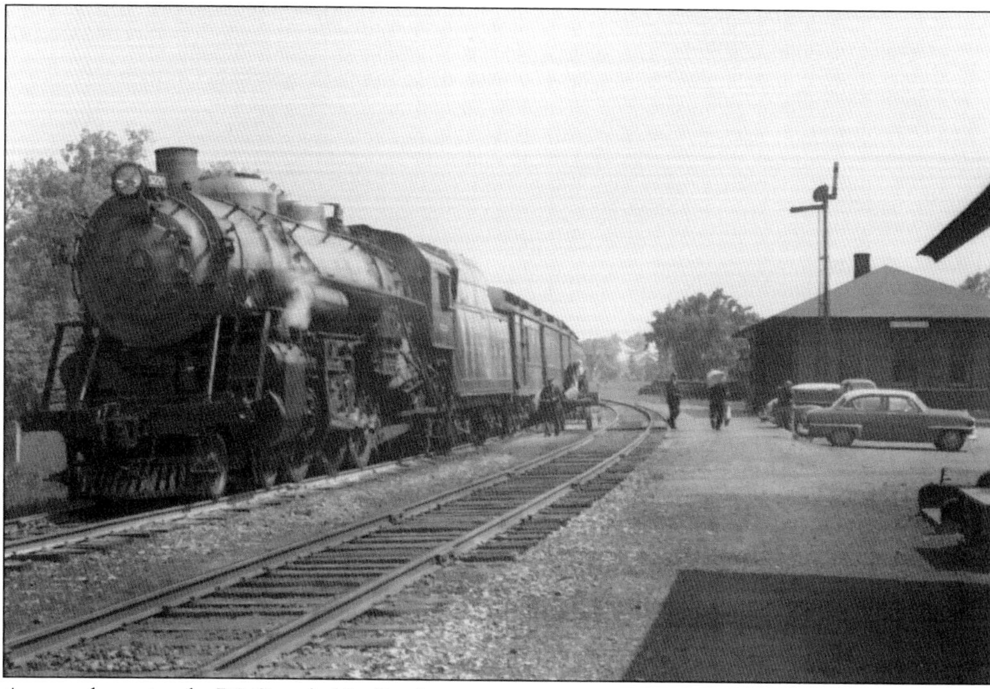

As noted previously, B&O ended its Rochester passenger service in 1953. In this photograph, the last B&O passenger train from Rochester is shown arriving in Scottsville. Again, a 4-6-2 class P-5a Pacific is on the headend. (Courtesy of Town of Wheatland historian.)

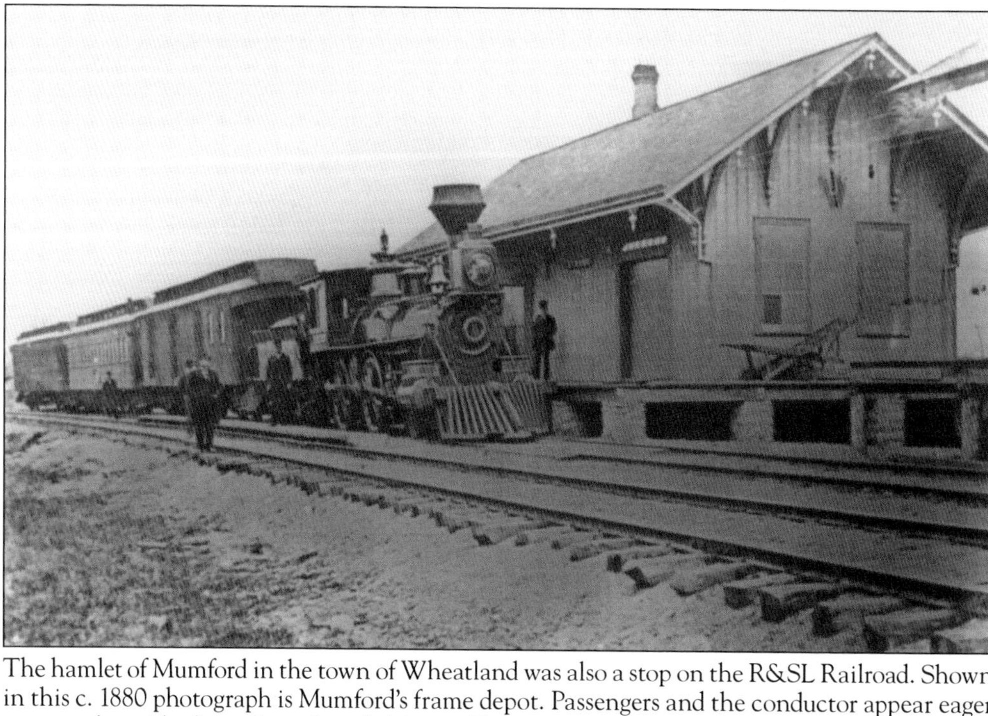

The hamlet of Mumford in the town of Wheatland was also a stop on the R&SL Railroad. Shown in this c. 1880 photograph is Mumford's frame depot. Passengers and the conductor appear eager to pose alongside the train and its 4-4-0 wood-burning steam locomotive. (Courtesy of Town of Wheatland historian.)

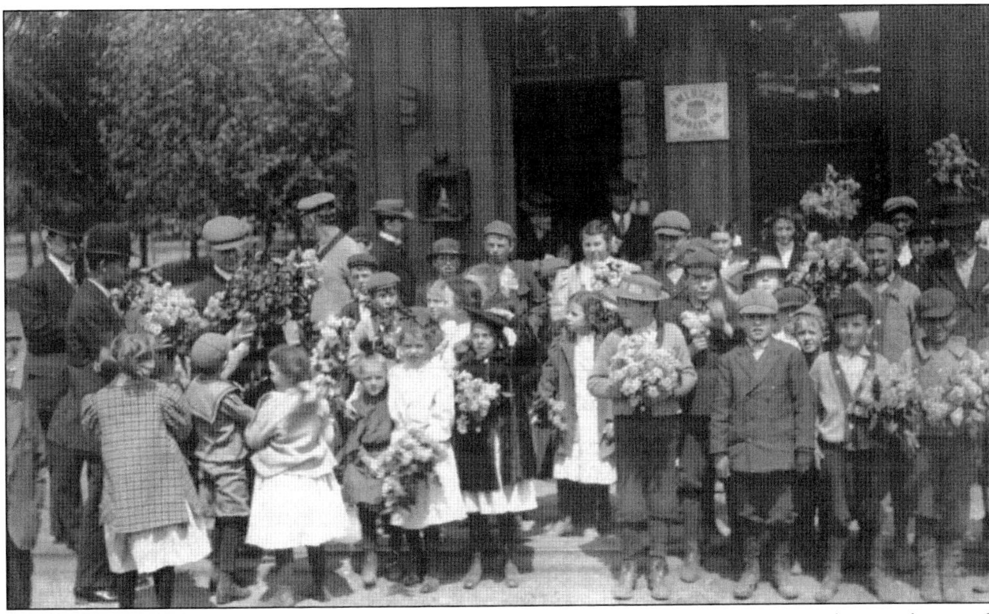

Mumford schoolchildren in this photograph appear to be a happy bunch as they gather with flowers at the depot on Arbor Day around 1900. (Courtesy of Town of Wheatland historian.)

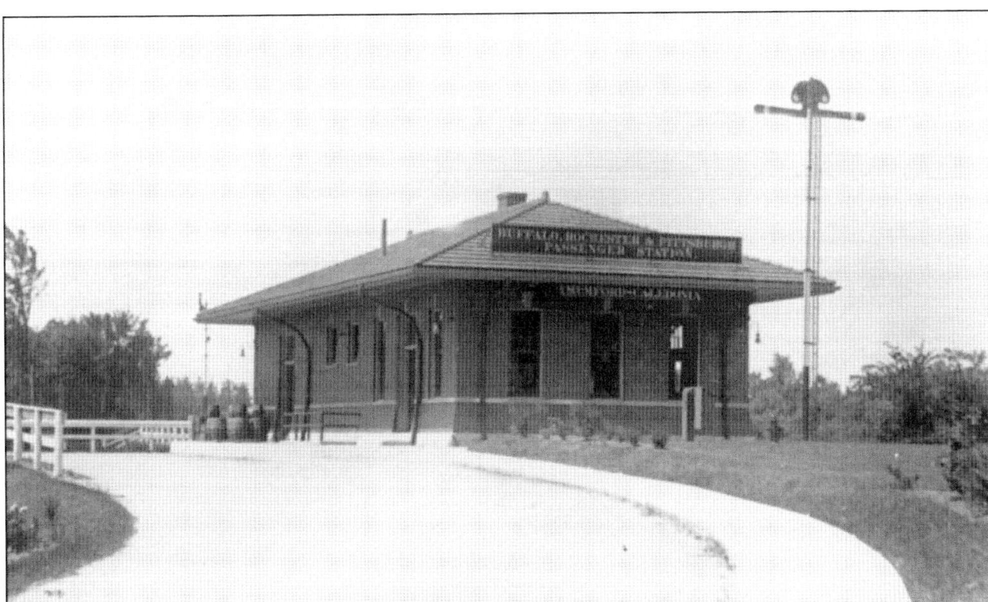

The BR&P replaced the original frame structure in Mumford with this 1911 brick depot. The depot remains today, but it is used for other purposes. (Courtesy of Town of Wheatland historian.)

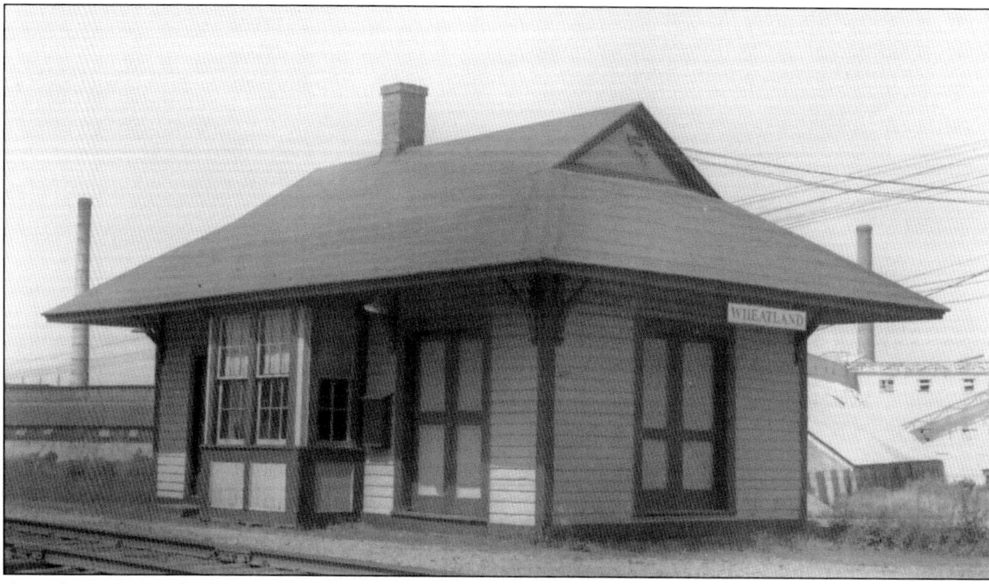

Another stop on the BR&P/B&O branch line was the hamlet of Garbutt in the town of Wheatland. The Garbutt depot was a busy place in the late 1800s. The gypsum that was mined in Garbutt was used for building construction, wallboard, and plaster as well as by farmers who wanted to enhance the fertility of the soil. To accommodate a changing economy, the Garbutt depot was moved in 1941 and became the Wheatland Center depot, shown in the photograph. The depot was demolished in 1972. (Courtesy of Town of Wheatland historian.)

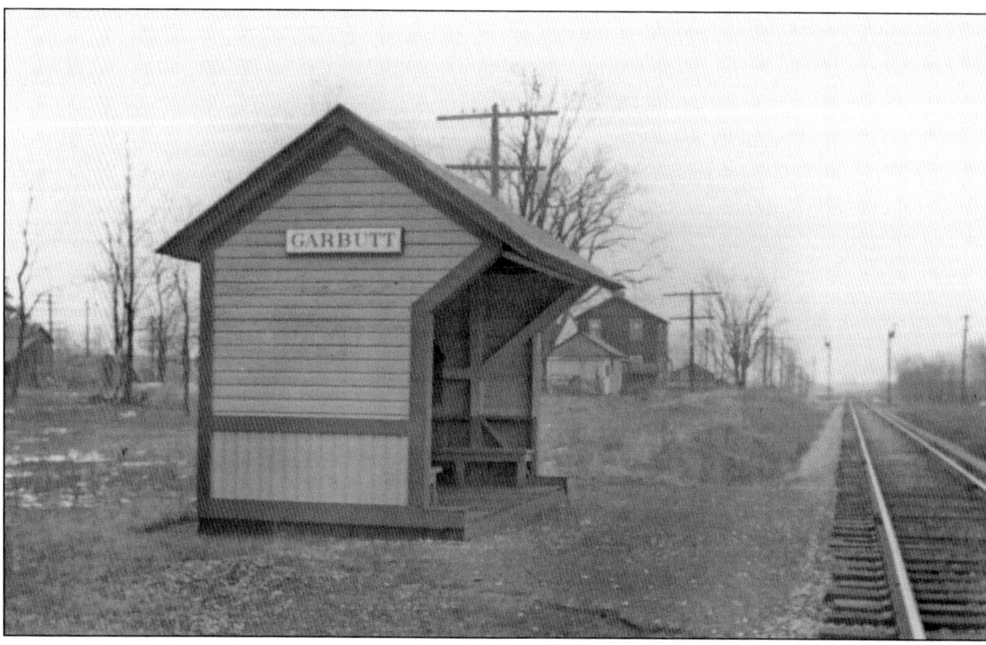

When the Garbutt depot was moved in 1941 to Wheatland Center, it was replaced by this small structure, which most likely was a flag stop on the B&O. (Courtesy of Town of Wheatland historian.)

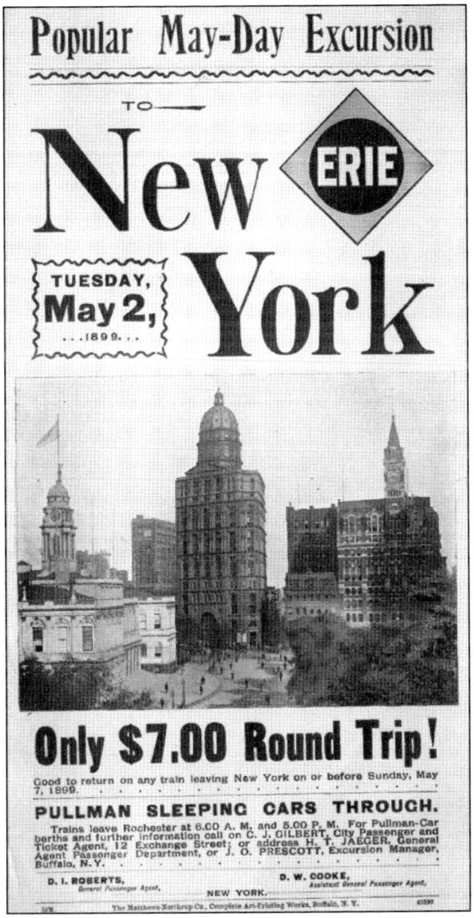

SEE-WAY BETWEEN NEW YORK

TABLE 12 ELMIRA-ROCHESTER

Westbound Read Down 5-463 Sat. o'ly	Westbound Read Down 7-467 Daily Ex. Sun.	Miles	Eastern Standard Time	Eastbound Read Up 468-8 Daily Ex. Sun.	Eastbound Read Up 464-8 Sun. o'ly
PM	PM		Leave — Arrive	PM	PM
7.25	......	......	NEW YORK Times Sq. Mtr. Coach Term. (Note ⊕)	11.45	11.45
7.10	11.55	0.0	West 23d St.	11.55	11.55
7.30	12.00	0.0	Chambers St.	11.54	11.54
7.45	12.25	1.0	Jersey City	11.30	11.30
Sun. only AM	Ex. Sun. AM			Ex. Sun. PM	Sun. o'ly PM
2.38	7.45	0.0	Elmira	5.10	5.10
3.07	8.18	17.4	Ar. Corning Lv.	4.39	4.39
3.30	8.22	17.4	Lv. Corning Ar.	3.54	3.50
3.37	8.29	19.3	Painted Post	3.44	3.40
3.43	f8.34	22.6	Cooper's	f 3.36	f 3.30
3.53	8.43	26.9	Campbell	3.10	3.01
4.02	8.52	31.5	Savona	3.04	2.54
4.16	9.01	37.7	Bath	2.54	2.44
4.23	9.11	41.4	Kanona	2.38	2.29
4.30	9.18	45.1	Avoca	2.26	2.08
4.35	9.24	48.0	Wallace	2.16	2.03
4.45	9.33	52.8	Cohocton	2.06	1.53
4.52	9.41	57.2	Atlanta	1.52	1.38
5.02	9.51	63.2	Wayland	1.42	1.28
5.10	9.59	67.9	Springwater	1.32	1.20
5.26	10.05	70.7	Websters	1.13	12.49
5.34	10.12	74.5	Conesus	1.07	f12.42
5.43	f10.18	78.3	So. Livonia	f 1.01	f12.36
5.51	10.25	81.9	Livonia	12.55	12.30
5.56	10.30	84.5	South Lima	12.48	f12.24
......	......	86.2	Conesus Lake Jct.	......	......
6.15	10.48	93.5	Avon	12.31	11.50
......	......	97.7	Golah	......	......
......	11.00	100.1	Industry	12.16	......
......	gc	103.3	West Henrietta	12.09	......
......	11.25	112.1	Ar. Rochester Lv.	11.55	......
AM	AM			AM	AM

Mixed Train

TABLE 13 SALAMANCA—DUNKIRK

Westbound Read Down 5-527 Daily Ex. Sun. & Hol.	Miles	Eastern Standard Time	Eastbound Read Up 540 Daily Ex. Sun. & Hol.
PM		Lv. — Ar.	
7.25	......	NEW YORK Times Sq. Mtr. Coach Term. (Note ⊖)	......
7.10	0.0	West 23rd St.	......
7.30	0.0	Chambers St.	......
7.45	1.0	Jersey City	......
6.09	413.6	Ar. Salamanca Lv.	......
AM			PM
7.20	0.0	Lv. Salamanca Ar.	5.00
7.55	8.3	Little Valley	4.40
8.50	15.7	Cattaraugus	4.05
......	21.9	Persia	f3.35
9.10	25.0	Ar. Dayton Lv.	3.25
10.55	......	Ar. Buffalo Lv.	......
9.40	25.0	Lv. Dayton Ar.	3.25
9.48	28.0	Perrysburg	3.15
f9.55	30.9	West Perrysburg	f3.05
f10.05	34.9	Smith's Mills	f2.55
10.13	38.8	Forestville	2.45
f10.28	42.6	Sheridan	f2.30
10.40	46.9	Ar. Dunkirk Lv.	2.15
AM			PM

Mixed Train (See Note Below)

LOCATE YOUR PLANT
WHERE YOU CAN
LOCATE MORE PROFITS
Ask us about industrial buildings and vacant land on Erie rails
GEO. F. WESTON
Industrial Commissioner
Erie Railroad, Midland Bldg., Cleveland, O.

TABLE 14 ROCHESTER—AVON

Eastbound Read Down N. B. 420 Daily Ex. Sun. & Hol.	N. B. 440 Daily	416 Daily Ex. Sun. & Hol.	N. B. 428 Sat. only	468 Daily Ex. Sun.	Mil.	Eastern Standard Time	Westbound Read Up N. B. 401 Daily Ex. Sun. & Hol.	N. B. 403 Daily	467 Daily Ex. Sun.	409 Daily Ex. Sun. & Hol.
PM	PM	PM	PM	AM			AM	AM	AM	PM
6.15	5.15	4.15	1.25	11.55	0.0	Lv. Rochester Ar.	7.45	8.45	11.25	1.05
6.25	5.25	4.25	1.35	......	4.6	Mortimer	7.30	8.27	......	12.52
6.32	5.33	4.34	1.43	12.09	8.8	W. Henrietta	7.22	8.18	gc	12.44
6.38	5.40	4.42	1.50	12.15	12.0	Industry	7.15	8.12	11.00	12.37
f6.43	f5.45	f4.47	f1.55	......	14.4	Golah	f7.10	f8.07	......	f12.32
6.57	5.55	5.08	2.04	12.25	18.6	Ar. Avon Lv.	7.02	8.00	10.48	12.25
PM	PM	PM	PM	PM			AM	AM	AM	PM

TRAINS between Avon and Rochester, except Trains 467, 468, will ...

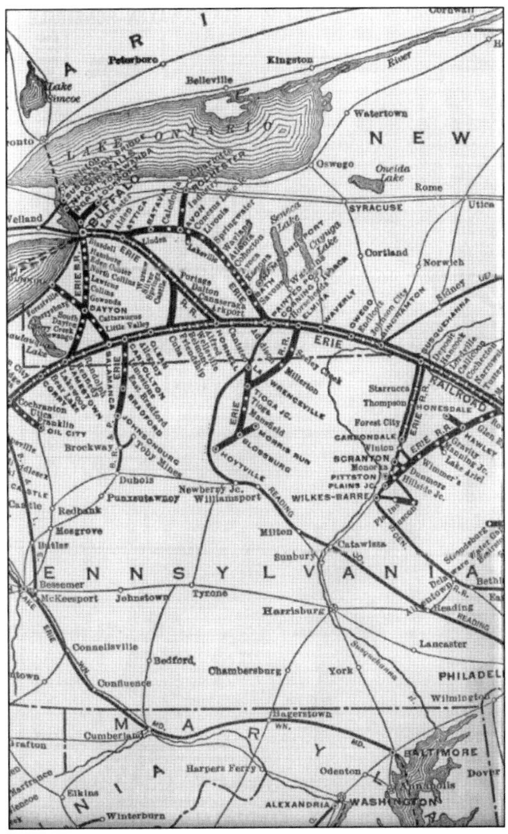

Another railroad serving the Genesee River valley was the Erie. As shown in this advertisement (above, left), the Erie was proud to announce its 1899 excursion to New York City. For the Rochester–New York City trip, the Erie connection to the main line was made at Corning in Steuben County. (Courtesy of *Rochester Images*: Rochester Library Local History Division.)

This map (right) of the Erie details the Rochester branch connection via Avon with the Chicago–New York City main line at Corning. As shown in the Erie 1940 timetable (above, right), the connections from Rochester allowed passengers to board the Atlantic Express for the trip to New York City. Erie also ran several local trains between Avon and Rochester for the commuters in the Genesee River valley. Passenger service to Rochester ended in 1941. (Both, author's collection.)

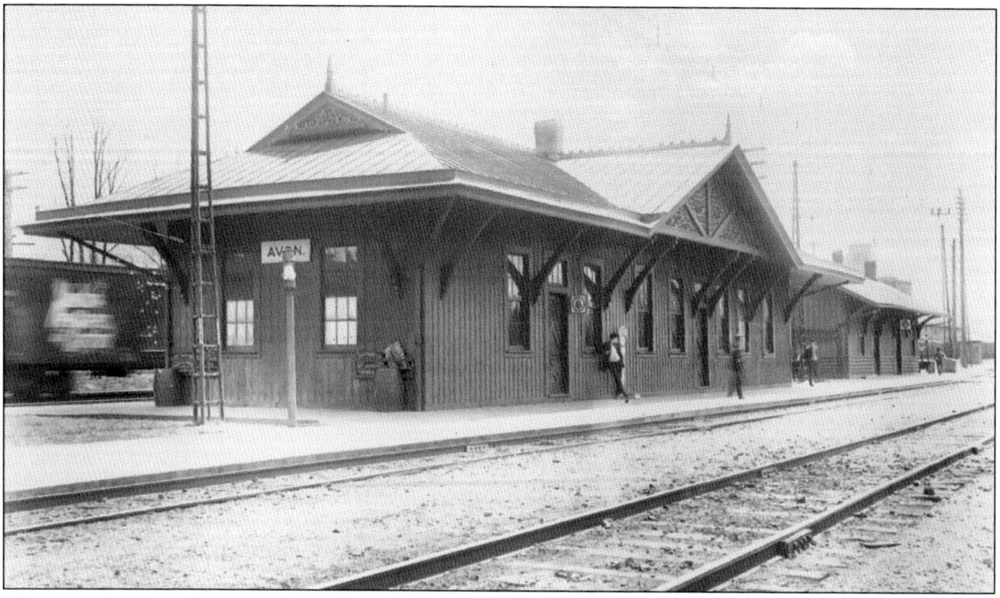

This c. 1875 Erie depot in the village of Avon, just over the Monroe County line in Livingston County, served as the starting point for many Genesee River valley residents and their commute to Rochester. Today, the former Erie depot houses one of Avon's eateries. (Courtesy of Steamtown National Historic Site.)

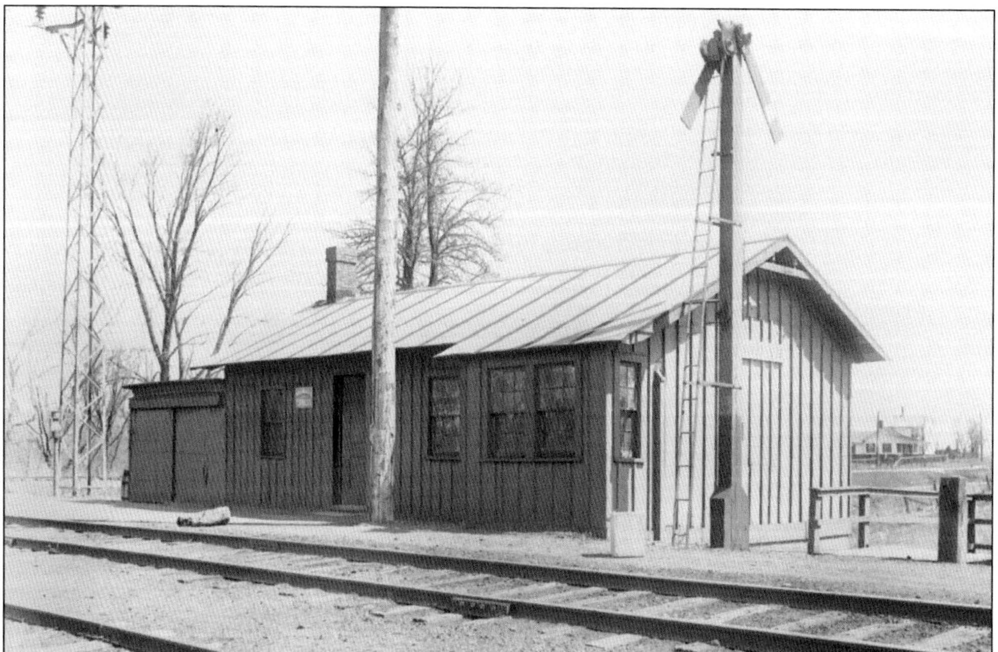

The hamlet of Golah in the town of Rush was the next stop on the Erie's morning commute to Rochester. Here, the Erie crossed NYC's "Peanut Line" that ran east-west from Tonawanda in Niagara County to Canandaigua in Ontario County. The 1850s Erie depot in Golah, shown in the photograph, was located near the Peanut Line crossing. (Courtesy of Steamtown National Historic Site.)

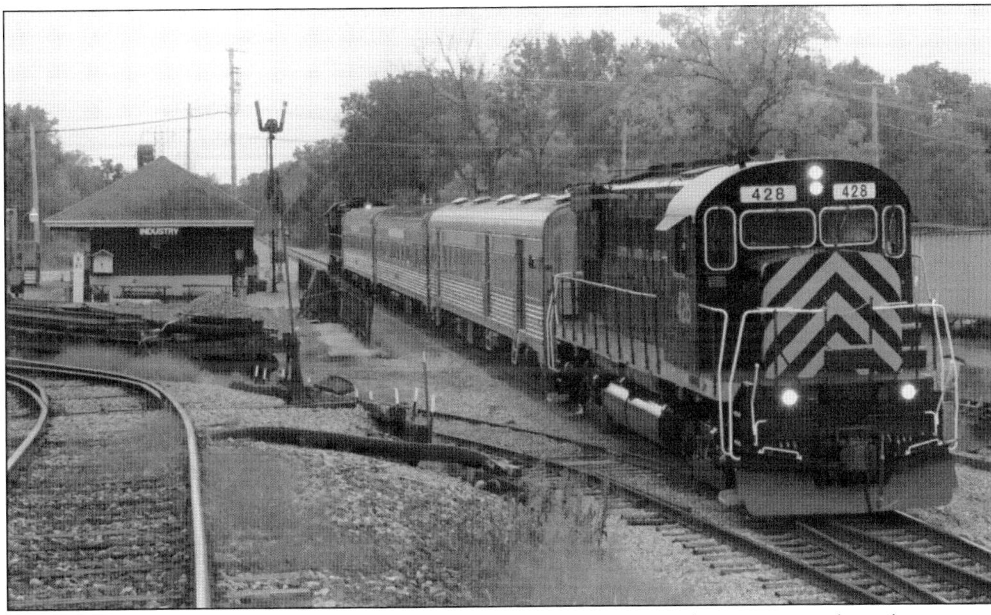

This Erie depot at Industry in the town of Rush was built in the early 1900s to replace the original 1850s depot. It was the next stop on the trip from Avon to Rochester. The former Erie tracks that ran north from Avon are now part of the Livonia, Avon & Lakeville Railroad (LAL). The Erie depot in Industry still stands and is home to the Rochester & Genesee Valley Railroad Museum. The LAL engine is an Alco C424 diesel road-switcher, a former Erie Lackawanna locomotive. Behind the engine are some of the museum's stainless steel Empire State Express cars. These cars were manufactured by the Budd Company and purchased in 1941 when NYC decided to streamline the Empire. It is interesting to note that the name Industry stemmed from New York State's Industry Residential Center located nearby. (Courtesy of Duncan Richards.)

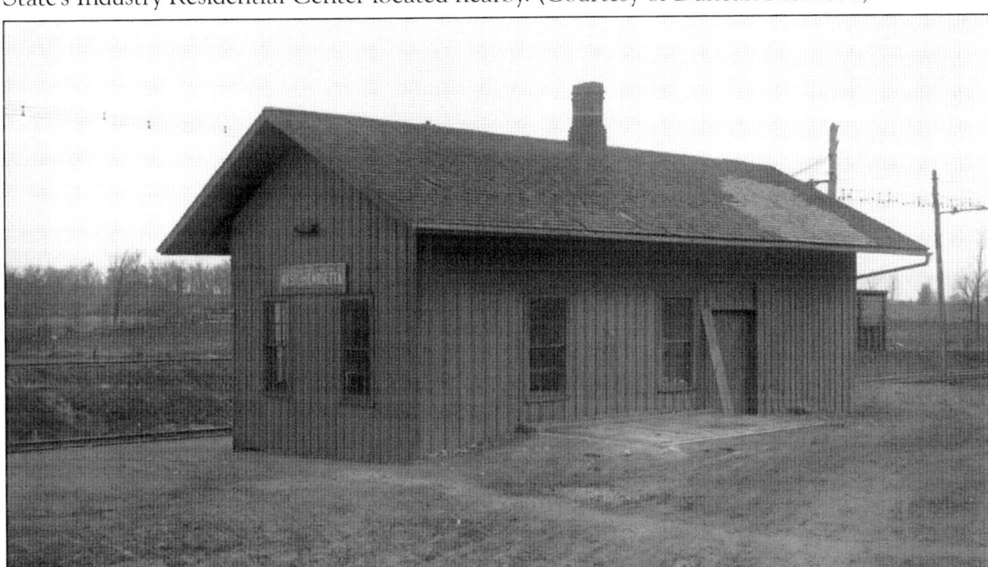

One of last stops before reaching Rochester was the hamlet of West Henrietta in the town of Henrietta. Like the other Erie depots on the Rochester branch line, it too was most likely built in the mid-1800s. (Courtesy of Steamtown National Historic Site.)

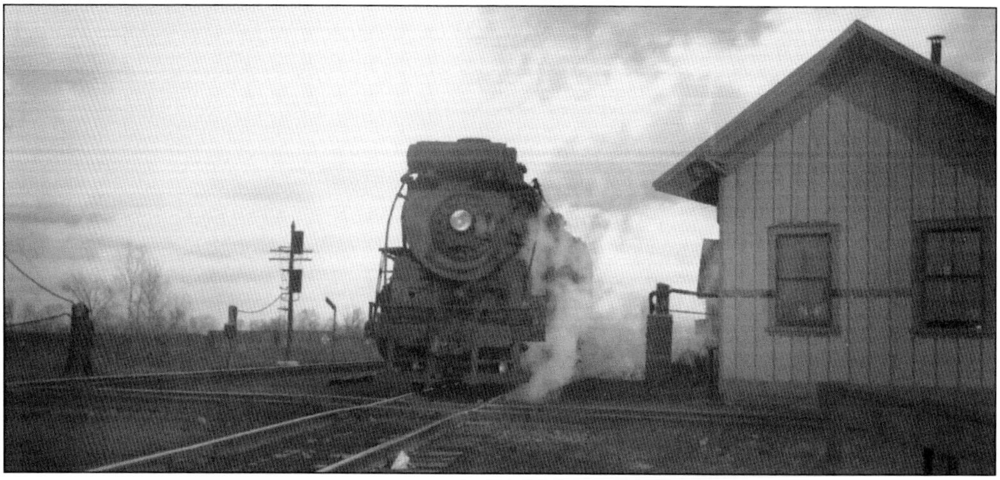

About a mile north of West Henrietta was the important Mortimer Junction where NYC's West Shore line, formerly the New York, West Shore & Buffalo that NYC acquired in the 1880s, interchanged with the Erie and the Lehigh Valley branch lines to Rochester. Just to the west of Mortimer Junction was the equally important Genesee Junction, where as mentioned previously, the West Shore line interchanged with both the B&O and the PRR branch lines to Rochester. This 1950 photograph, most likely taken at Mortimer Junction, shows a class L2a Mohawk about to enter the diamonds that enabled the busy West Shore line running east-west to cross the north-south Rochester branch lines noted above. (Photograph by Robert Gerling, courtesy of Jeff Hands.)

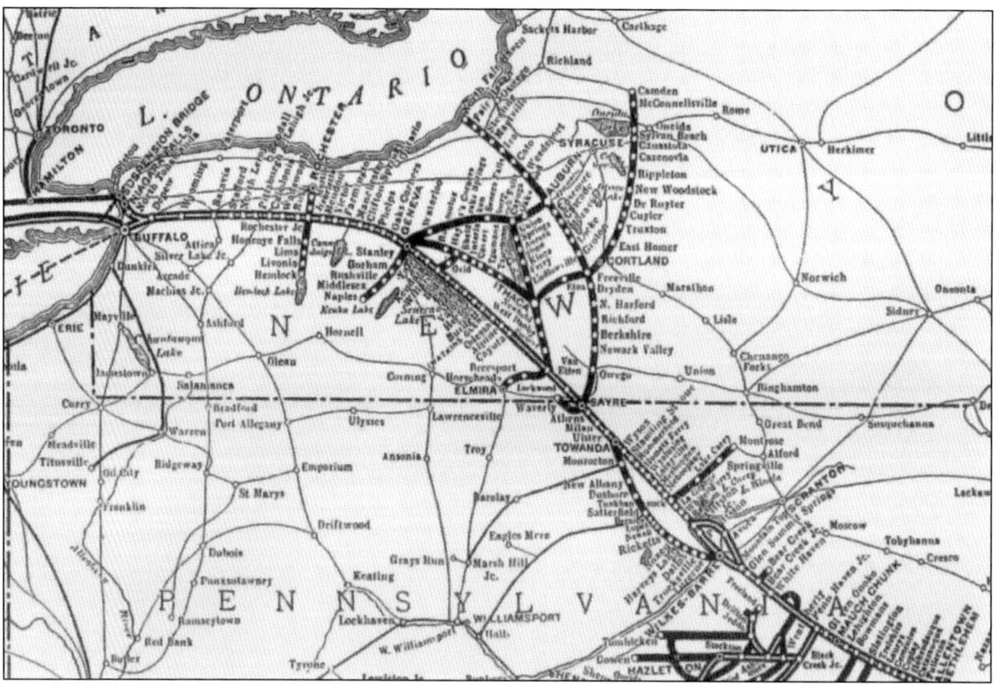

South of Mortimer Junction on the Lehigh Valley was Rochester Junction in the town of Mendon. As shown on this Lehigh Valley Railroad map, Rochester Junction, about 15 miles south of Rochester, was the location of the interchange between the Lehigh Valley's Buffalo–New York City main line and the branch line to Rochester. (Author's collection.)

This menu reflects the pride that the Lehigh Valley had in its passenger service particularly that of its crack passenger train, the Black Diamond Express, which ran between Buffalo and New York City. Interestingly, the Lehigh Valley called itself "the Route of the Black Diamond" named after the anthracite coal it transported. (Courtesy of *Rochester Images*: Rochester Library Local History Division.)

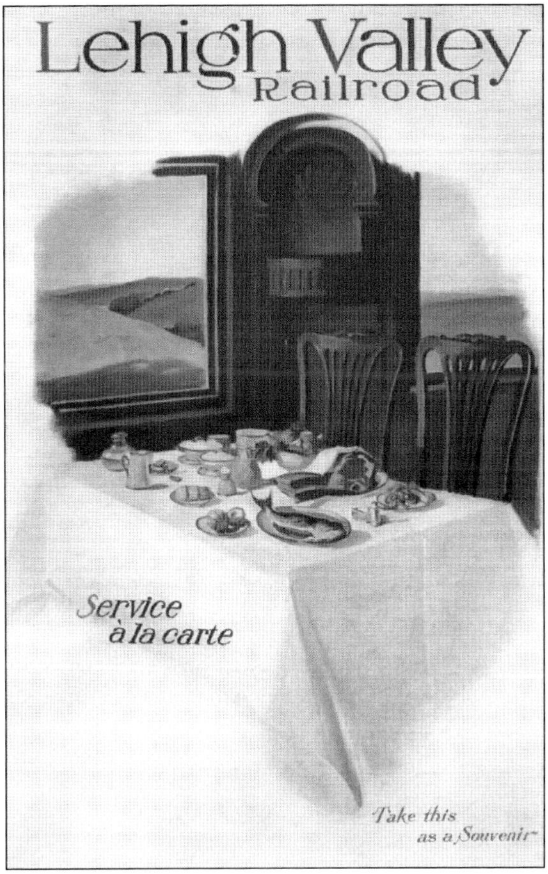

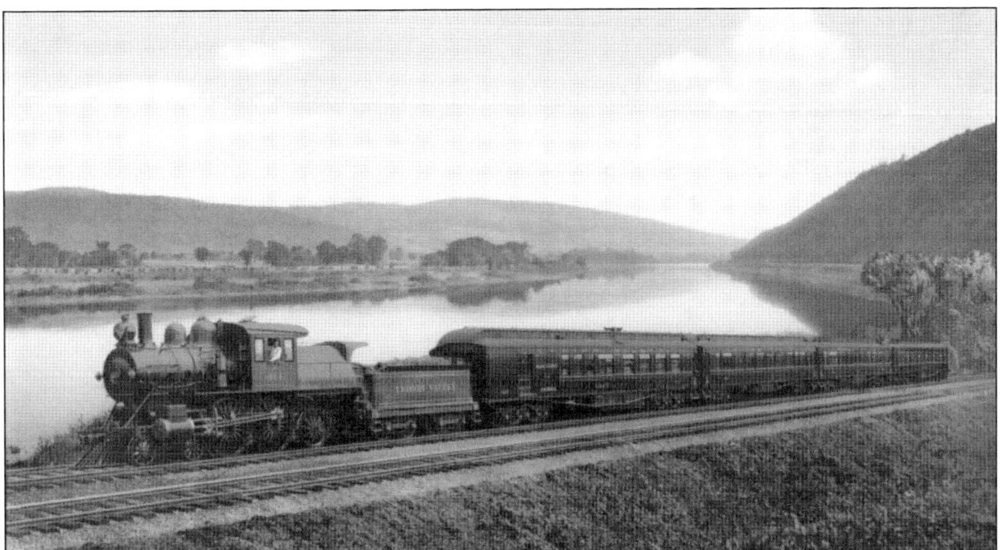

The first run of the Black Diamond Express in 1896 is captured in this postcard. Note that even the combination baggage/café car reflects the train's name. (Courtesy of Town of Mendon historian.)

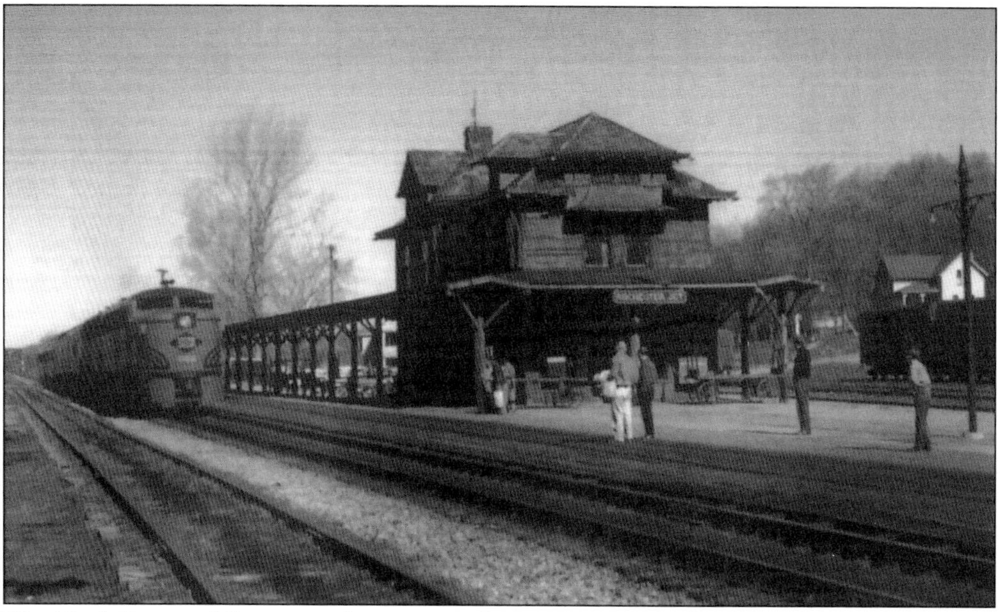

The Black Diamond Express is shown on its last run in 1959 at Rochester Junction (town of Mendon). With a Lehigh Valley Alco PA diesel on the headend and a baggage car and two coaches, it seemed to be a shadow of the train it once was. (Courtesy of Town of Mendon historian.)

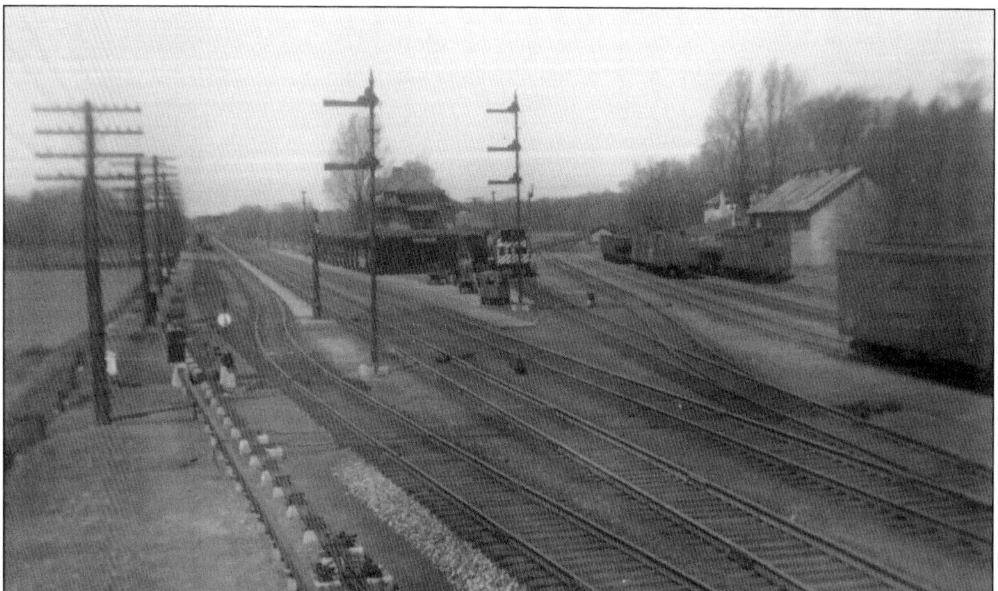

This 1936 photograph shows the interlocking at Rochester Junction. The Lehigh Valley main line is to the left of the depot. Note the doodlebug to the right of the depot. This self-propelled baggage-coach car was used by Lehigh Valley on the Rochester branch line. As noted in chapter 1, doodlebug service to and from Rochester ended in 1950. (Photograph by Ed Van Leer, courtesy of Jeff Hands.)

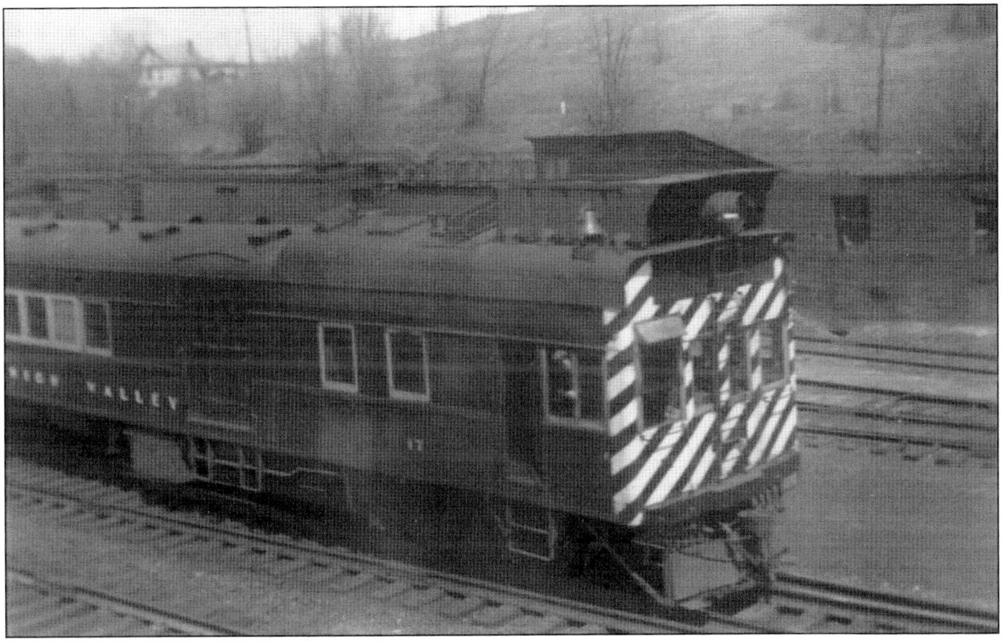

Features of the doodlebug railcar No. 17 can be seen in this 1936 photograph taken at Rochester Junction. In chapter 1, this same doodlebug is shown after it had collided with a hopper car near the University of Rochester in 1940. (Photograph by Ed Van Leer, courtesy of Jeff Hands.)

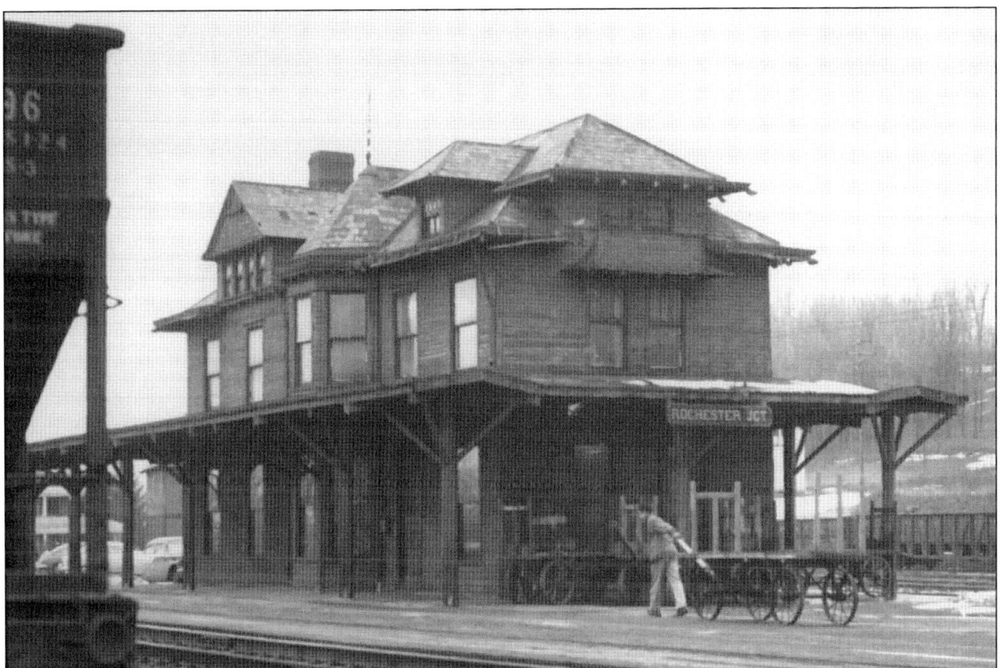

A closer look at the Rochester Junction depot reveals the architectural beauty of this 1896 Victorian-style building. It was fitting that such a structure was a stop for the Black Diamond Express. Sadly, the depot was destroyed by fire in 1973. (Courtesy of Town of Mendon historian.)

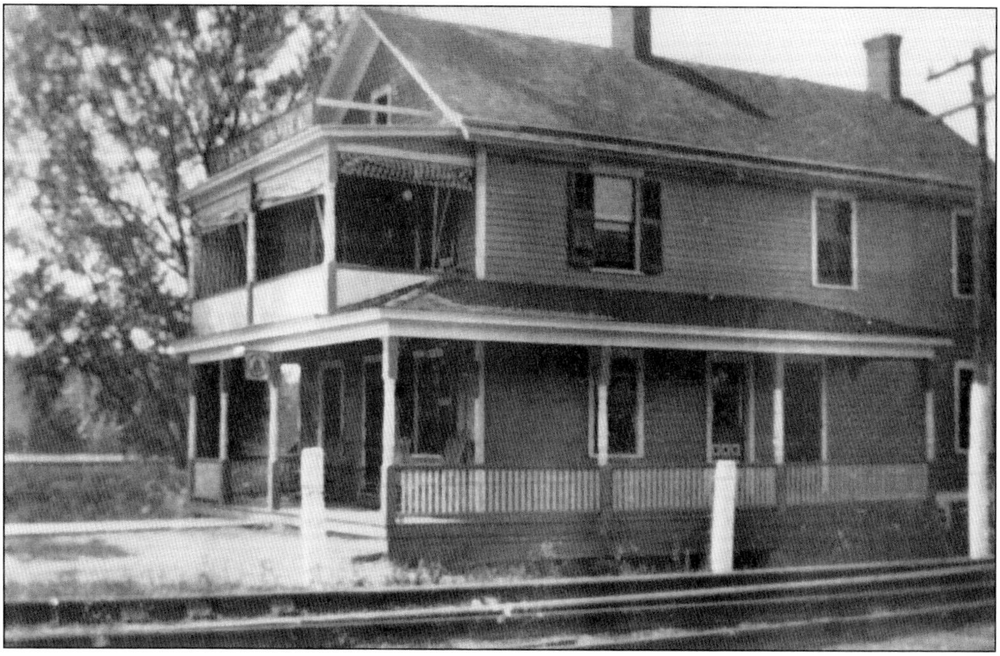

Passenger trains that stopped at Rochester Junction made the depot a very busy place. As a result, William Terry and his wife built the Terry Hotel in 1899. The building remains today and can be seen across the road from the site of the former passenger depot. (Courtesy of Town of Mendon historian.)

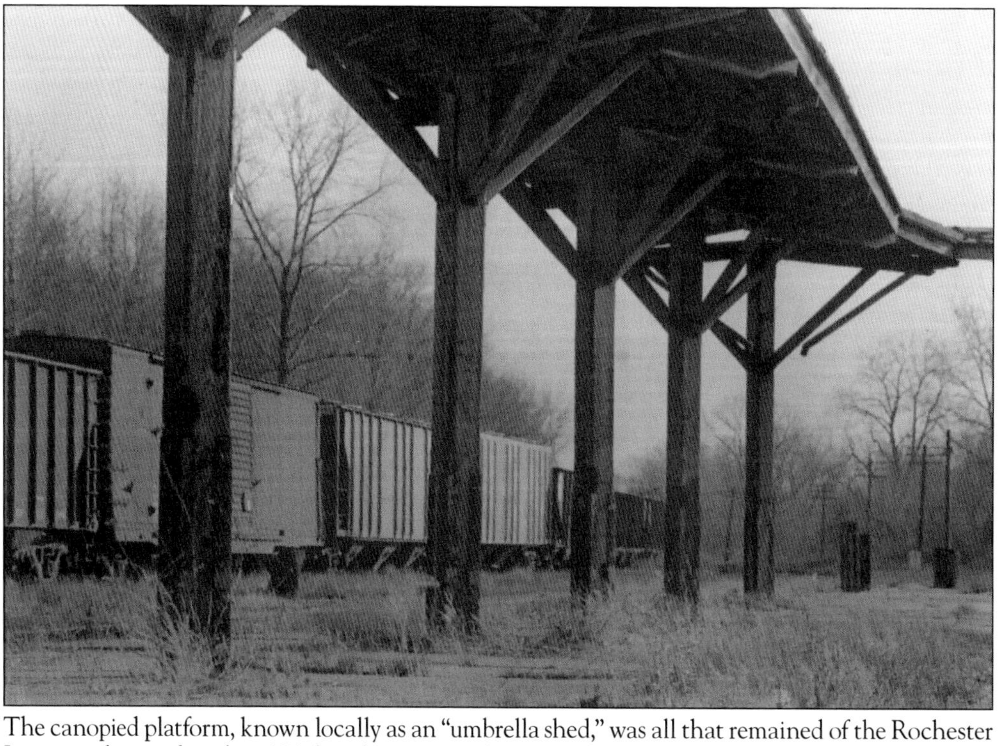

The canopied platform, known locally as an "umbrella shed," was all that remained of the Rochester Junction depot after the 1973 fire. (Courtesy of Town of Mendon historian.)

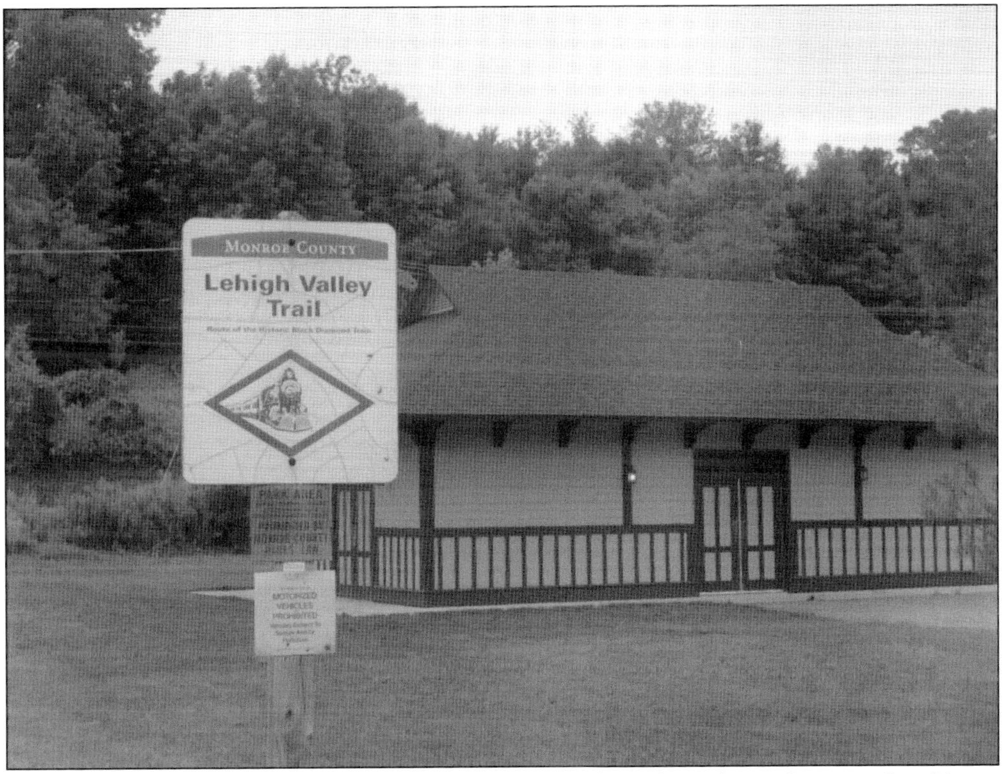

Today, there are reminders of the Lehigh Valley that ran through Rochester Junction. In addition to the reconstructed freight house in the background, the Lehigh Valley Trail that follows the former main line is also a reminder of "the Route of the Black Diamond." (Author's collection.)

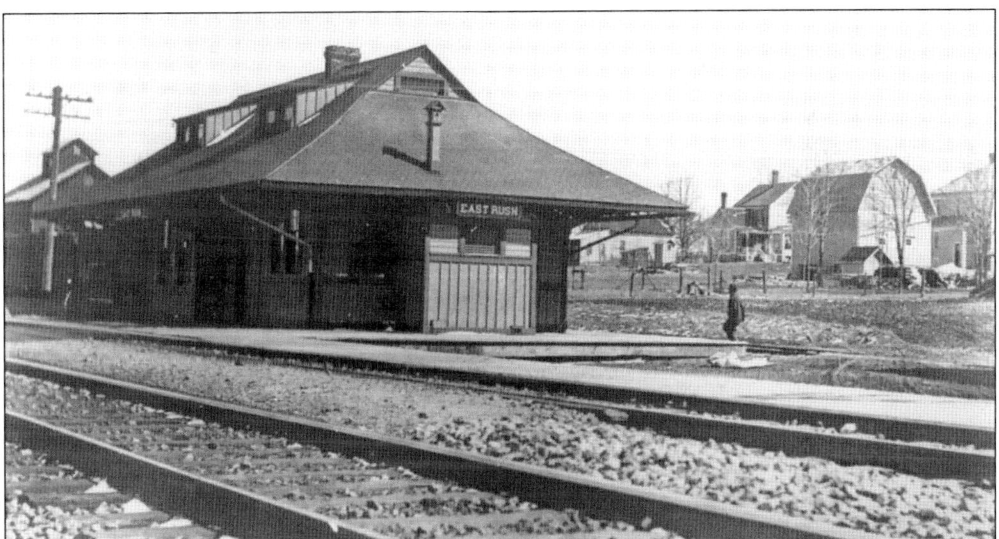

This depot, built in 1892, served the hamlet of Rush in the town of Rush located west of Rochester Junction on the Lehigh Valley main line. The depot was taken down around 1950. (Courtesy of Town of Mendon historian.)

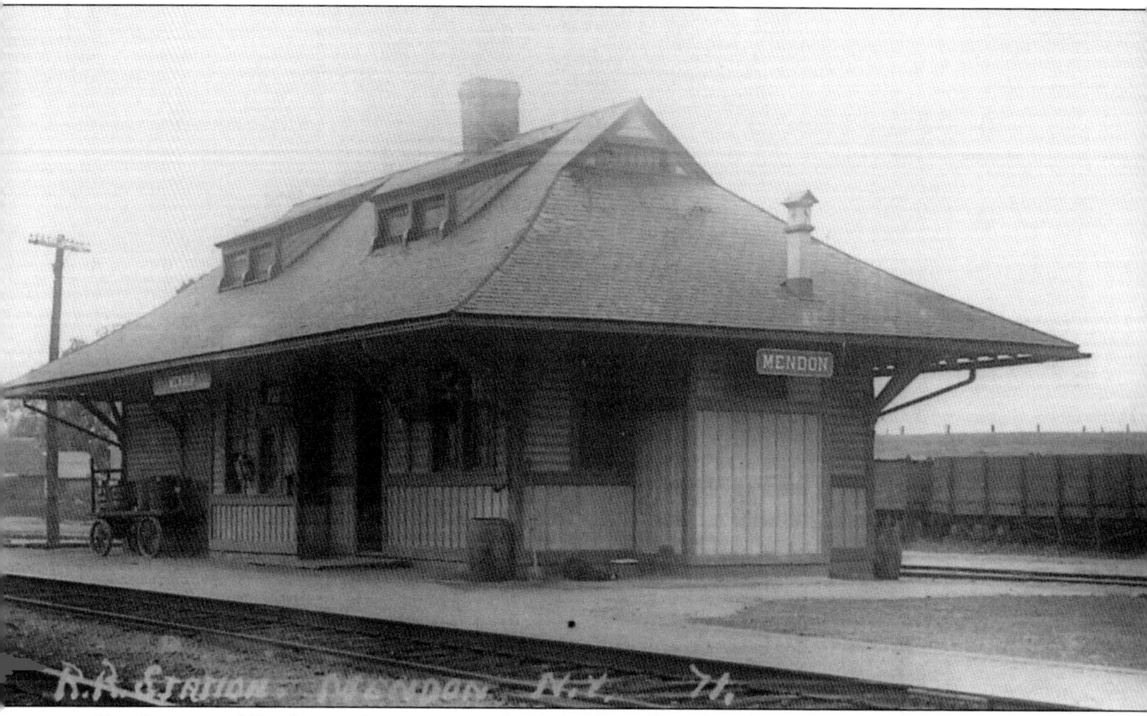

To the east of Rochester Junction on the Lehigh Valley main line is the hamlet of Mendon in the town of Mendon. The Mendon depot, shown in the photograph, was built in 1896 and was taken down in the early 1950s. (Courtesy of Town of Mendon historian.)

Five

Producing Freight Cars in East Rochester

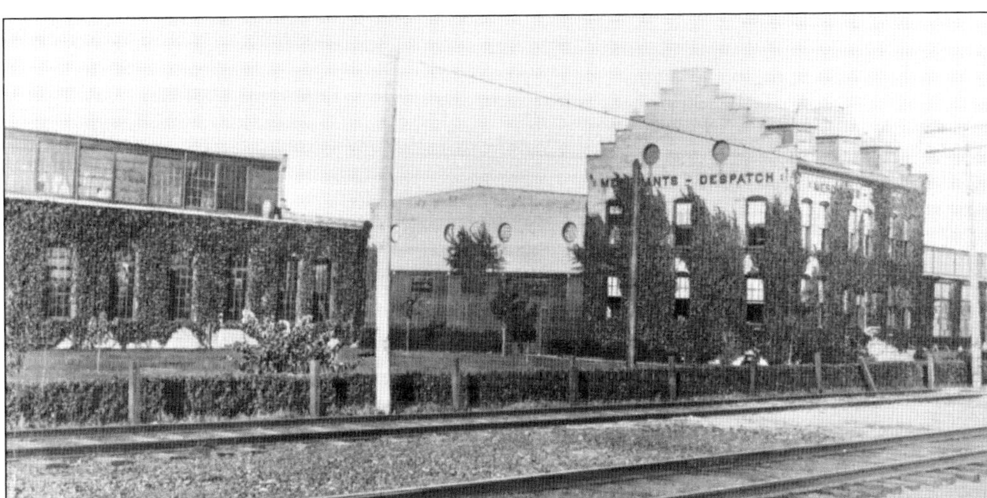

In the 1880s, the Merchants Despatch Transportation Company entered the business of manufacturing refrigerated freight cars and built a facility in an area southeast of the city of Rochester, in the present-day village of East Rochester in the town of East Rochester. Some of the company's first buildings constructed along the New York Central main line are shown in this early-1900s photograph. (Courtesy of Village of East Rochester historian.)

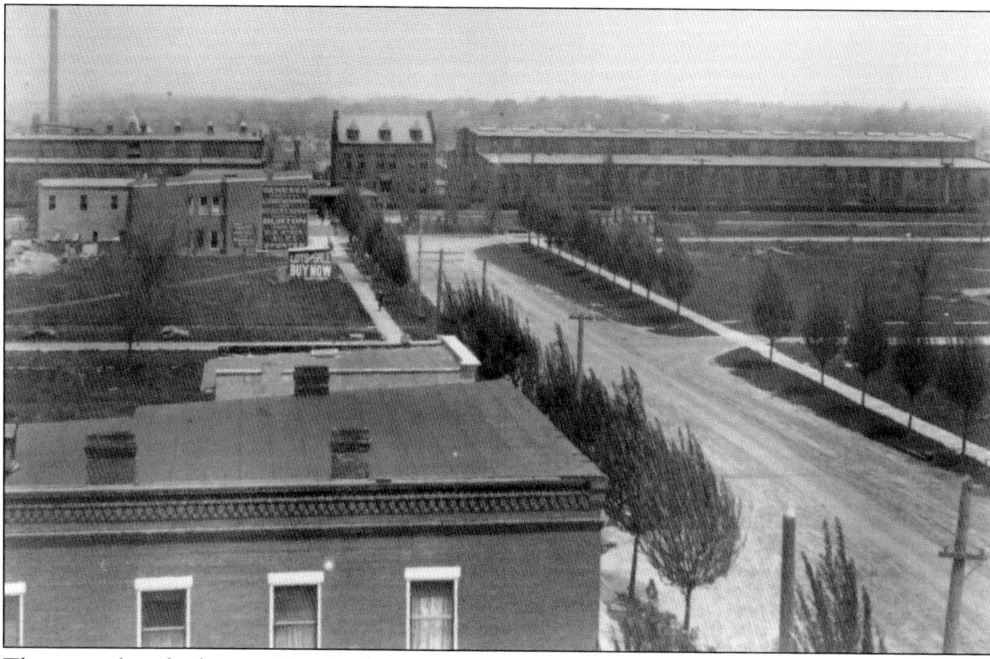

The expanding facilities in East Rochester are shown in the background of this c. 1910 photograph. The "Lots for Sale-Buy Now" sign is indicative of the fact that East Rochester was growing and attracting people and businesses. Eventually, the Merchants Despatch plant, also known as the carshops, occupied about 50 acres and employed nearly 1,000 people. (Courtesy of Village of East Rochester historian.)

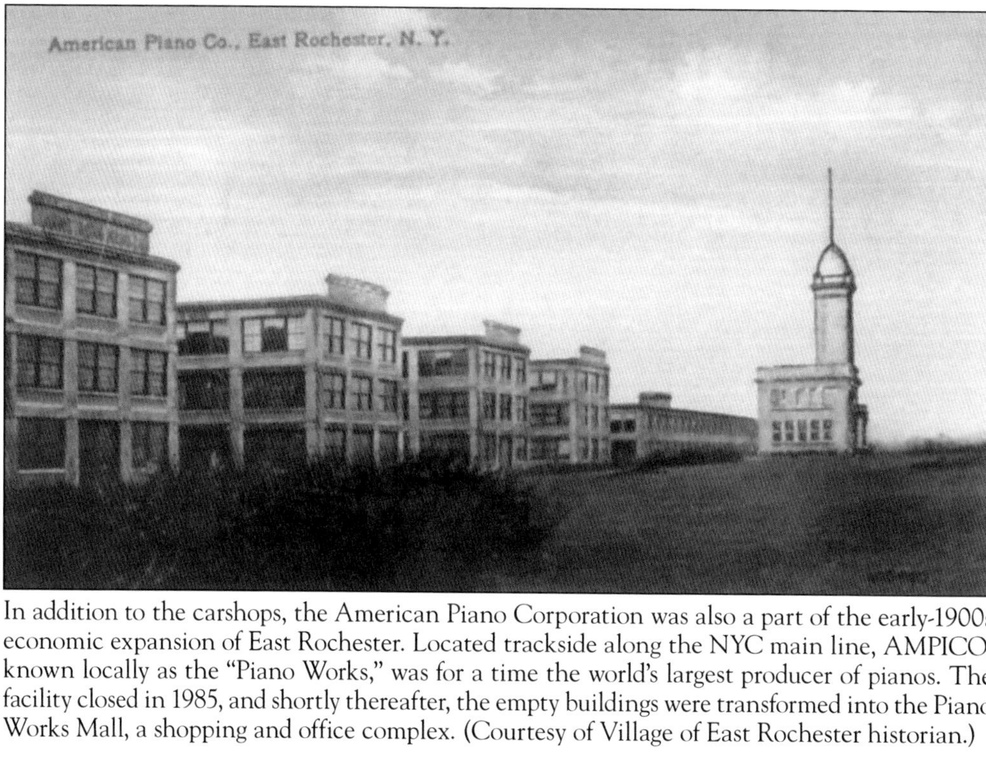

In addition to the carshops, the American Piano Corporation was also a part of the early-1900s economic expansion of East Rochester. Located trackside along the NYC main line, AMPICO, known locally as the "Piano Works," was for a time the world's largest producer of pianos. The facility closed in 1985, and shortly thereafter, the empty buildings were transformed into the Piano Works Mall, a shopping and office complex. (Courtesy of Village of East Rochester historian.)

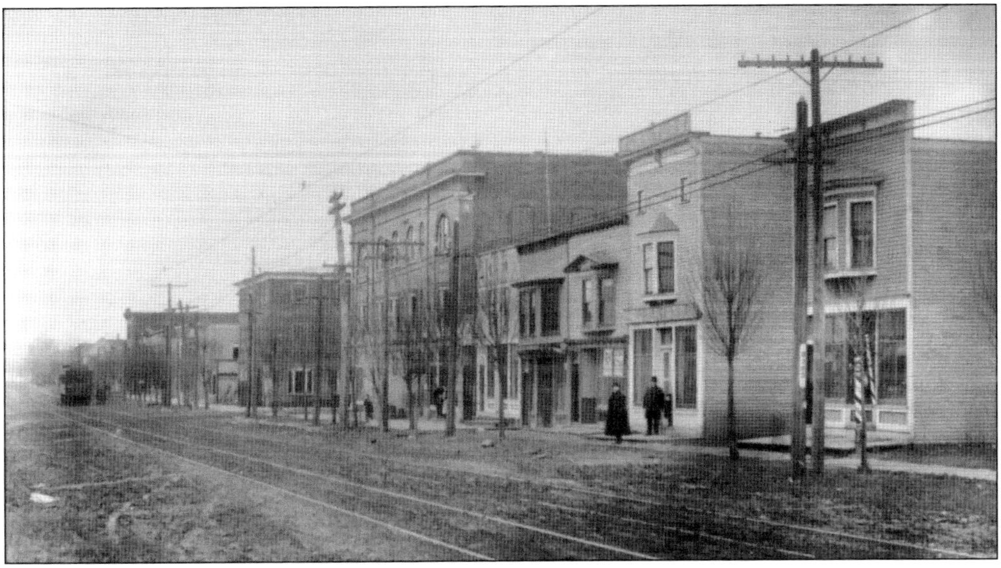

As shown in this c. 1910 photograph, East Rochester, with its increased economic activity, saw electric streetcars on East Commercial Street as part the Rochester, Syracuse & Eastern Railway line. The line ceased its operation in 1931. (Courtesy of Village of East Rochester historian.)

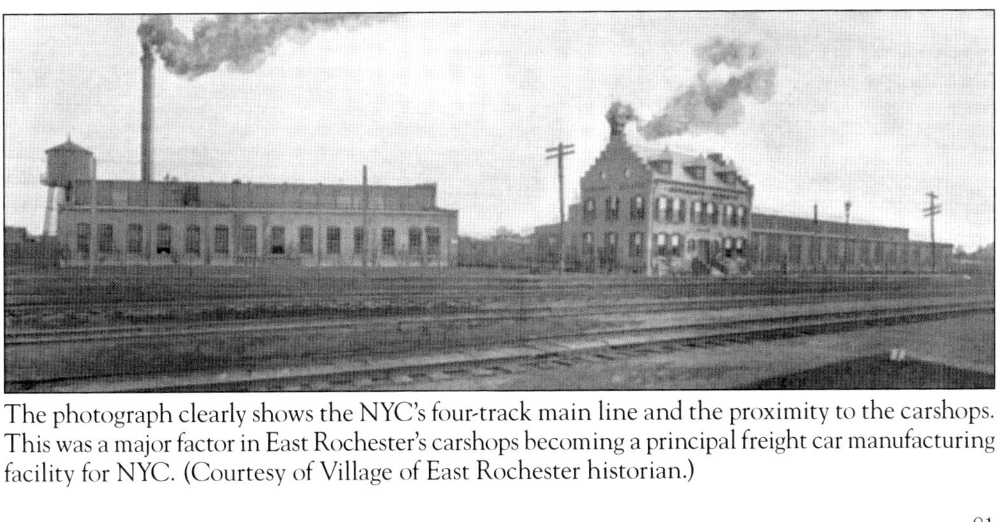

The photograph clearly shows the NYC's four-track main line and the proximity to the carshops. This was a major factor in East Rochester's carshops becoming a principal freight car manufacturing facility for NYC. (Courtesy of Village of East Rochester historian.)

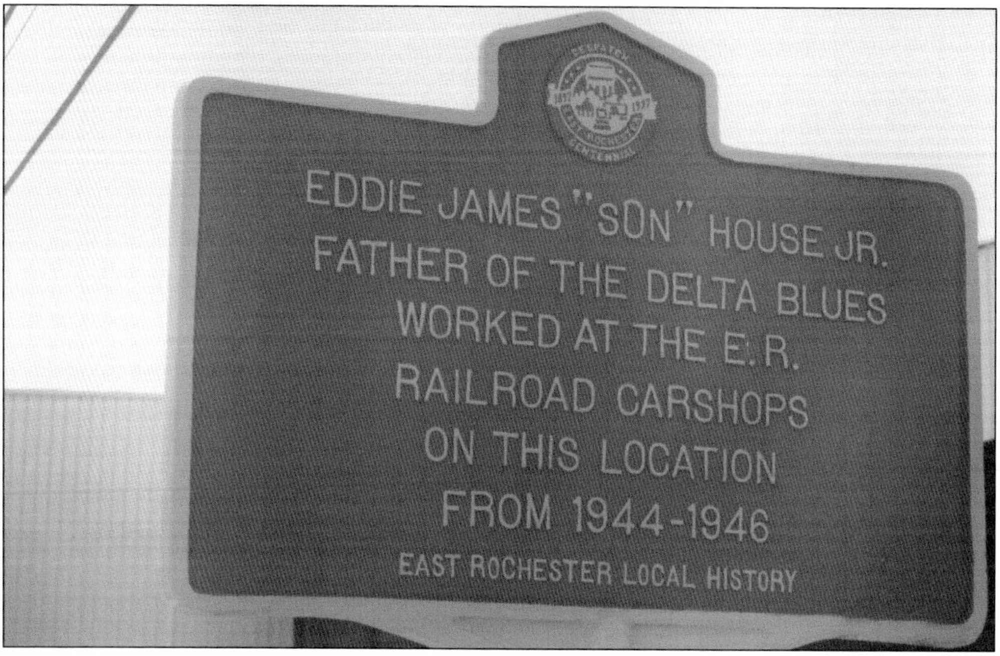

While Eddie James worked at the carshops for only a short while, he was nonetheless recognized for his musical talent. Despite being a noted blues singer and guitarist in the 1930s, "Son," as he was known, fell on hard times and had to leave Mississippi in the 1940s to look for work in the North. He found it at the carshops. (Author's collection.)

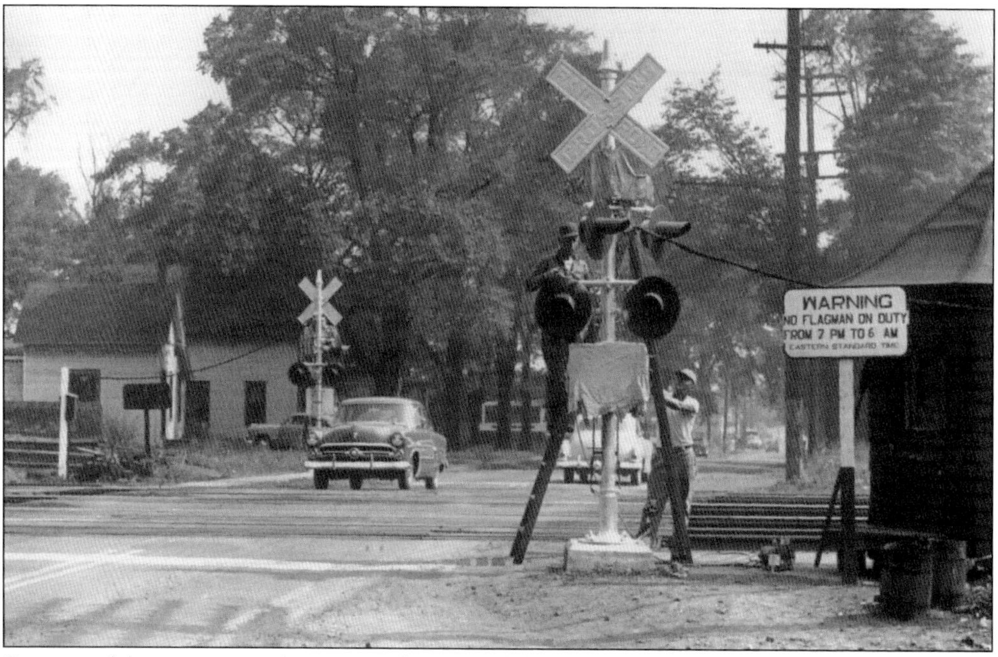

Because of the many main line trains that passed through East Rochester, it was very important to keep crossings like this one on Washington Street in working order. However, as the sign in this 1950s photograph warns, the flagman was not on duty overnight. (Courtesy of *Rochester Images*: Rochester Public Library Local History Division.)

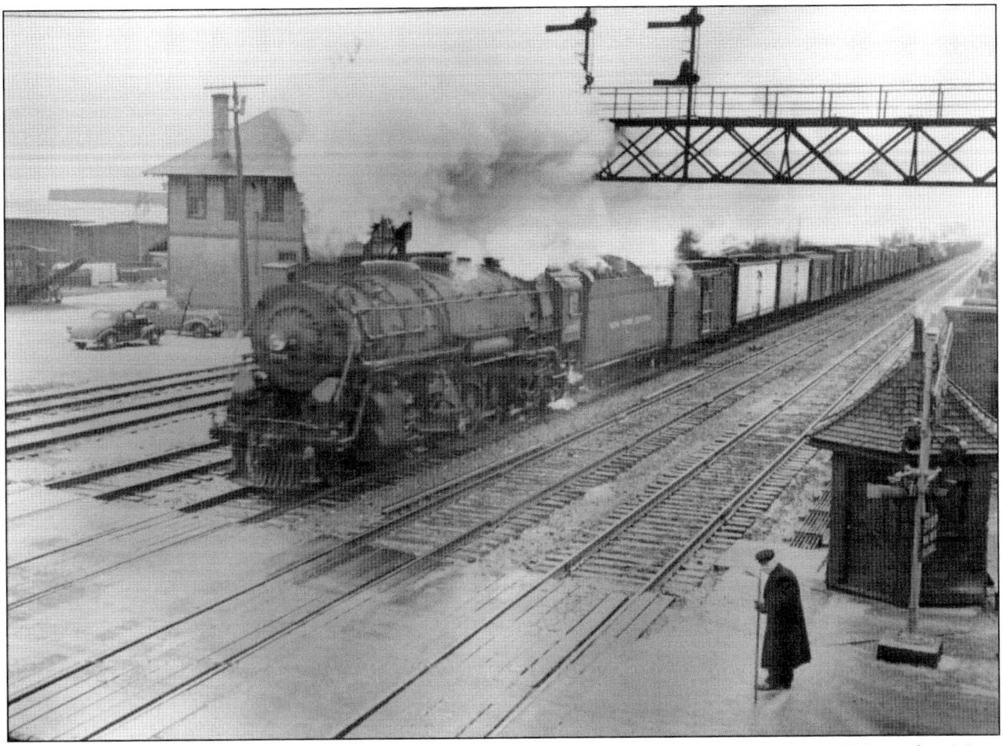

Passing through East Rochester at the busy Washington Street crossing in the 1940s is this New York Central freight with a class L2d Mohawk 4-8-2 on the headend. There is a good chance that the two refrigerated freight cars, known as "reefers," behind the locomotive were manufactured in East Rochester. (Courtesy of Jeff Hands.)

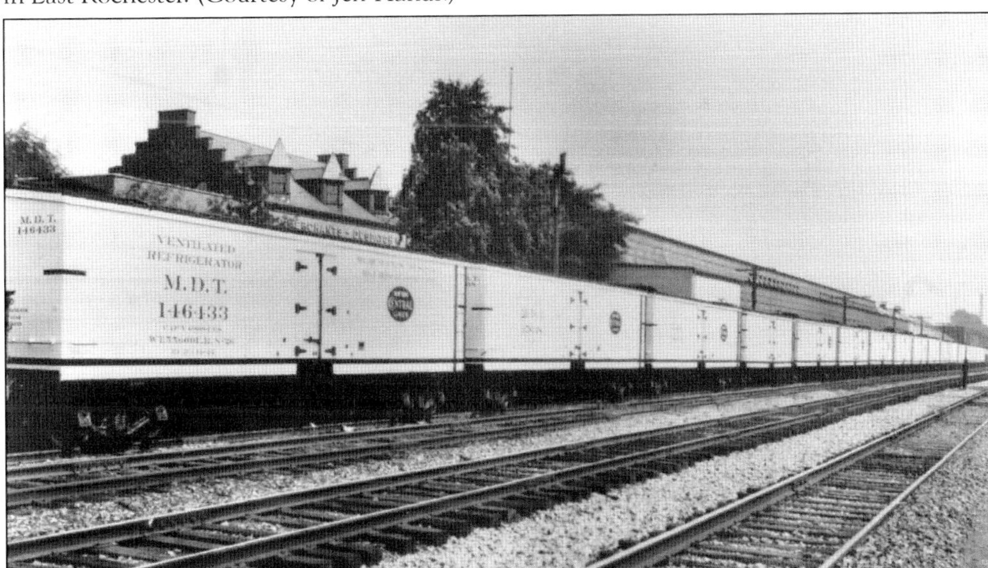

The East Rochester carshops were well known for the manufacture of reefers. The photograph shows a day's production of reefers ready to be rolled out. Markings on the side indicate that these cars were manufactured in the 1920s. (Courtesy of Village of East Rochester historian.)

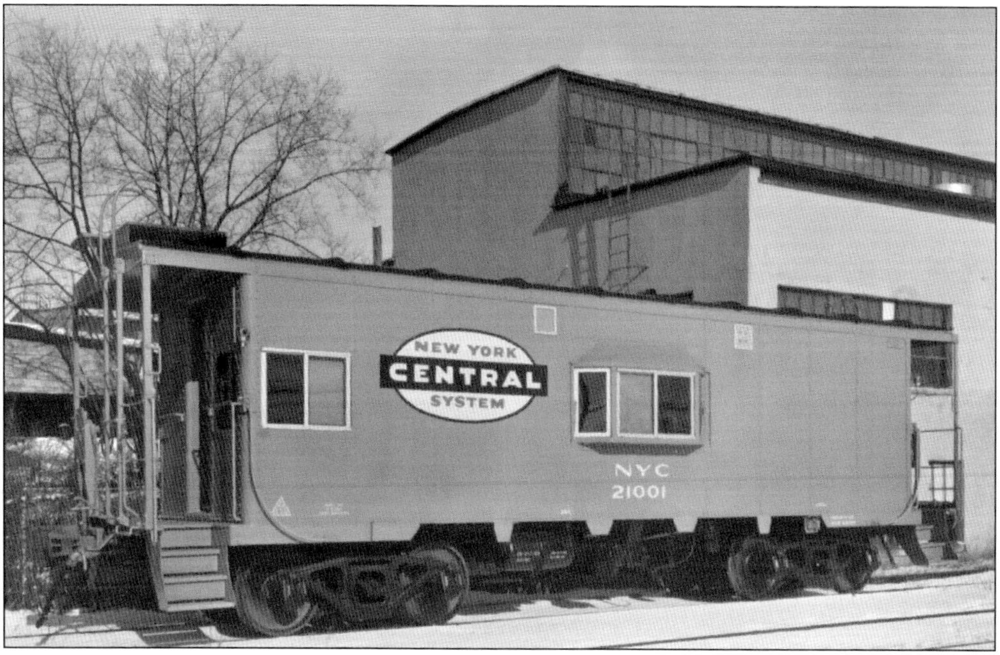

In addition to reefers, the carshops produced other types of cars such as this c. 1960 bay-window caboose. Located at the end of the train, this type of caboose allowed the crew to easily monitor the sides of the moving train. (Courtesy of Village of East Rochester historian.)

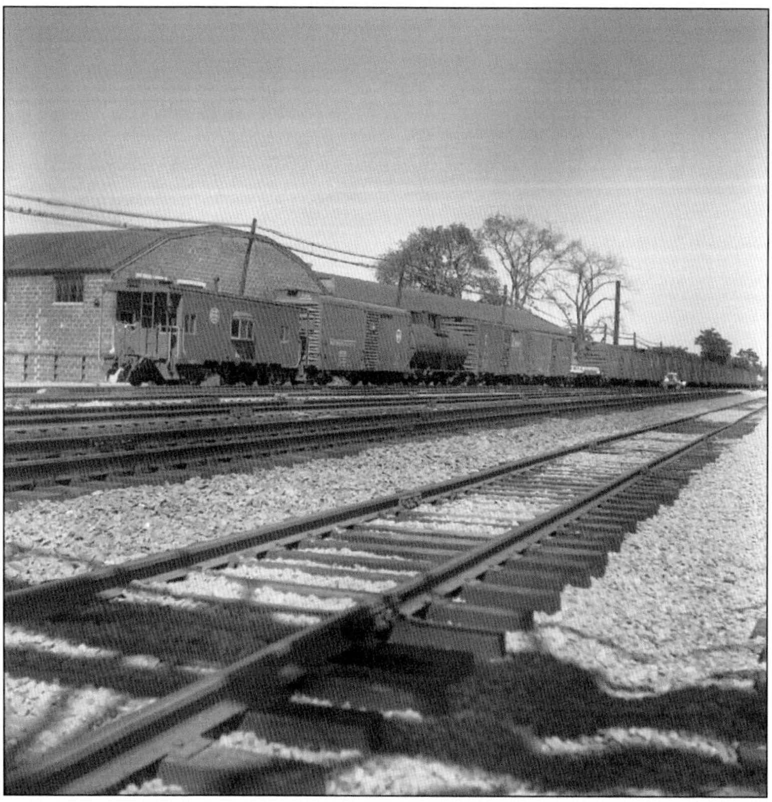

The bay-window caboose seen in this early-1950s photograph shows exactly how crewmen observed the sides of a moving freight train. This scene is along the NYC main line near West Avenue on Rochester's west side. (Photograph by Robert Carper, courtesy of Jeff Hands.)

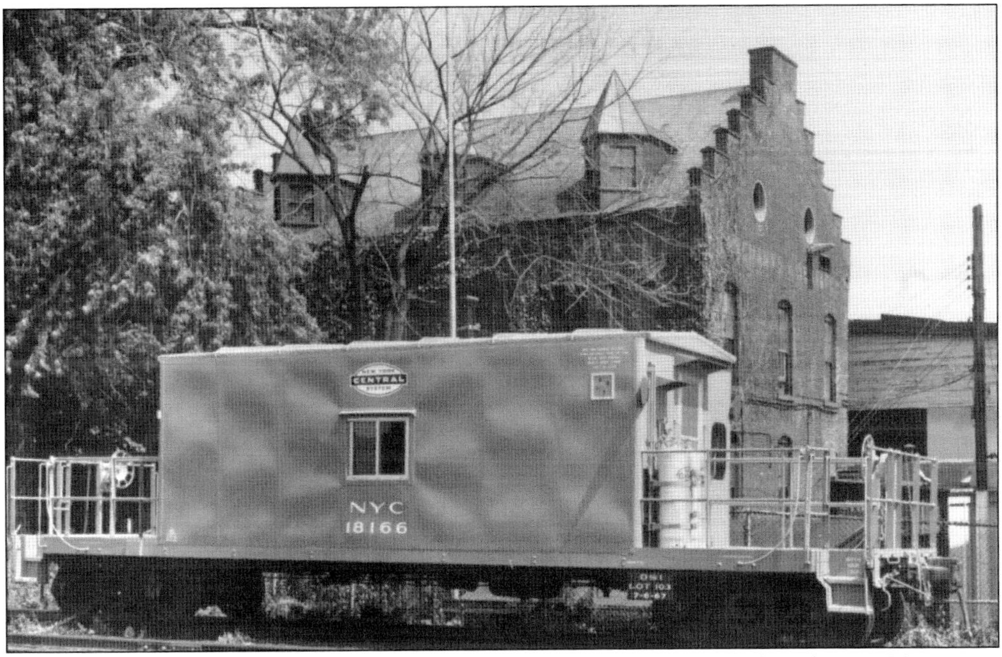

Another type of caboose manufactured by the carshops was the transfer caboose. These cars provided a location to store needed tools and materials for men to work trackside. Shown in this 1967 photograph is a new transfer caboose ready to be deployed on the NYC. In a year or so, it would belong to Penn Central as a result of the NYC and PRR merger. (Courtesy of Village of East Rochester historian.)

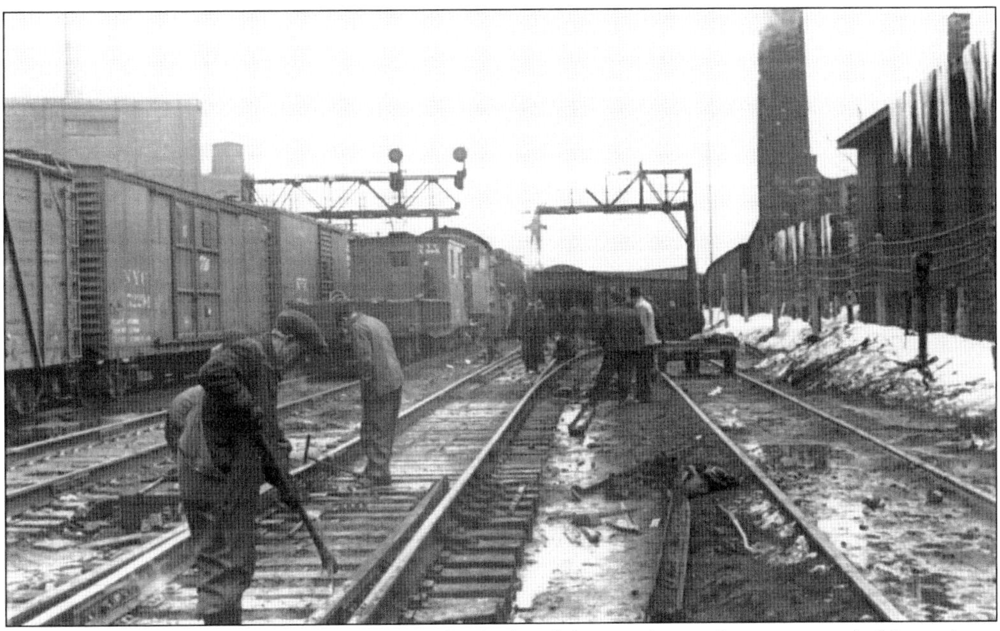

Here is a transfer caboose in action. From the looks of things, the trackmen are probably working to deal with a derailed hopper car as well as a frozen switch in the dead of a 1950s winter at NYC's Goodman Street Yards in Rochester. In the background, there appears to be one of NYC's cranes ready to tackle the derailed hopper car. (Courtesy of Robert Pastorkey.)

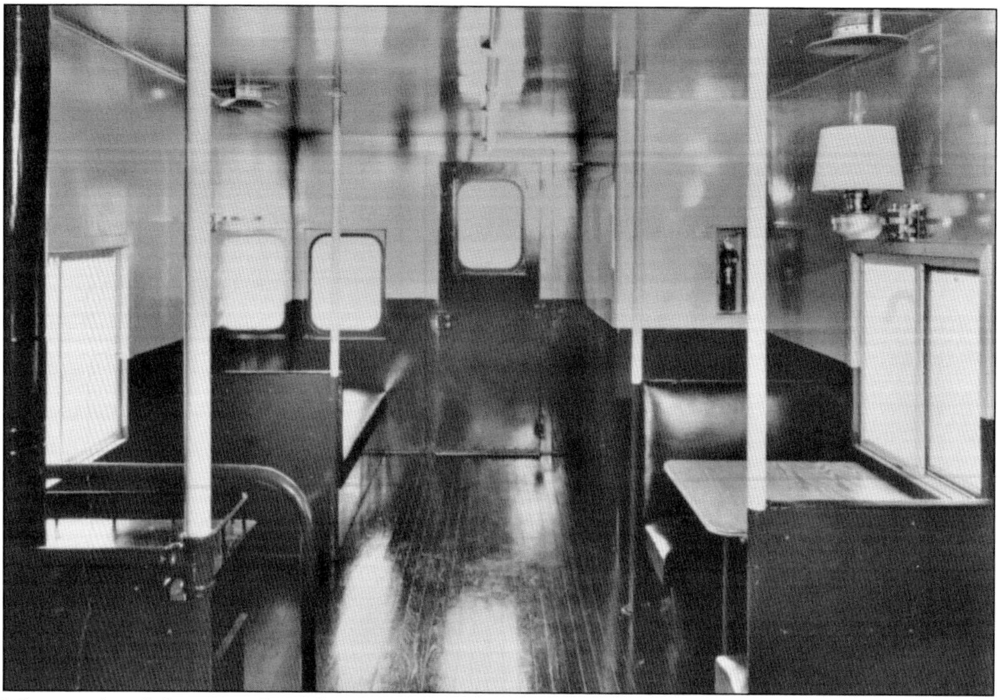

The inside of this transfer caboose is shown in this photograph. Unlike in the regular bay-window caboose, sleeping and cooking space are in short supply. (Courtesy of Village of East Rochester historian.)

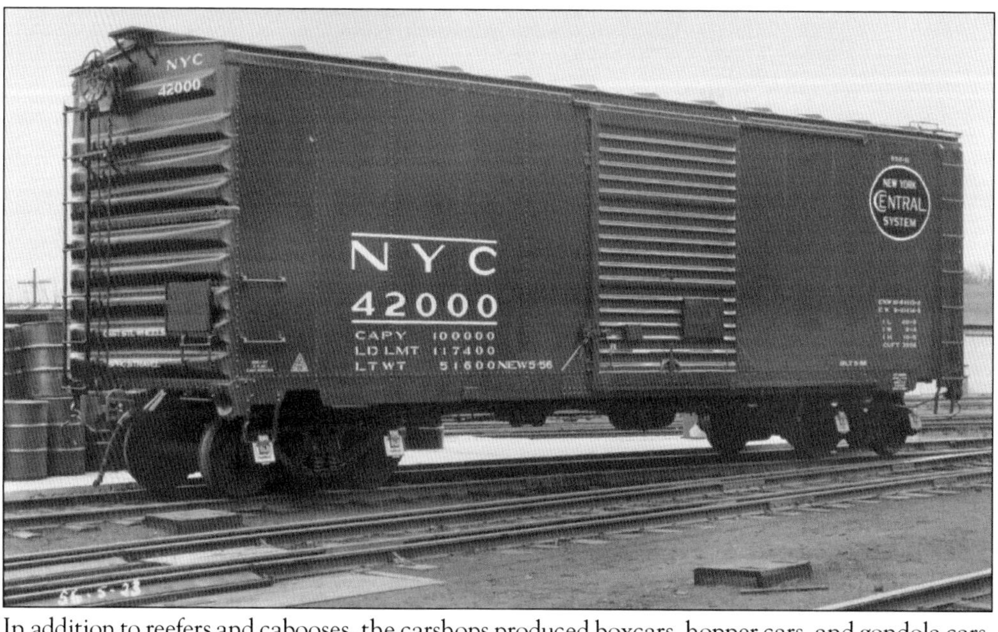

In addition to reefers and cabooses, the carshops produced boxcars, hopper cars, and gondola cars. Shown here is a new boxcar ready for main line action. Note the 1956 date clearly visible on the lower-left side of the boxcar. (Courtesy of Village of East Rochester historian.)

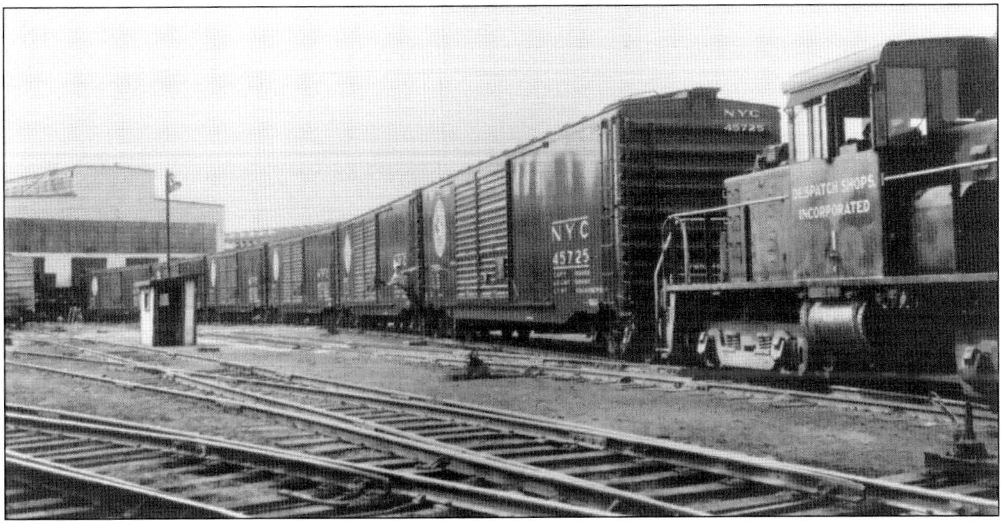

For larger cargo, the carshops also produced a double-door boxcar. Shown in the late-1950s photograph is a brand-new set of double-doors being pulled along by a recently purchased GE center-cab diesel switcher. Note that the "Early Bird for Progress" faster freight service logo has replaced the traditional NYC oval on the side of each boxcar. (Courtesy of Village of East Rochester historian.)

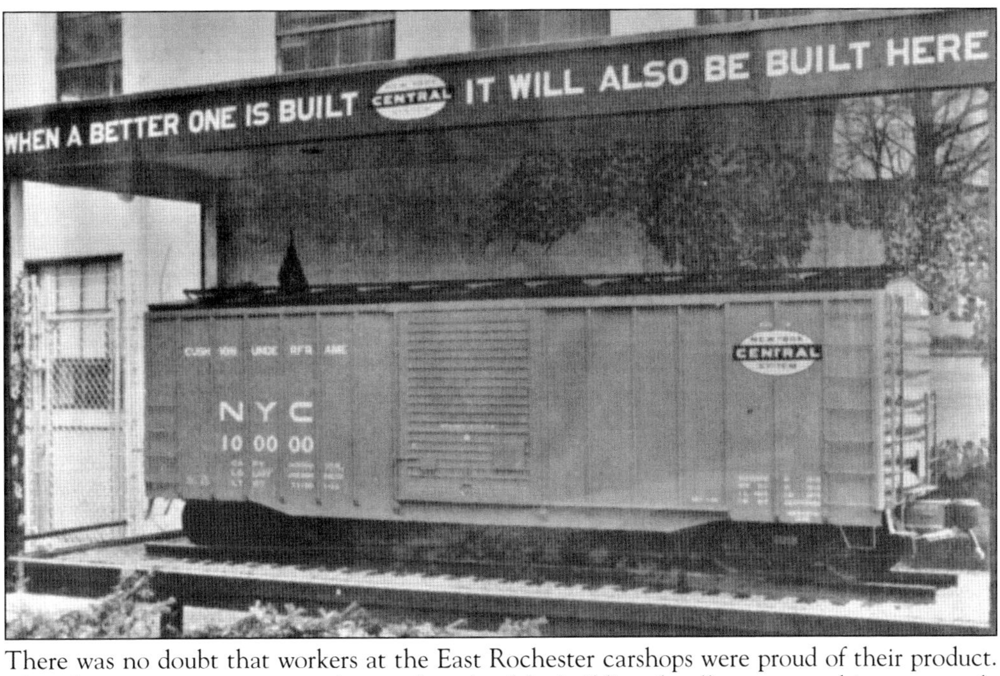

There was no doubt that workers at the East Rochester carshops were proud of their product. Therefore, it was not surprising that on the side of the building, for all to see, was this quarterscale model of a mid-1960s boxcar. The sign above the model says it all. (Courtesy of Village of East Rochester historian.)

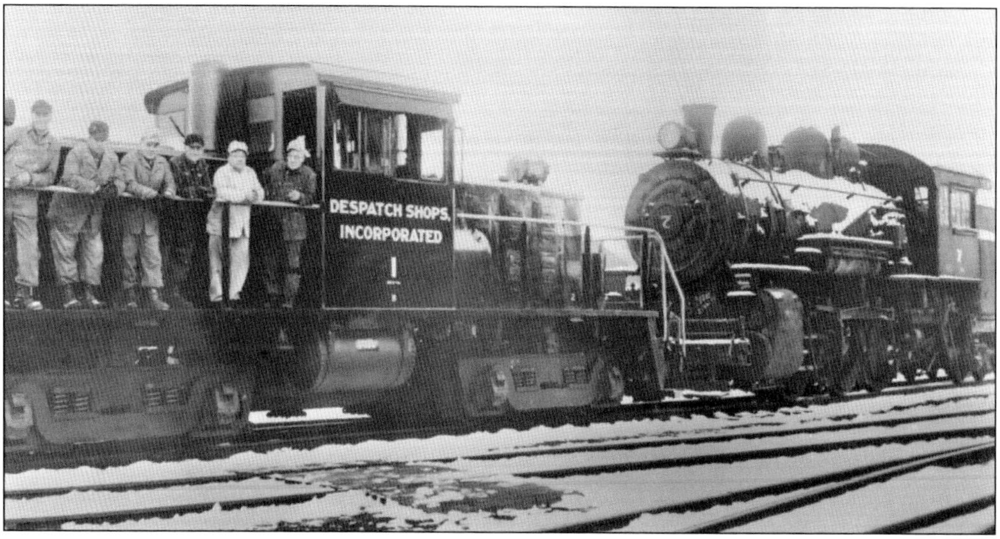

These men look quite happy to exchange their 0-6-0 yard switcher for the recently delivered center-cab diesel switcher. This event occurred in the mid-1950s when three such engines were received. (Courtesy of Village of East Rochester historian.)

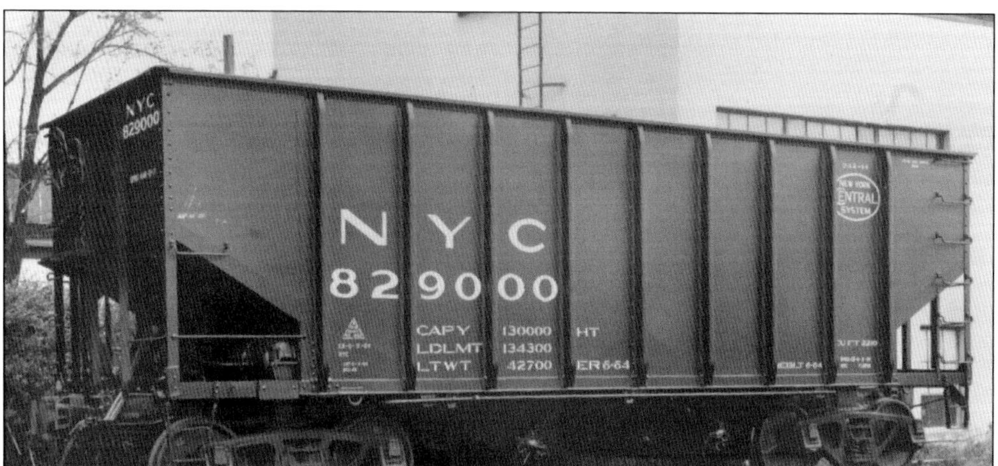

The carshops also rebuilt freight cars. Shown in this photograph is a hopper car rebuilt for NYC in 1964. (Courtesy of Village of East Rochester historian.)

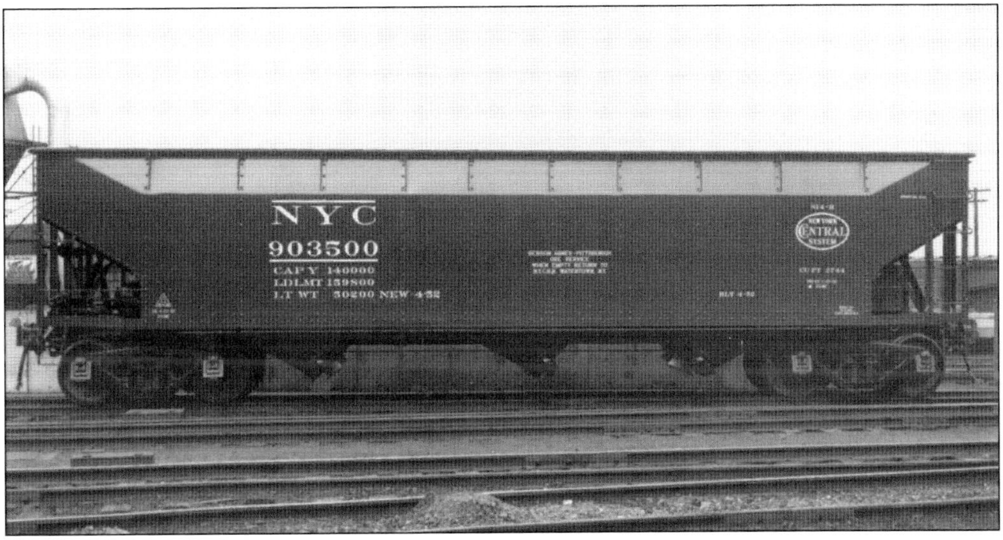

In 1952, NYC turned to the carshops to build special 70-ton hopper cars for the shipment of iron ore from Benson Mines in the Adirondack Highlands of New York State to the steel mills of Pennsylvania. Note that the instructions on the side of the car request a return of the empty hopper to Watertown, New York, and the Massey Yards located there. (Courtesy of New York Central System Historical Society.)

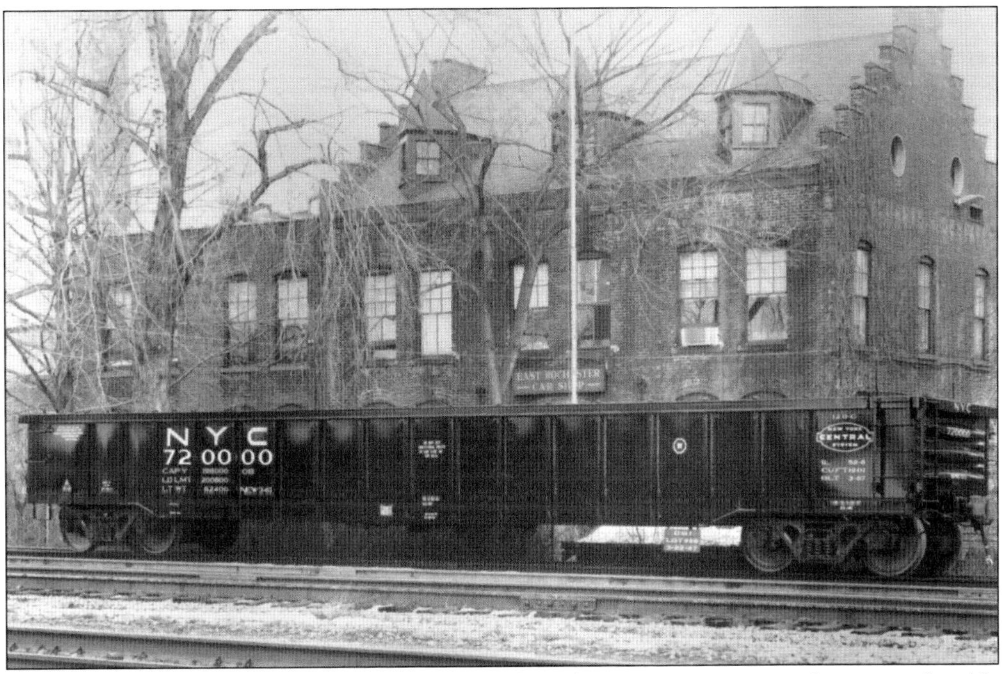

The name "the carshops" was familiar to all, so much so that management seemed quite comfortable to display the sign on the building behind this shiny 1967-built gondola car. As noted previously, this building was one the first buildings to be constructed by the Merchants Despatch Transportation Company. (Courtesy of Village of East Rochester historian.)

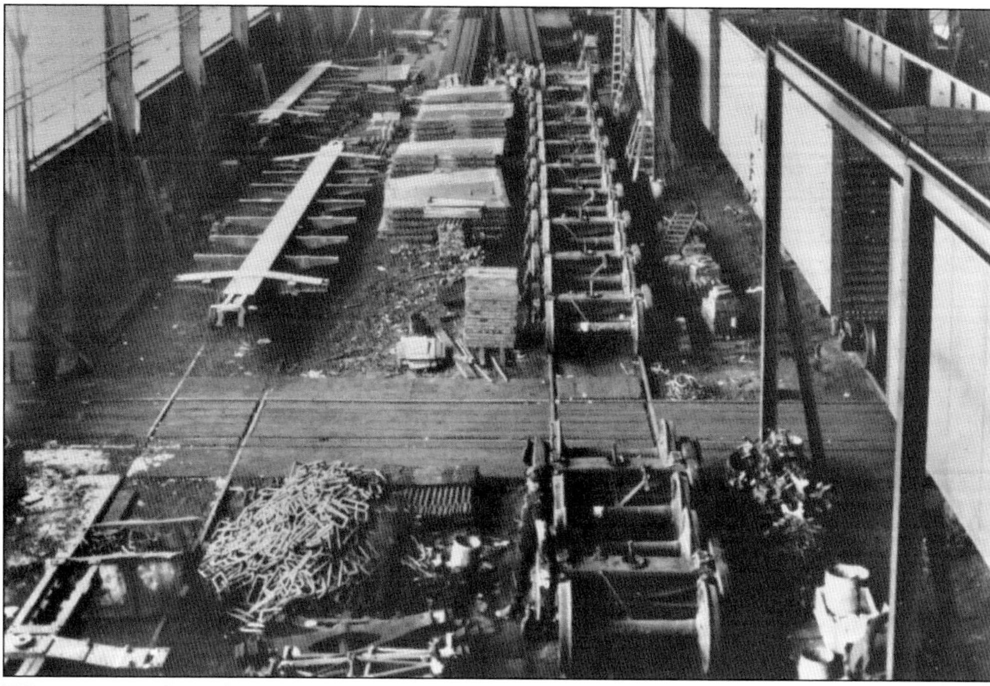

Efficiency was the order of the day inside the carshops plant. Here, the assembly line of wheels and axles is being readied for the undercarriage frames shown on the left. Note that the frames rest on small rail carts for movement around the shop floor. (Courtesy of Village of East Rochester historian.)

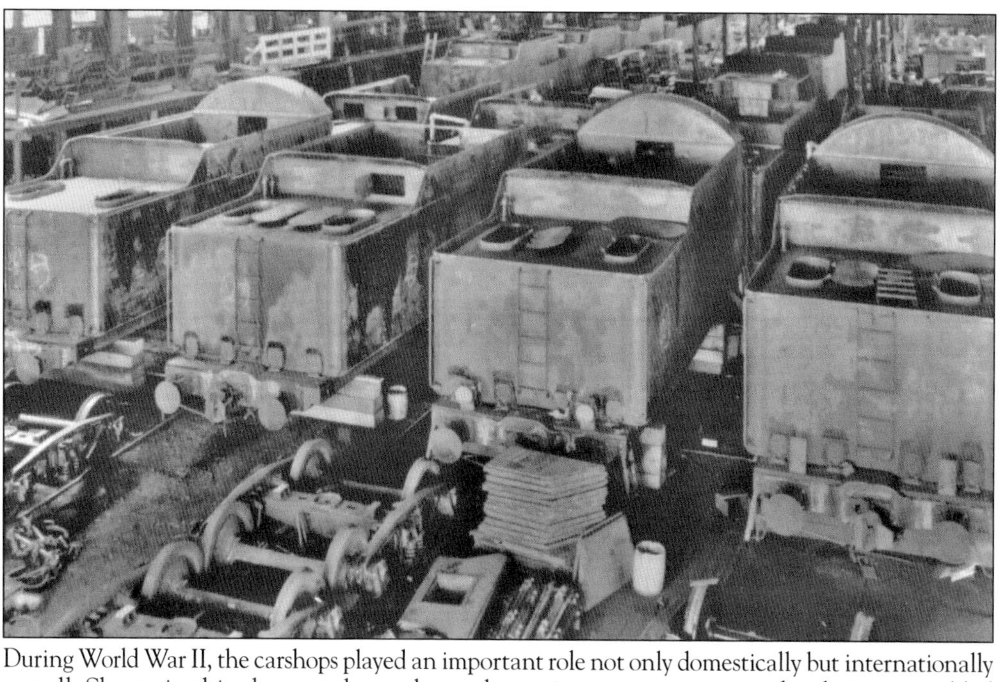

During World War II, the carshops played an important role not only domestically but internationally as well. Shown in this photograph are the coal-carrying steam engine tenders being assembled for shipment to the Soviet Union. (Courtesy of Village of East Rochester historian.)

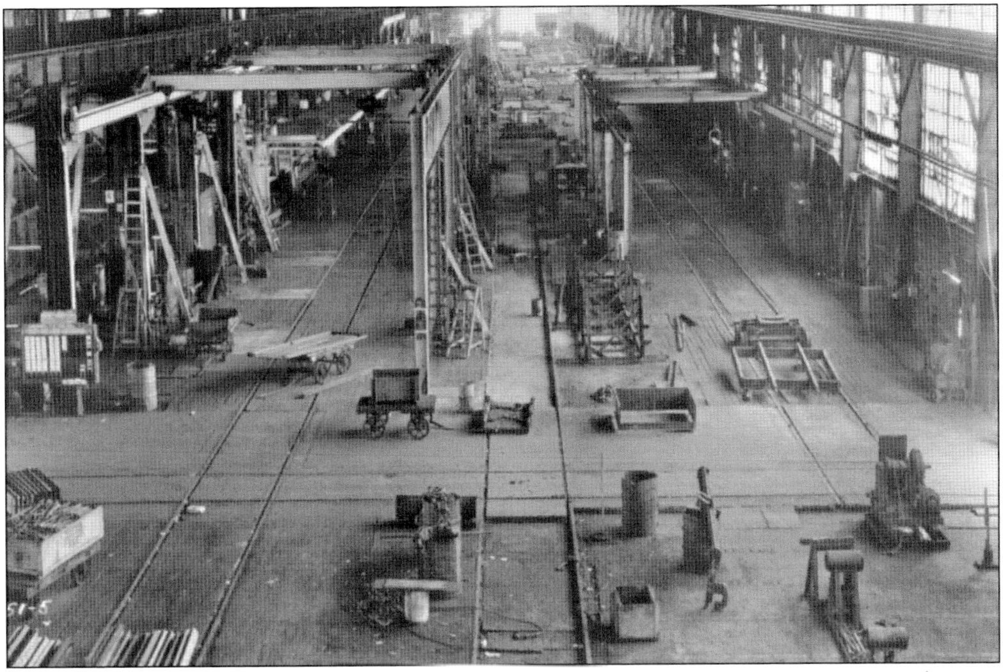

This view of the shop floor shows both the small rail carts and pushcarts as important features of the production process. They enabled rapid movement of parts to and from different areas of the shop floor. (Courtesy of Village of East Rochester historian.)

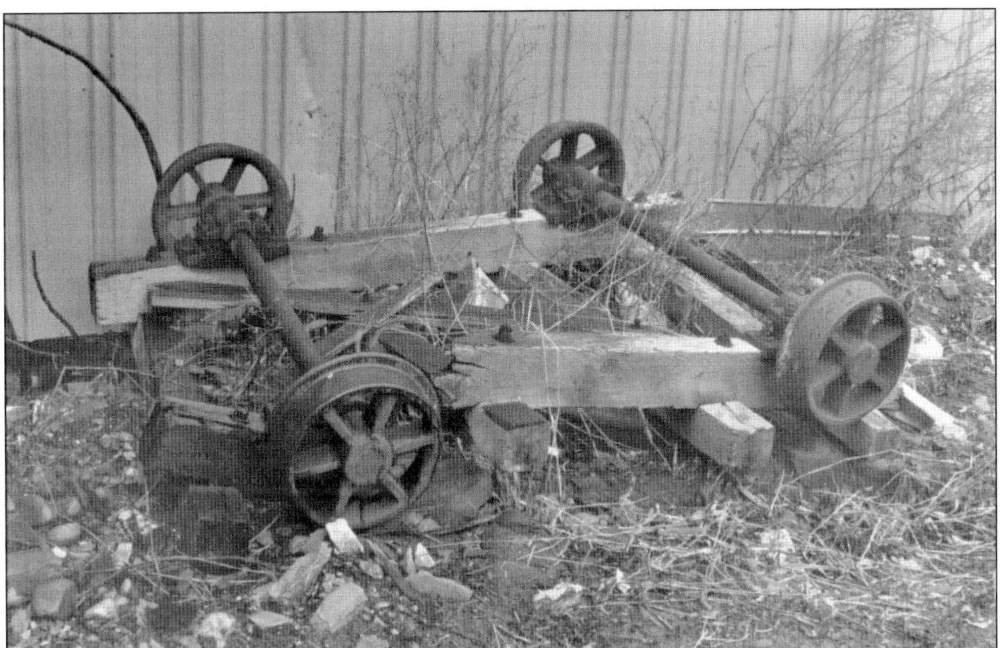

The carshops closed in the early 1970s. Discarded were items such as this small rail cart that at one time was so important to the production line efficiency. (Courtesy of Village of East Rochester historian.)

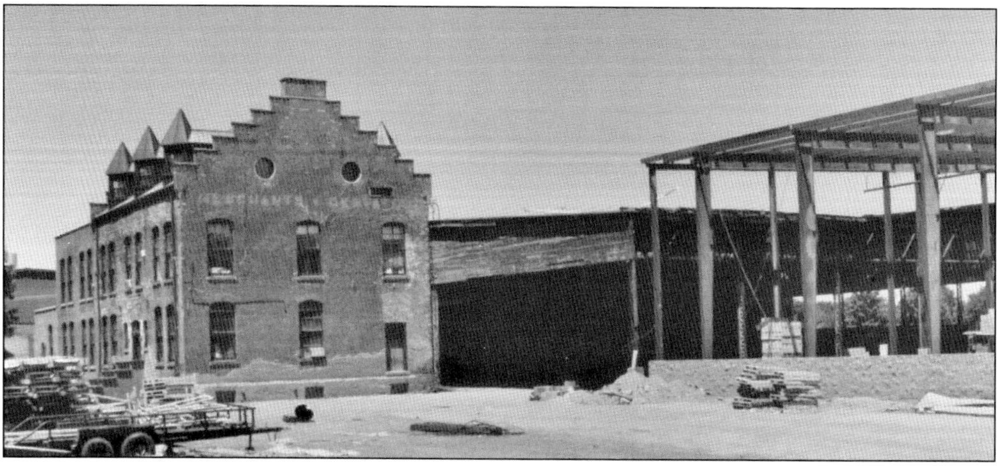

The last of original Merchants Despatch Transportation Company structures is shown in this 2012 photograph. This is the same building that appears in several previous photographs. Note that the name Merchants Despatch is still visible on the side of the building. (Courtesy of Village of East Rochester historian.)

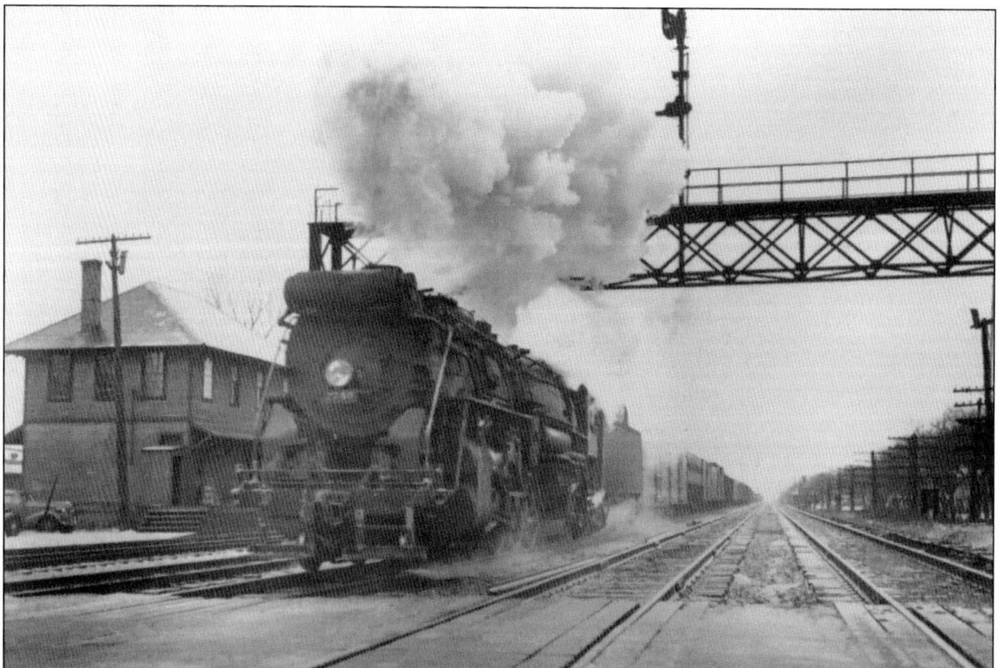

This 1940s photograph shows a class L2a Mohawk speeding through East Rochester on the NYC main line near the carshops. The building on the left was erected in the mid-1800s and served as a freight station until the late 1940s. The structure was then converted to a bar and grill, appropriately called the Freight House, and in the mid-1980s, it became home to the Despatch Junction hobby shop. Sadly, the entire building was destroyed by fire in 2014. However, the owner made many people happy by vowing to rebuild his popular hobby shop. (Courtesy of Jeff Hands.)

Six

Getting Around by Streetcar

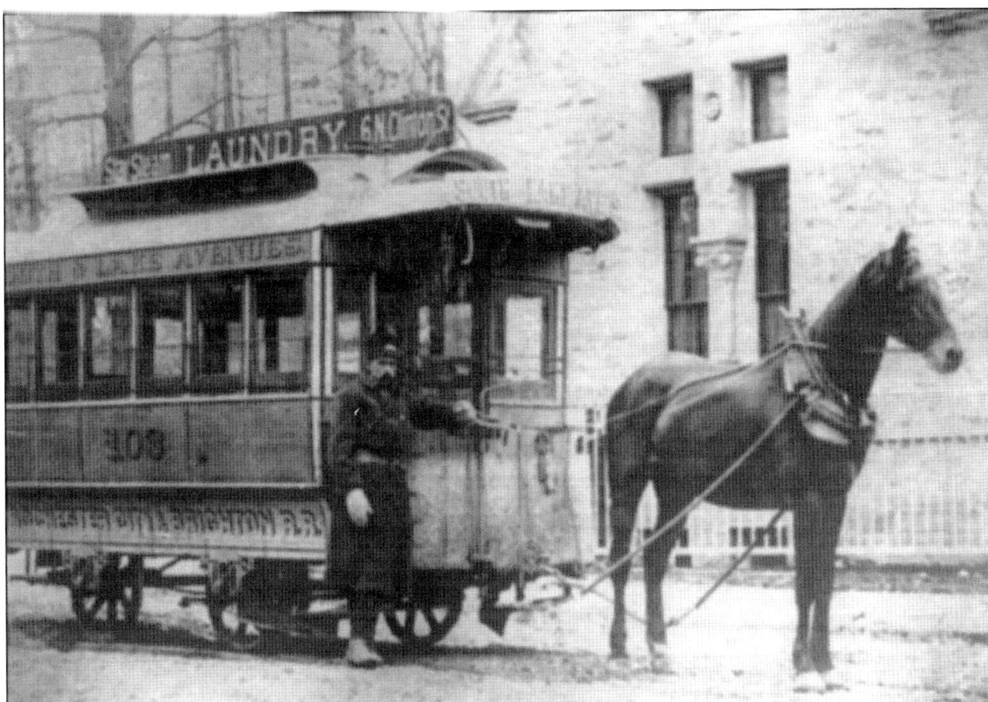

The Rochester City & Brighton Railroad started as a railway transit company in 1862 using horse-drawn streetcars. It expanded its service throughout the city of Rochester, and before its sale to the Rochester Railway Company in 1890, it planned to convert from horses to electricity to power its streetcars. One of the company's last horse-drawn streetcars, complete with its rooftop advertisement for a steam laundry, is shown in this 1889 photograph. (Courtesy of *Rochester Images*: Rochester Library Local History Division.)

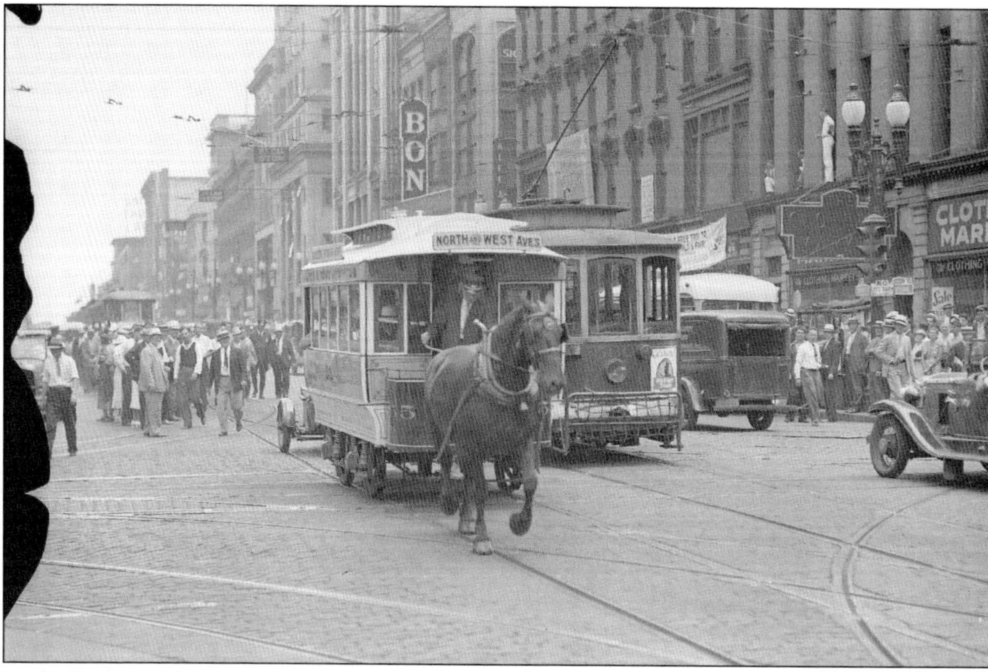

Both the horse-drawn and the electric streetcar are shown in this photograph taken on Main Street at South Avenue. They are probably part of a 1934 Rochester Centennial Celebration Parade that people have gathered to watch. (Courtesy of Rochester Museum & Science Center, Albert R. Stone Collection.)

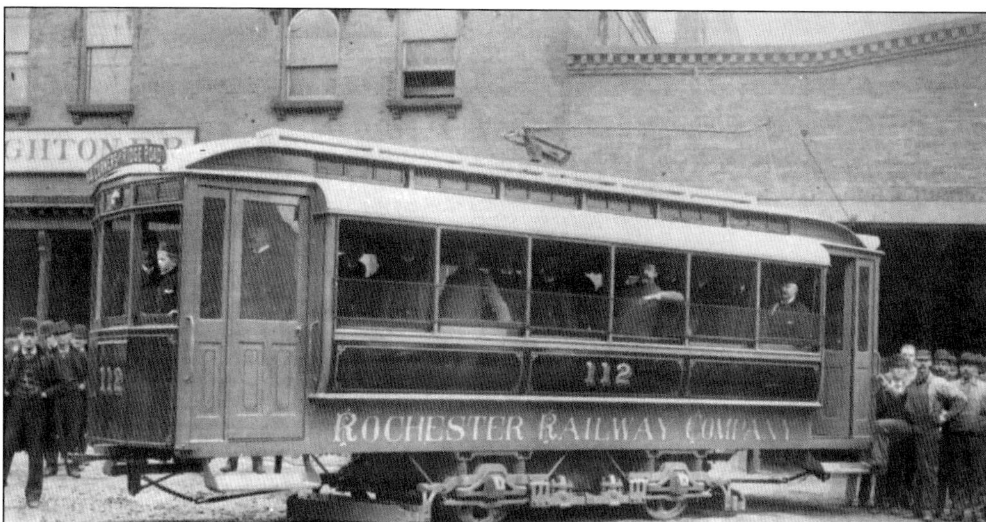

In 1890, with the Rochester Railway Company leading the way, electric streetcars started operating in Rochester. The streetcars were very popular with Rochesterians, as seen in the photograph. The company continued to grow, leasing several lines that extended its service to additional city and county locations. In 1909, it became the Rochester Lines, part of the larger New York State Railways group. With the bankruptcy of the parent company, Rochester Lines was reorganized in 1938 as the Rochester Transit Company. (Courtesy of *Rochester Images*: Rochester Library Local History Division.)

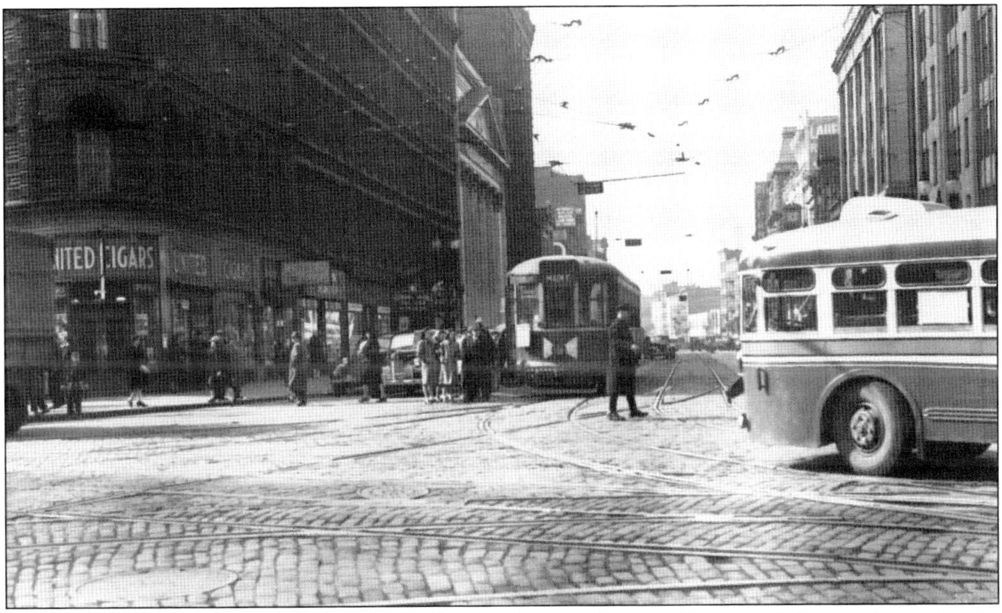

In this interesting 1941 photograph, both a Rochester Transit Company's bus and an electric streetcar are shown at the busy corner of State and Main Streets. During this time period, urban transportation in Rochester was undergoing a change from streetcars to buses. By March 3, 1941, the transition was complete. (Courtesy of the City of Rochester, New York.)

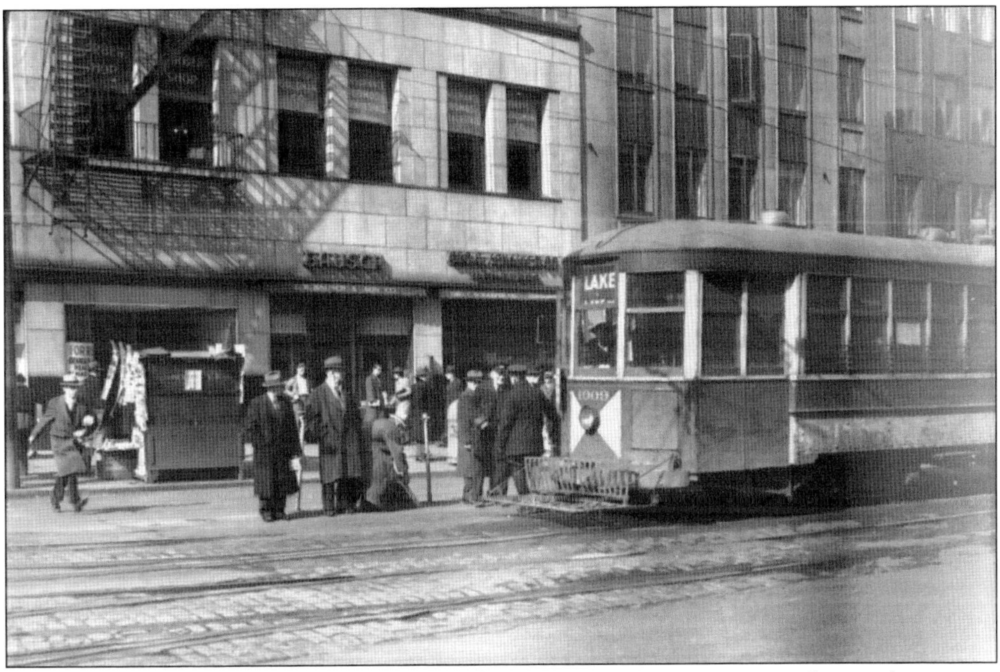

Many streetcar routes served Rochester providing convenient transportation for people to get to and from work. In this 1941 photograph, passengers are seen getting on the Lake Avenue streetcar, homeward bound from a day's work at one of the many companies in Rochester. (Courtesy of the City of Rochester, New York.)

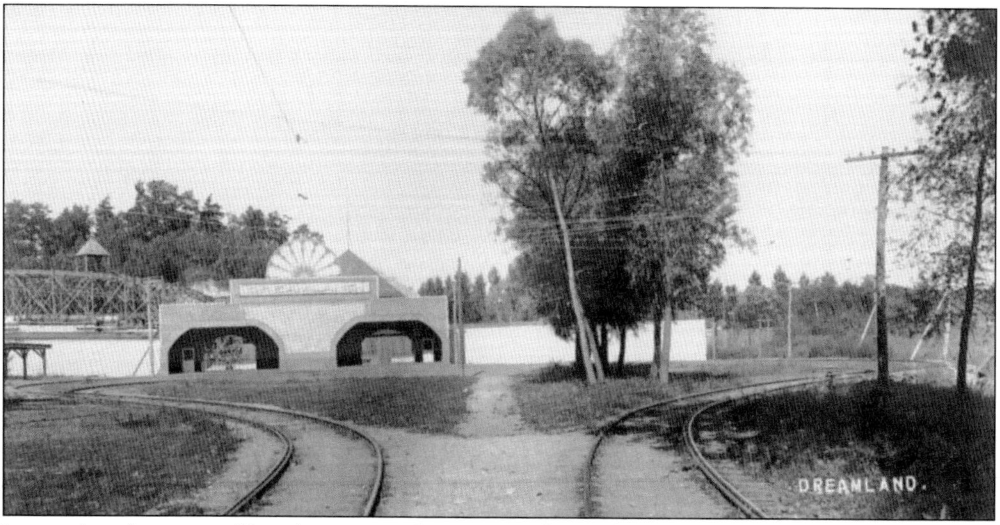

Located in the town of Irondequoit on the western shore of Irondequoit Bay was one of Monroe County's most popular amusement parks, Dreamland Park, known originally as Glen Haven Park. Shown in the c. 1908 photograph is the Rochester and Sodus Bay Railroad trolley stop at the Dreamland Park entrance. (Courtesy of *Rochester Images*: Rochester Library Local History Division.)

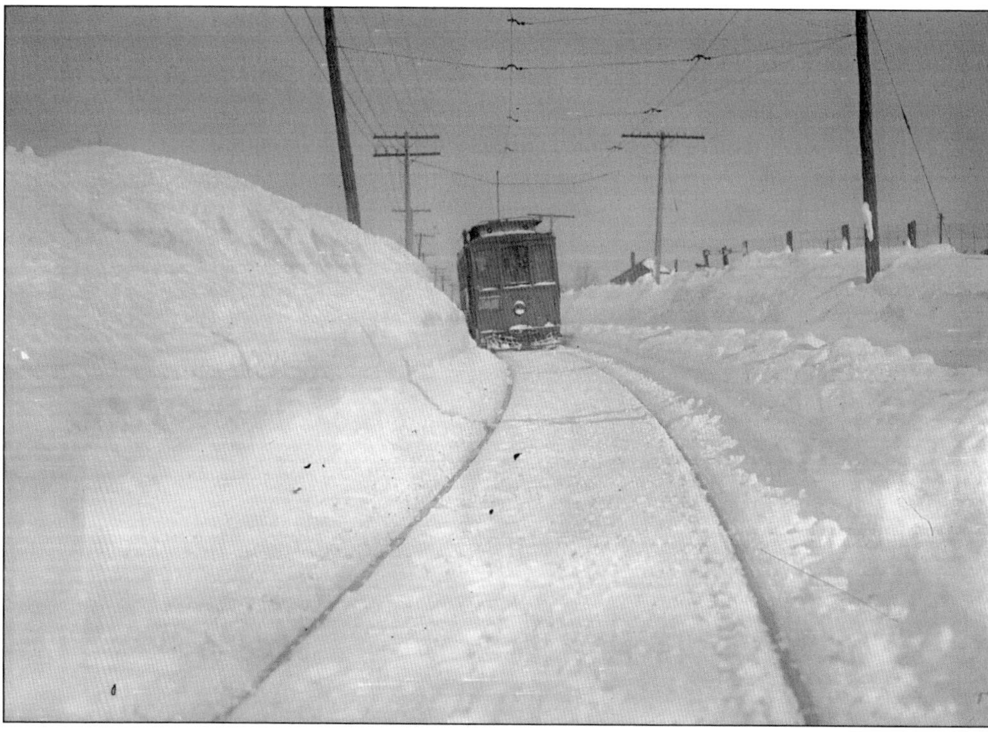

Sea Breeze, with its well-known Jack Rabbitt roller coaster, was another amusement park located in the town of Irondequoit east of Durand-Eastman Park. With Sea Breeze located close to Lake Ontario, it was not surprising to see that lake-effect snowdrifts posed problems. In this 1916 photograph, plows have had to tier the snowdrifts to keep the Sea Breeze line clear. (Courtesy of Rochester Museum & Science Center, Albert R. Stone Collection.)

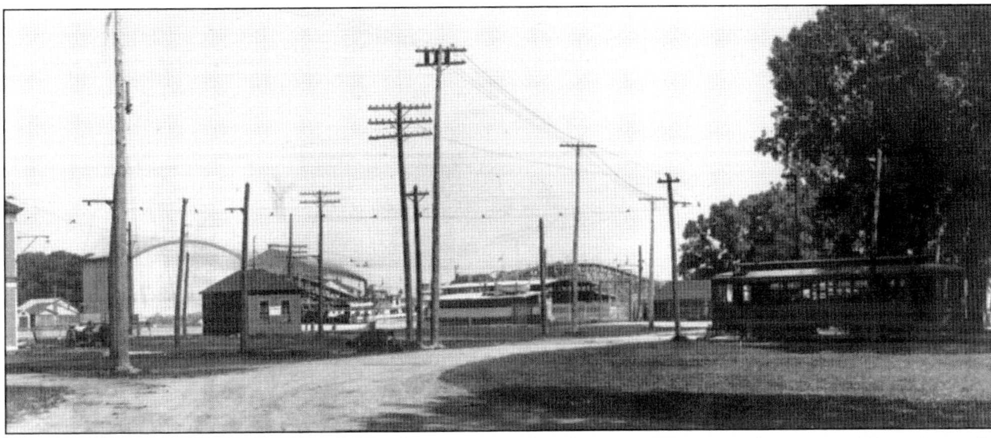

Summerville, located just east of Charlotte across the Genesee River in the town of Irondequoit, was a gathering spot that was reachable by the streetcars of the Rochester & Irondequoit Railway, under lease to Rochester Railway Company. Both the ferry on the Genesee River and Ontario Beach Park in the background are indications that the photograph was probably taken in Summerville, with a view looking to the west across the river toward Charlotte. Adjacent to the Summerville trolley loop in the photograph is the popular Summerville Garden restaurant that was built in 1882. The Charlotte-Summerville Ferry Company began operating in 1894, shuttling people across the Genesee River for a day of food and drink. (Courtesy of *Rochester Images*: Rochester Library Local History Division.)

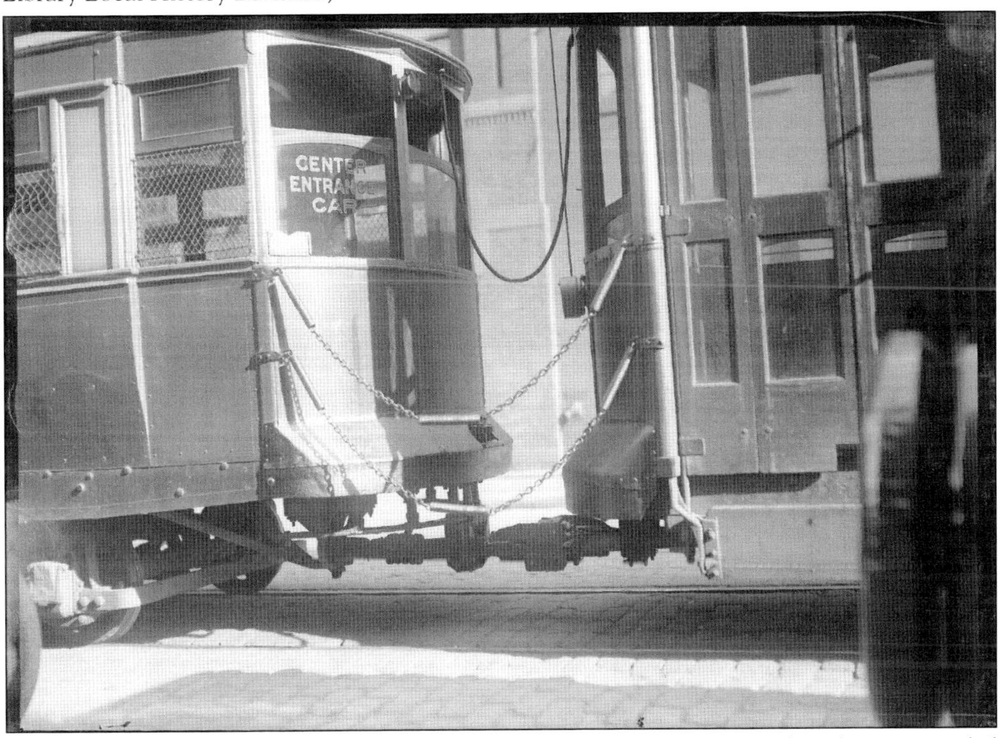

To handle rush-hour passenger loads, the Rochester Railway Company used trailer cars coupled to powered streetcars. This 1922 photograph shows the company's concern with safety, with safety chains on the boarding side to keep passengers away from the space between the cars. (Courtesy of Rochester Museum & Science Center, Albert R. Stone Collection.)

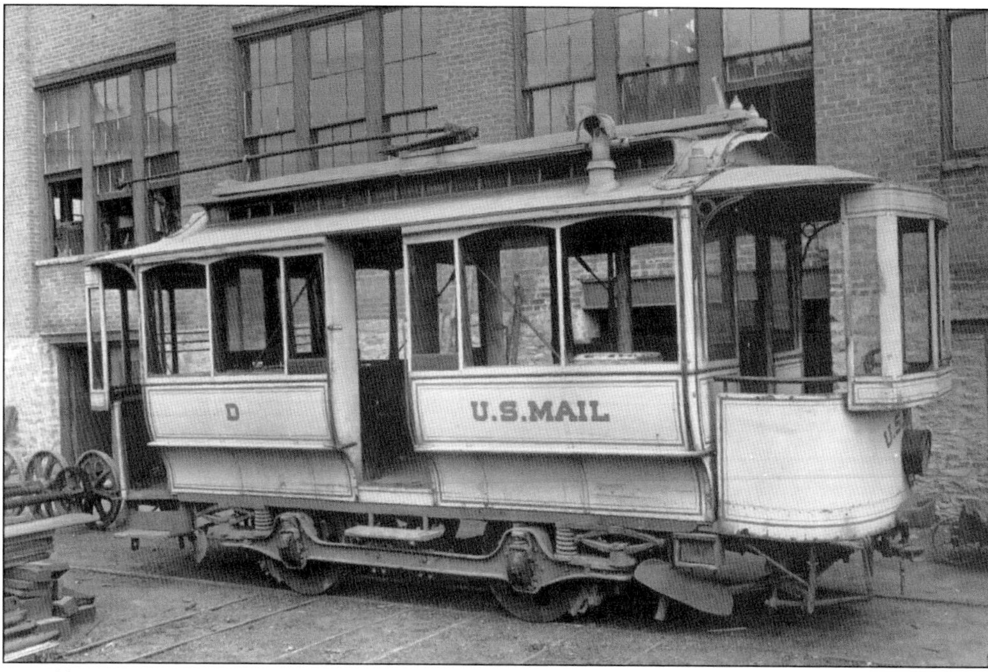

In addition to providing excellent transportation for the people of Rochester, the Rochester Railway Company also carried mail for a time. The company operated mail cars B, C, and D between 1896 and 1909. The cars made five trips daily, collecting mail at special holding boxes. (Courtesy of *Rochester Images*: Rochester Library Local History Division.)

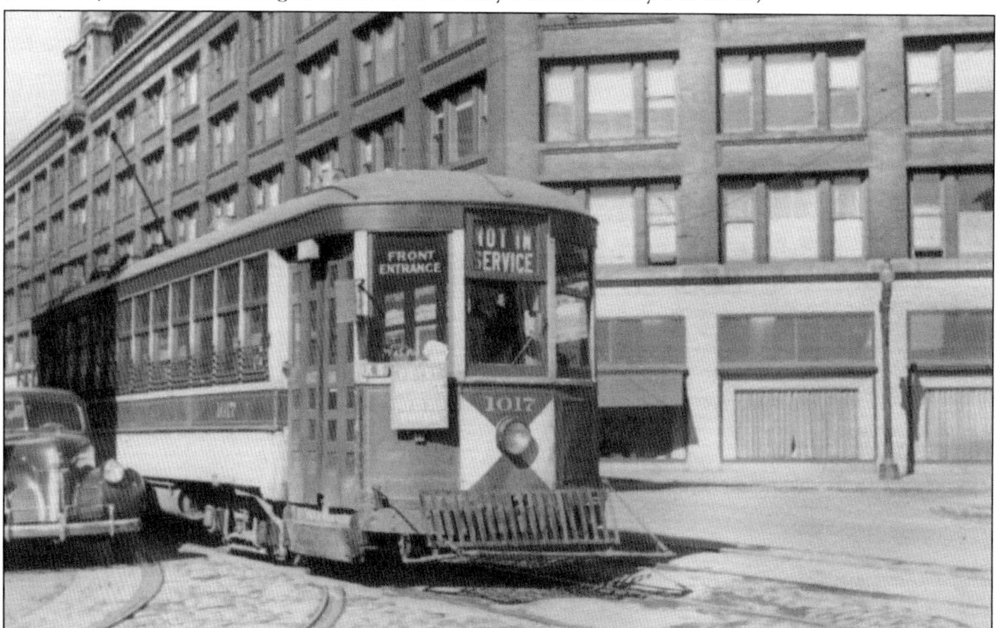

In the early 1940s in Rochester, the transition from streetcars to buses was well underway. The photograph, taken on Main Street near the popular Sibley's department store, shows a streetcar displaying a "not in service" sign indicating it is on its way back to the East Main Street carbarns. (Courtesy of *Rochester Images*: Rochester Library Local History Division.)

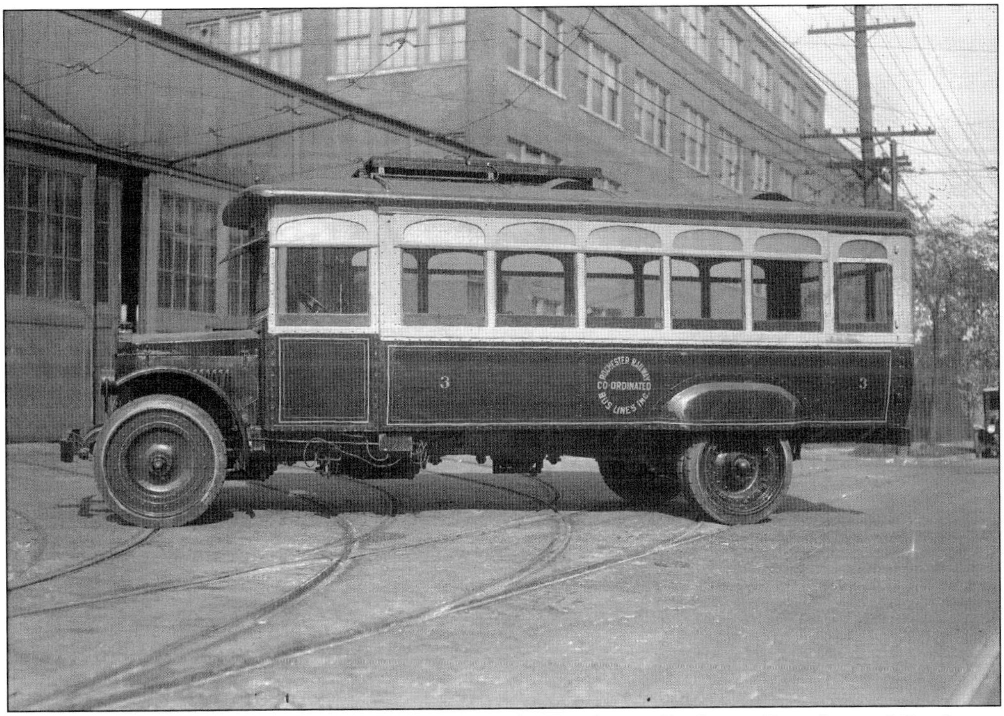

Prior to the transition from streetcars to buses, the Rochester Railways Coordinated Bus Lines installed a "track-less trolley" on Driving Park Avenue in 1923. Because these vehicles ran on rubber wheels and received their power from overhead transmission lines, another overhead wire was needed for the electric current return. It appears that vehicle No. 8 has just come from the factory and has yet to have the two trolley poles mounted on the roof. The company ceased operations in 1932. (Courtesy of Rochester Museum & Science Center, Albert R. Stone Collection.)

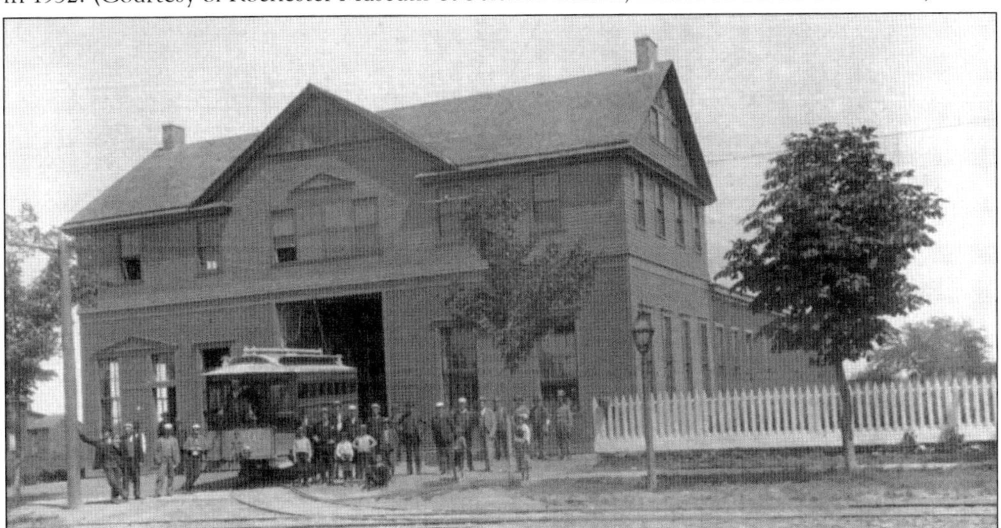

Besides the Sea Breeze line and Summerville line, there was also service to Charlotte and the Ontario Beach Park. The carbarn shown in this c. 1890 photograph was very close to the Genesee River Lighthouse presented in chapter 2. (Courtesy of *Rochester Images*: Rochester Library Local History Division.)

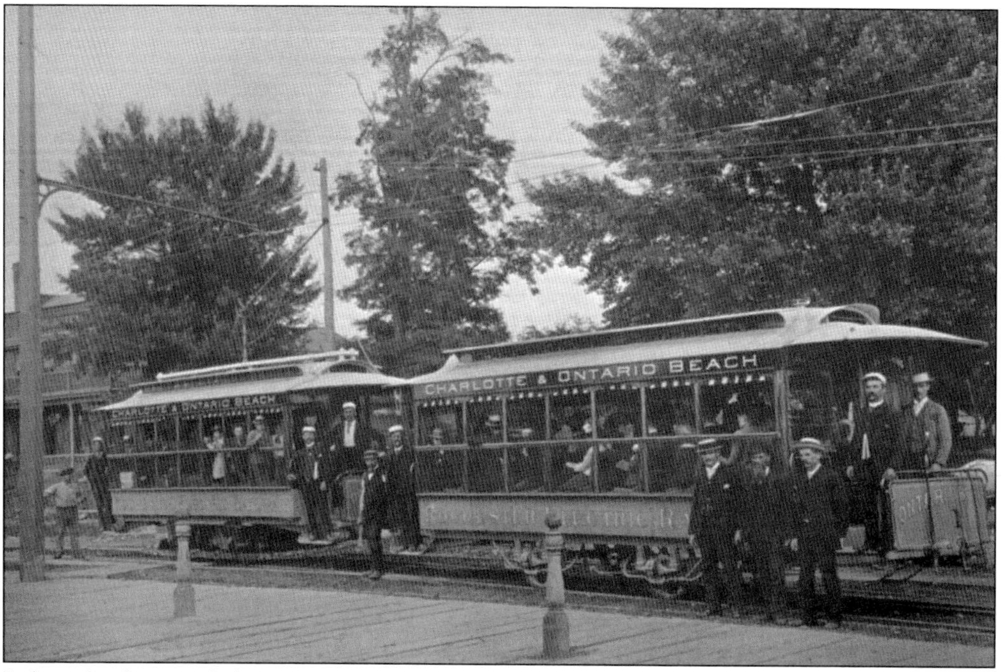

Judging by the crowded streetcar in this c. 1890 photograph, the line to Ontario Beach Park, part of the Rochester Electric Railway, was a very popular route, especially in the summer. (Courtesy of the City of Rochester, New York.)

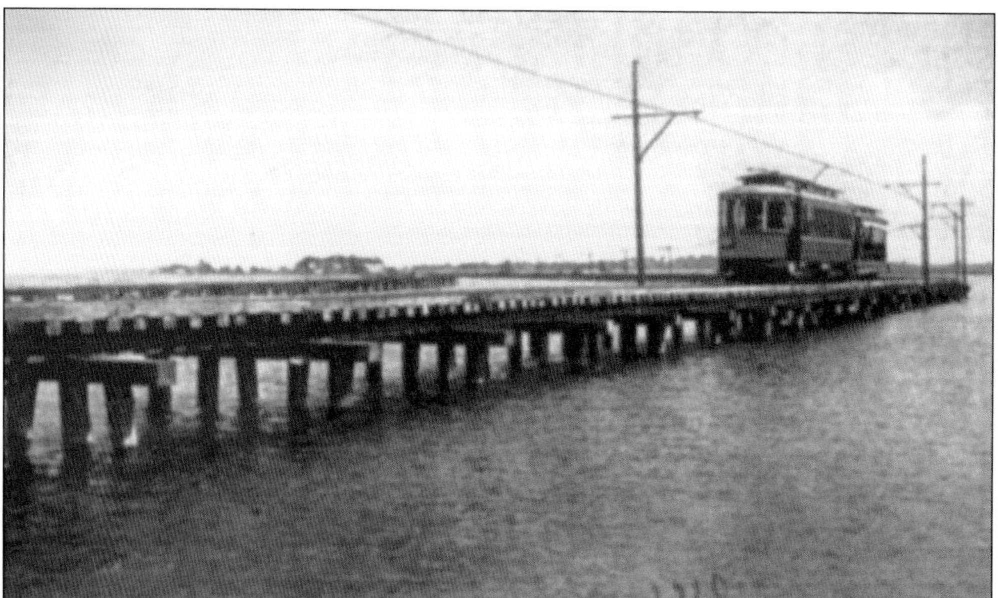

Also popular in the summer was the Rochester & Manitou Railroad that served the summer resorts along Lake Ontario west of Charlotte. The trolley in this c. 1910 postcard is shown crossing Braddock Bay in the town of Greece. (Courtesy of *Rochester Images*: Greece Municipal Historian Collection.)

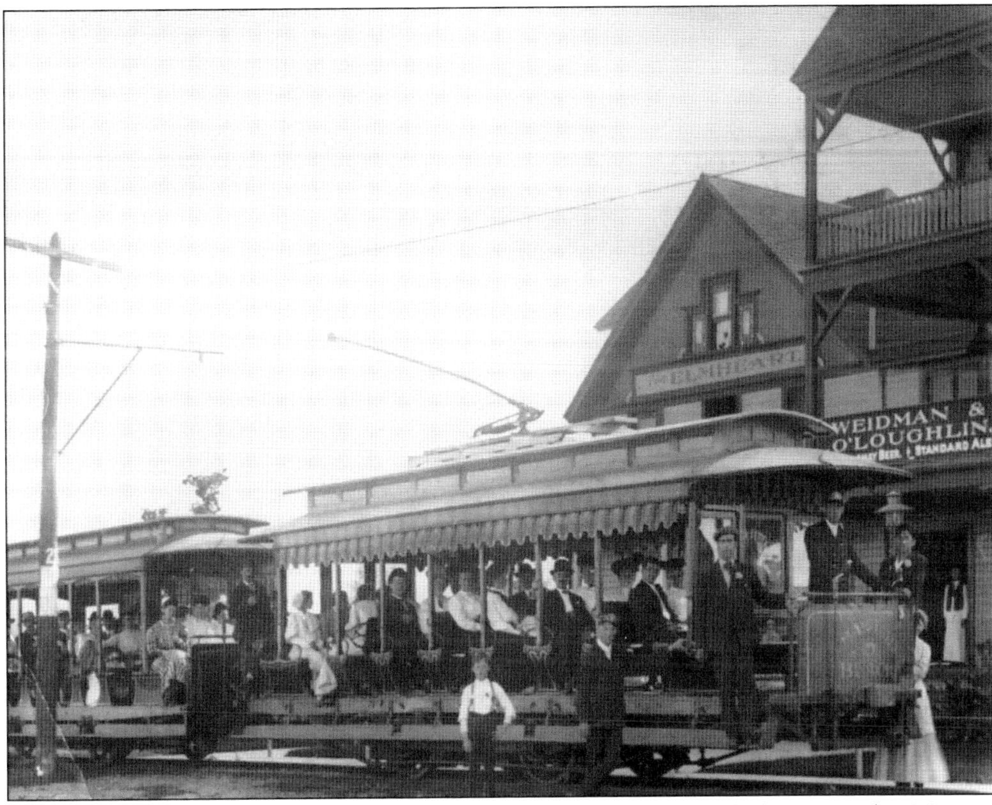

One of the hotels served by the Rochester and Manitou line was the Elmheart Hotel in Manitou Beach in the town of Greece. In the late 1930s, it ceased operating as a hotel and became a restaurant. In 1992, the restaurant was destroyed by fire. (Courtesy of *Rochester Images*: Greece Municipal Historian Collection.)

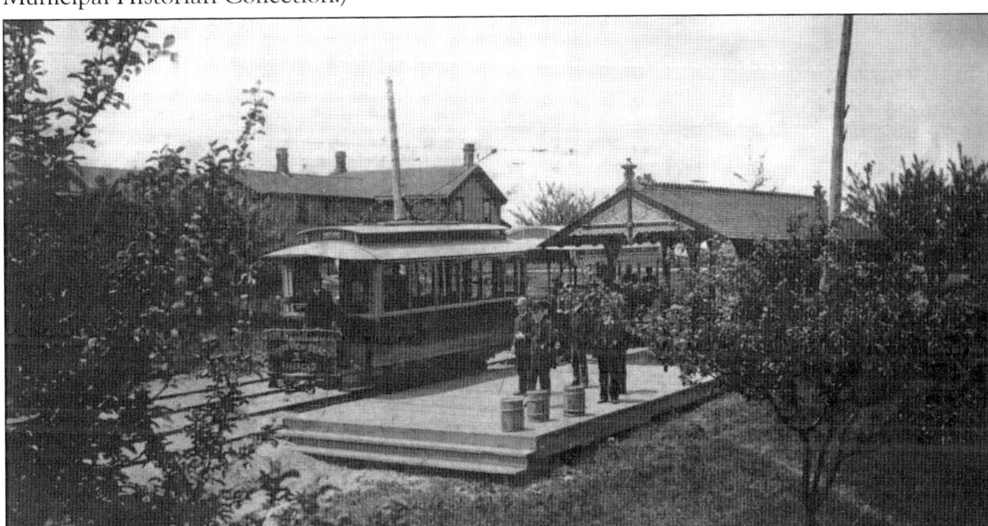

For a brief time, from 1891 to 1895, the line to Manitou Beach was operated by the Grand View Beach Railroad. The photograph shows the station at Manitou Beach during this time period. (Courtesy of *Rochester Images*: Rochester Library Local History Division.)

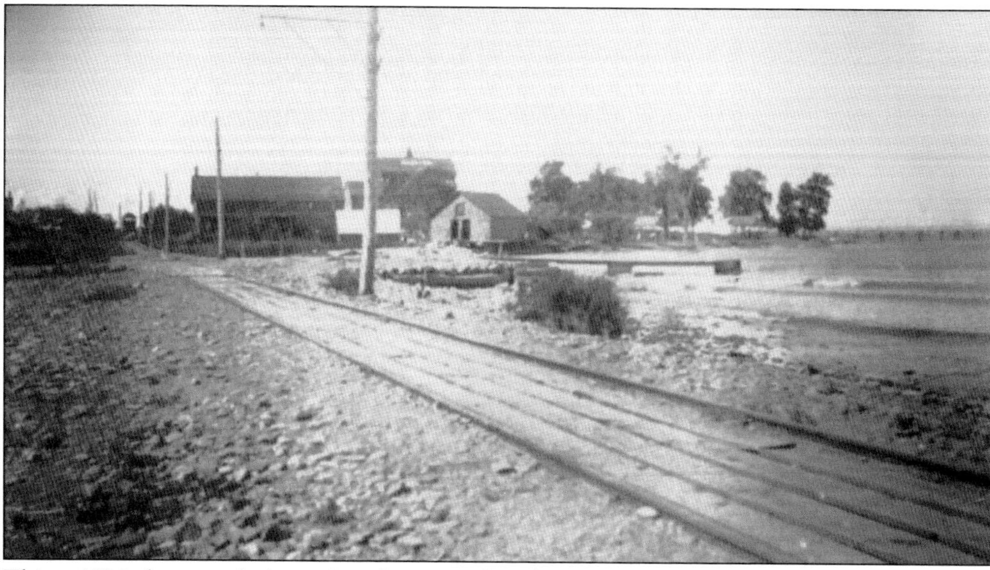

This c. 1900 photograph shows that there were hotels to visit at the Manitou beaches. In addition to the Elmheart Hotel, there was the Manitou Hotel, shown in the center of the photograph. (Courtesy of *Rochester Images*: Rochester Library Local History Division.)

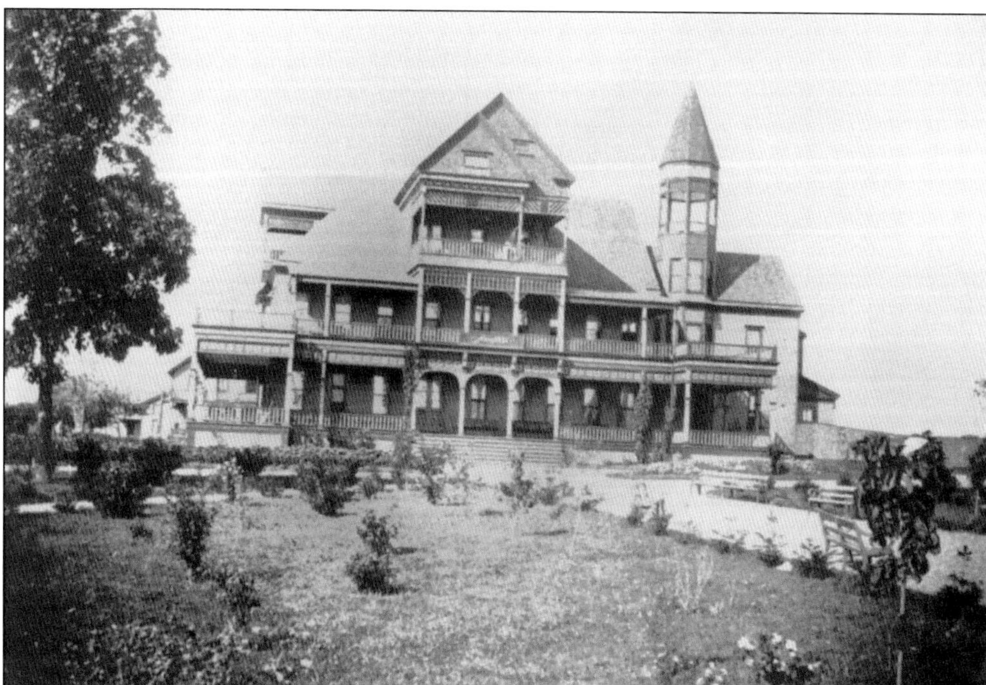

The photograph shows the grandeur of the Manitou Hotel. Its extensive grounds only added to its beauty. The Manitou Hotel opened in 1889 and operated as a hotel until the 1950s. (Courtesy of *Rochester Images*: Rochester Library Local History Division.)

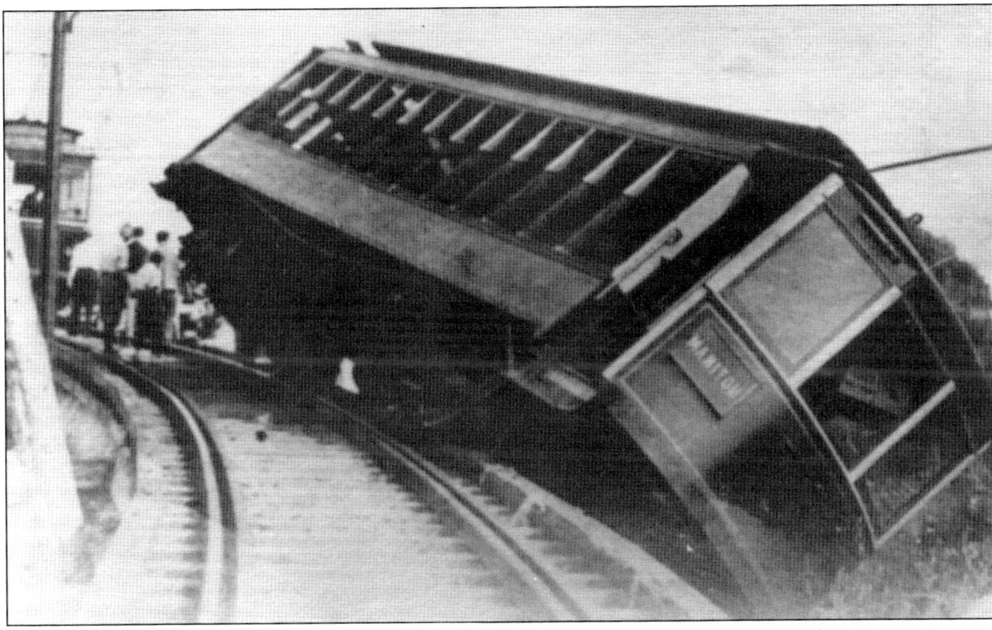

This derailment on the Manitou Beach line occurred during the early 1900s. The two companies that operated the line during this period were the Manitou Beach Railway (1895–1908) and the Rochester & Manitou Railroad (1908–1925). (Courtesy of *Rochester Images*: Rochester Library Local History Division.)

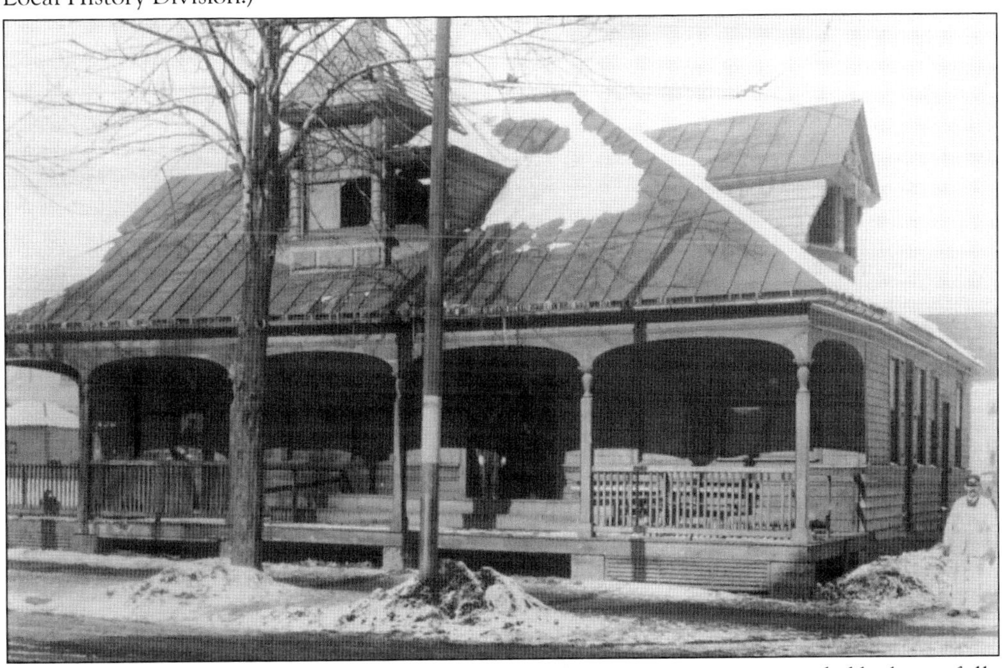

The Glen Haven Hotel was another grand resort. Built in 1899, it was surrounded by beautifully landscaped gardens, and its dining rooms and large verandas could seat over 400 people. By 1902, the Rochester and Sodus Bay Railroad was running cars directly from the center of Rochester to Glen Haven. By 1930, thing changed. The line was discontinued and the hotel was destroyed by fire. (Courtesy of *Rochester Images*: Rochester Library Local History Division.)

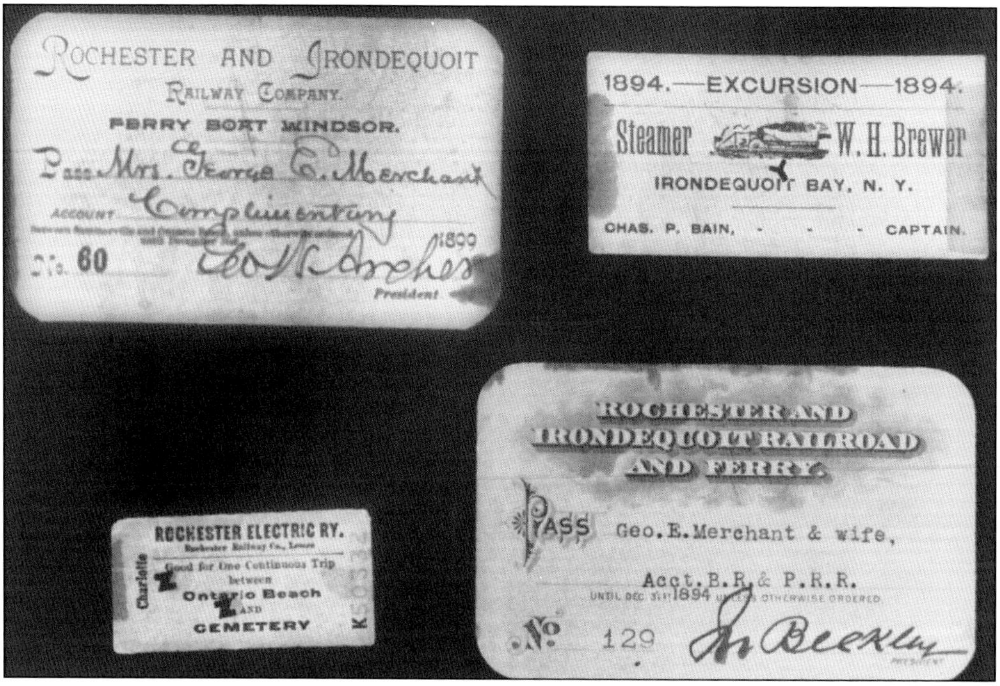

While some trolley riders needed tickets for regular service (lower left) and for excursions (upper right), favored customers and company officials were issued passes such as those shown (upper left and lower right). (Courtesy of *Rochester Images*: Rochester Library Local History Division.)

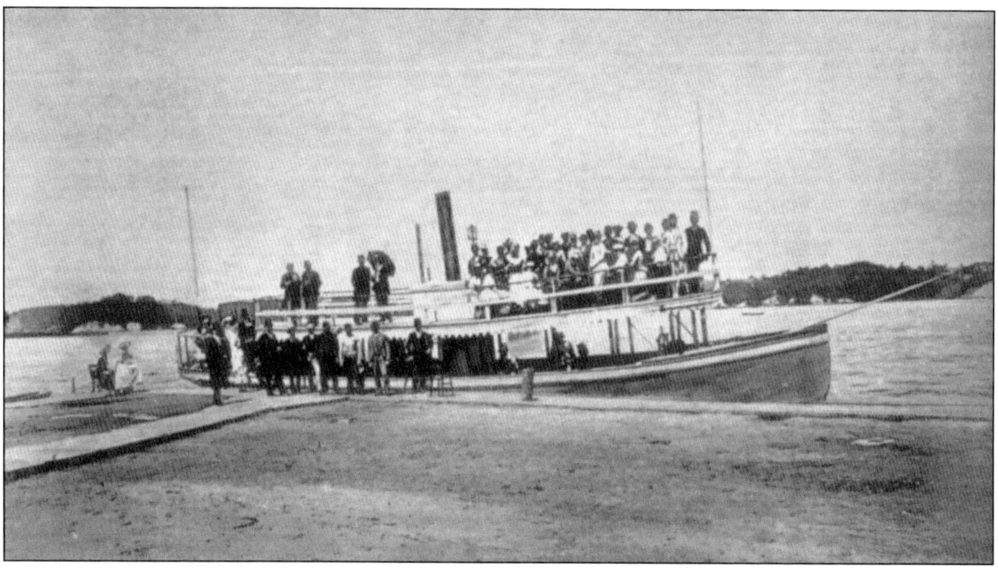

After arriving in Sea Breeze by trolley, it was possible to get to Irondequoit Bay by excursion steamer operating along the Lake Ontario shoreline. In this 1889 photograph, a steamboat from Sea Breeze is shown at the dock of the Bay View Hotel on Irondequoit Bay. (Courtesy of *Rochester Images*: Rochester Library Local History Division.)

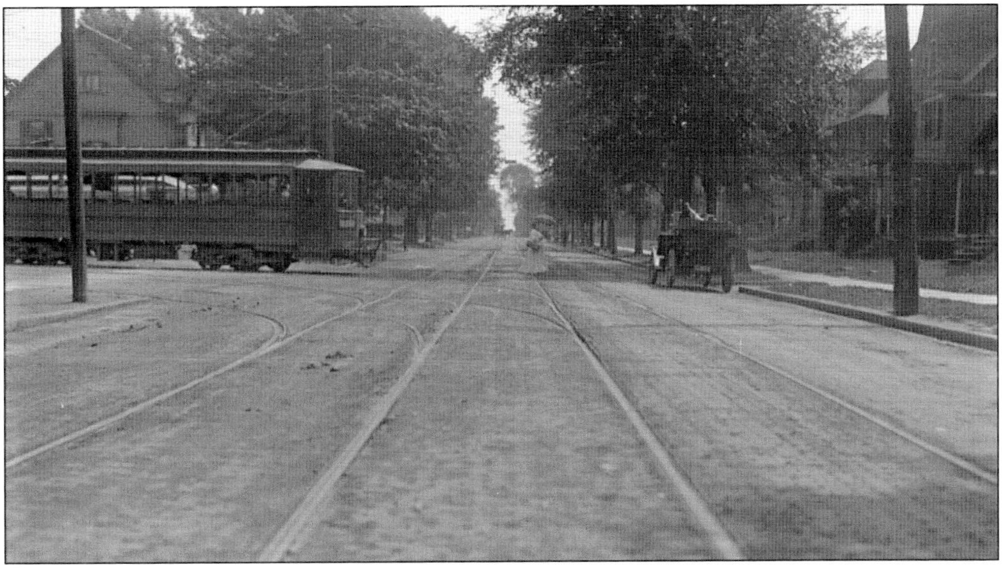

For those who wanted to venture a bit farther for recreation, it was possible to travel to Sodus Bay in Wayne County east of Rochester. Shown in this 1913 photograph is the East Main Street intersection of the Rochester and Sodus Bay Railway with the Main Street streetcar line. At the time of the photograph, the Rochester and Sodus Bay line was part of the New York State Railways. The line ceased operation in 1929. (Courtesy of the City of Rochester, New York.)

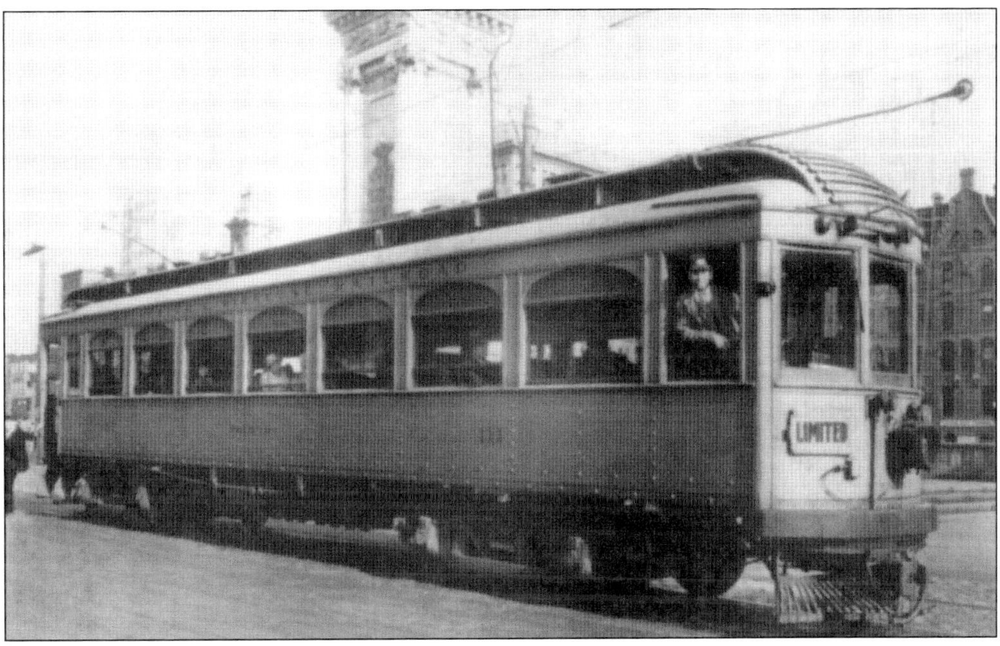

Travel between major cities was also available on an electric interurban line. This photograph shows a Rochester & Syracuse interurban leaving Clinton Square in Syracuse, in Onondaga County, on June 25, 1931, just two days before the line was abandoned. The line provided service to not only Monroe County and Onondaga County but also to those counties in between, namely Wayne and Cayuga. (Courtesy of *Rochester Images*: Rochester Library Local History Division.)

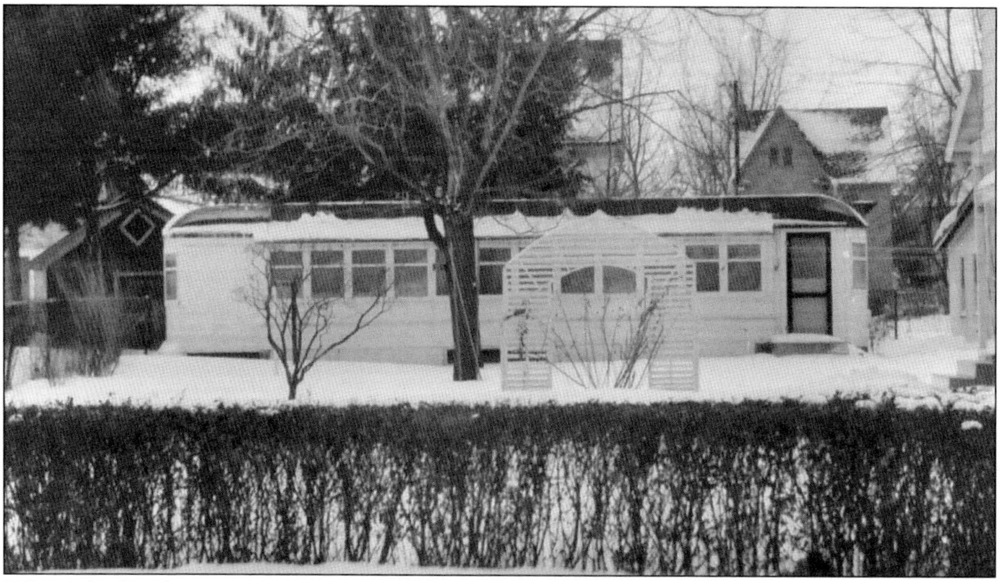

When the Rochester & Syracuse Railroad ceased operations in 1931, its cars were a surplus commodity. Shown in this photograph is how some residents of the village of East Rochester put the unwanted cars to good use. (Courtesy of the Village of East Rochester historian.)

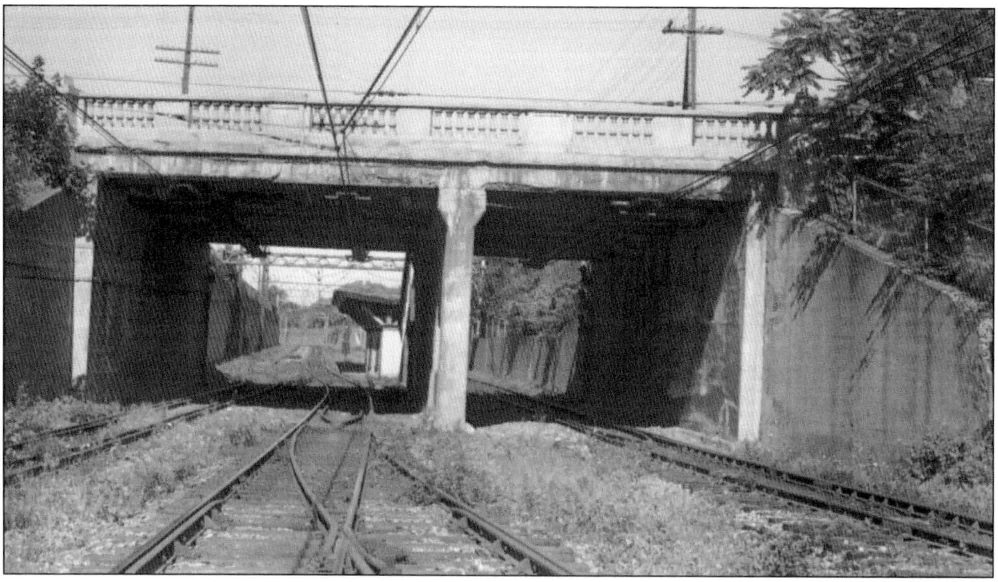

In 1927, an effort was initiated in Rochester to reduce traffic on city streets by funding the Rochester Industrial and Rapid Transit Railway, an electric line more commonly known as the "Rochester Subway." Locating a key section in the old Erie Canal bed allowed the railway to run through Rochester's downtown area without disruption by city street traffic. This 1940s photograph shows a close-up view of the railway's tracks and overhead electric wires on the approach to the Winton Road station. Both the tracks and overheads of the system appear to be well maintained. Economic factors forced the railroad to cease operations in 1956. Today, portions of Rochester's Interstate 490 and Interstates 590 that use the former track bed are reminders of the route taken by the Rochester Subway. Also, memorabilia of the Rochester Subway system can be seen at the New York Museum of Transportation. (Courtesy of the City of Rochester, New York.)

Seven

Iron Horses on the New York Central Main Line

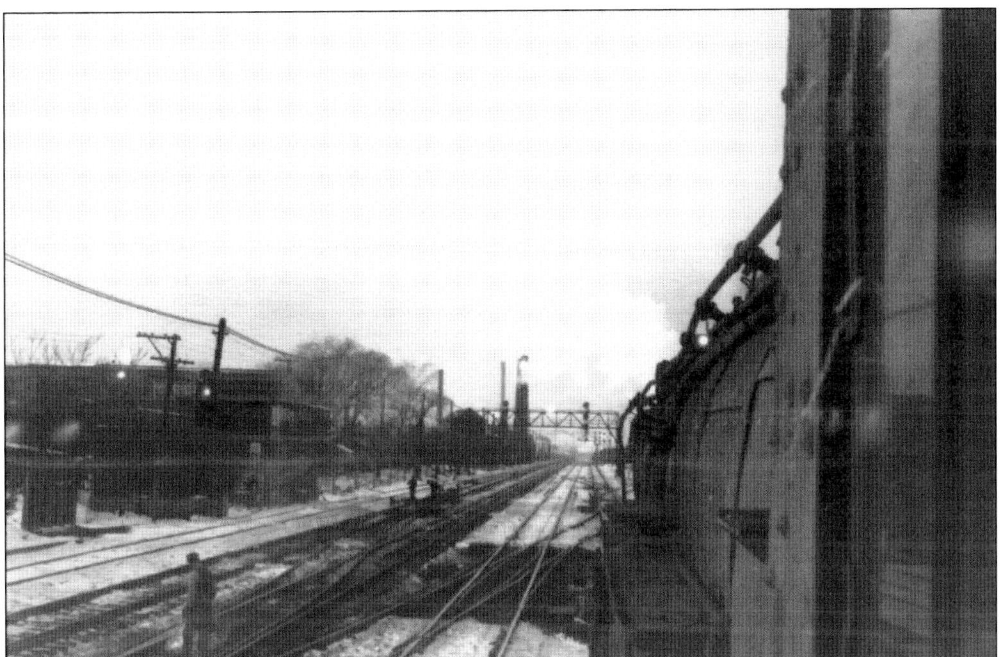

Looking from the fireman's seat in the cab, one would have this view of the New York Central main line at Culver Road on Rochester's east side. With the main line as well as important branch lines of the NYC going through Rochester and parts of Monroe County, there were many vantage points for viewing the many classes and types of NYC steam engines. (Photograph by Bill Chapin, courtesy of Jeff Hands.)

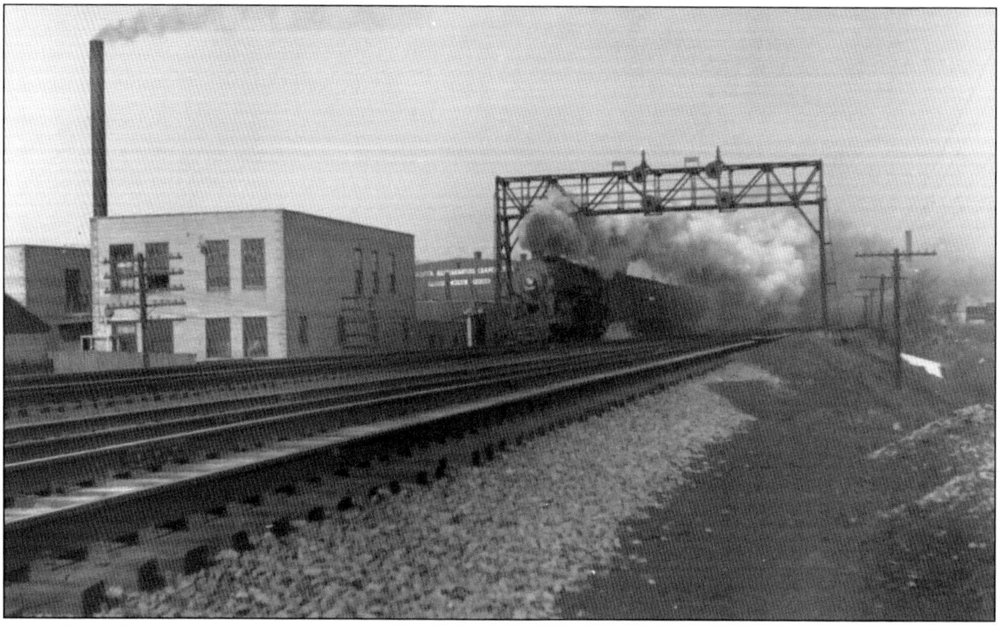

Probably NYC's most famous steam engine was the Hudson class 4-6-4 that was used to power many of NYC's long-distance passenger trains. There were several different subclasses of the Hudson during its production years, which ran from the late 1920s to the late 1930s. Shown in this photograph is a class J1c Hudson headed eastbound near Winton Road, also on Rochester's east side. (Photograph by Robert Carper, courtesy of Jeff Hands.)

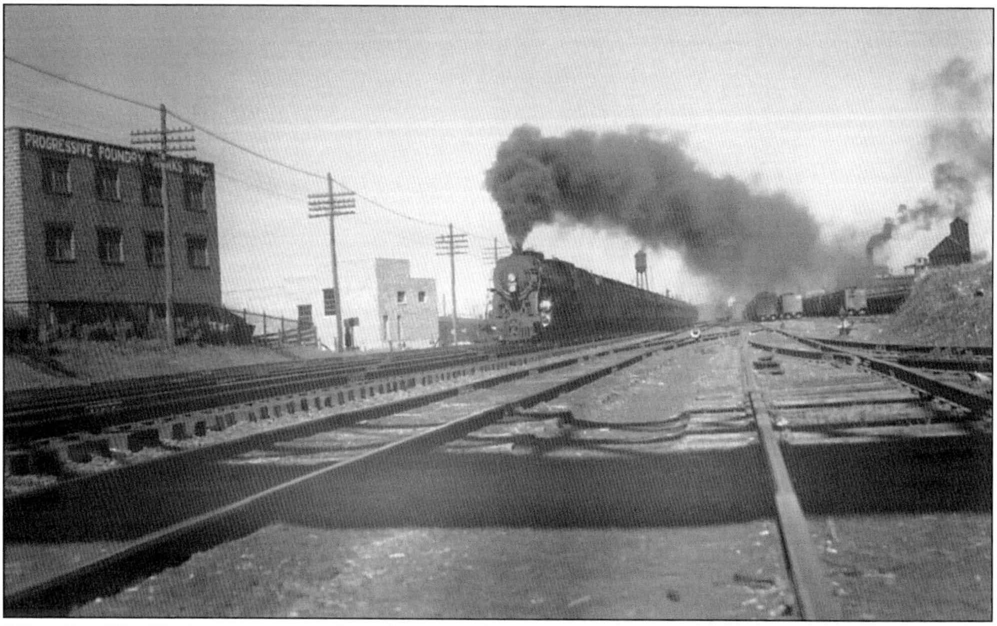

The class J3a Hudson, seen in this photograph passing Ames Street on Rochester's west side, was produced in the late 1930s. The J3a, capable of increased speed that resulted from several modifications, was called the "Super Hudson." It has been said that the Super Hudson was "pound-for-pound" NYC's best steam engine. (Photograph by Ed Van Leer, courtesy of Jeff Hands.)

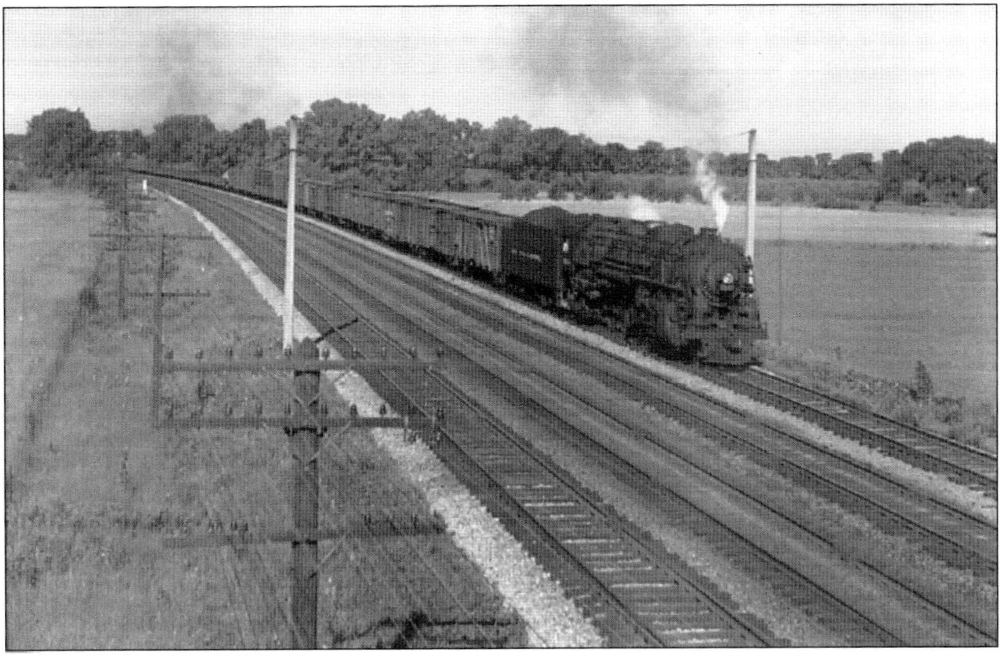

In the 1920s to the 1940s, NYC turned from the 2-8-2 Mikado to the 4-8-2 Mohawk to power many of its main line freights. Shown near Howard Road in the town of Gates is an eastbound freight with a class L2d Mohawk on the point. From the looks of the freight's consist, it may very well be headed to a meatpacking company. (Photograph by Robert Carper, courtesy of Jeff Hands.)

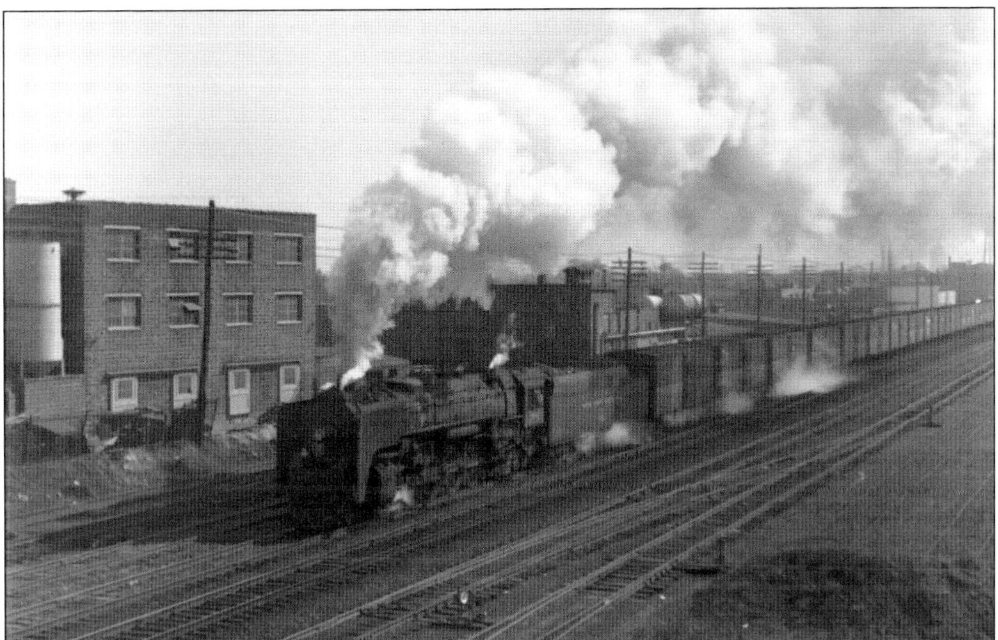

Mohawks also powered the Pacemaker freights, NYC's fast freight service dedicated to less-than-a-carload merchandise. The photograph shows a class L4a Mohawk on the headend of this westbound Pacemaker freight at West Avenue in Rochester. Note the Pacemaker logo on the boxcars. (Photograph by Robert Carper, courtesy of Jeff Hands.)

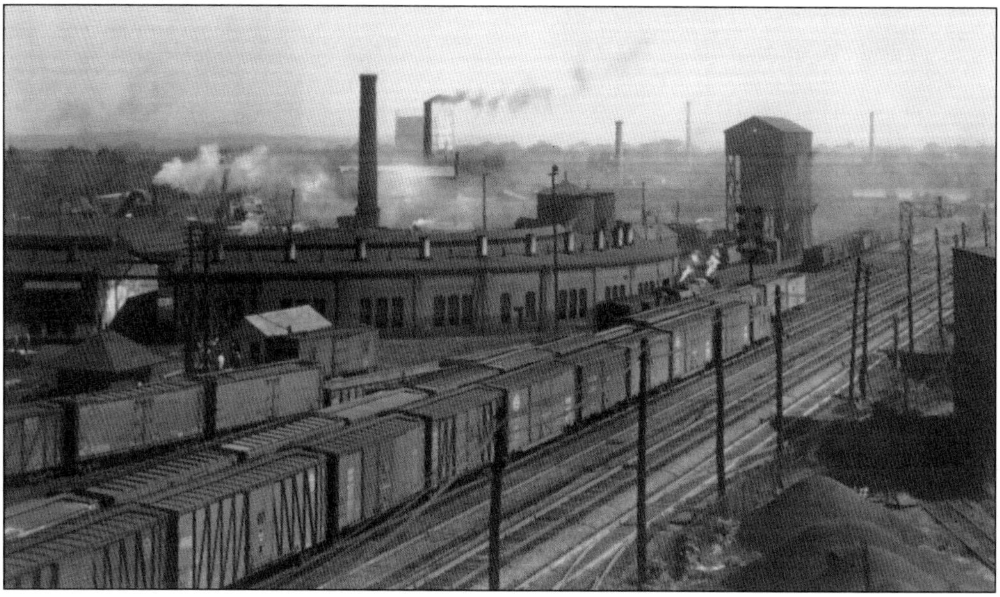

In the 1870s, NYC began construction of Rochester's Goodman Street Yards as a main switching and classification yard. Since that time, it has played a major role in the economic development of Rochester and Monroe County. Taken in the 1940s from the adjacent Gleason Works on Rochester's University Avenue, this photograph provides an excellent view of the Goodman Street Yards. Front and center is the roundhouse, and to its right are the water and coaling towers. Today, Goodman Street Yards is operated by CSX, and it is still a busy place. However, the roundhouse, and the water and coaling facilities are no more. (Courtesy of Ron Amberger.)

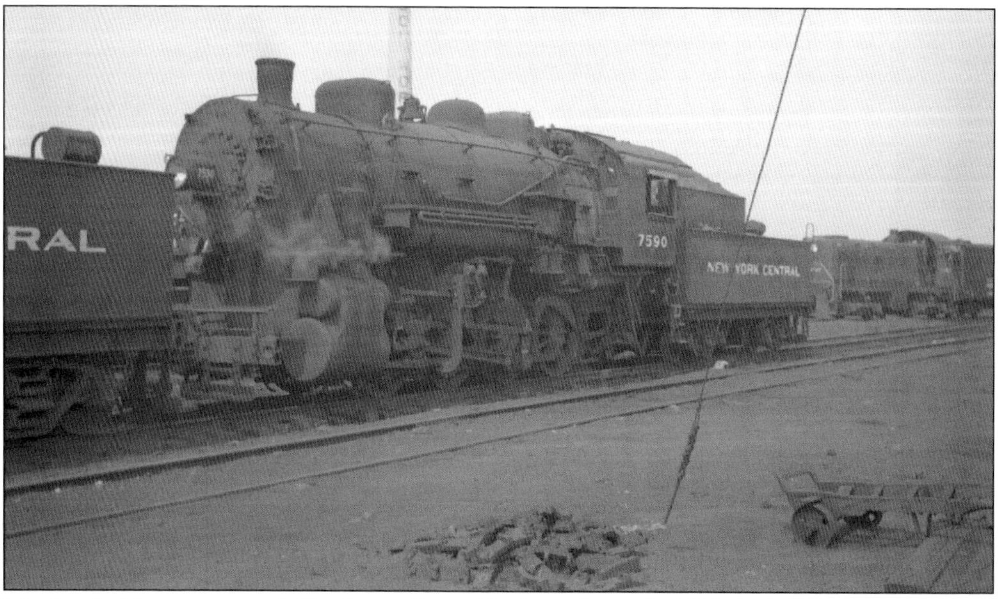

Moving freight cars around Goodman Street Yards in the early 1900s was the responsibility of this class U2f, an eight-wheeled 0-8-0 switcher, shown near the yard's roundhouse. The Alco diesel switcher in this 1940s photograph is a good indication that the U2f's days are numbered. Note the smokestack of Gleason Works, world-famous producer of high-performance gears, in the background. (Photograph by Robert Gerling, courtesy of Jeff Hands.)

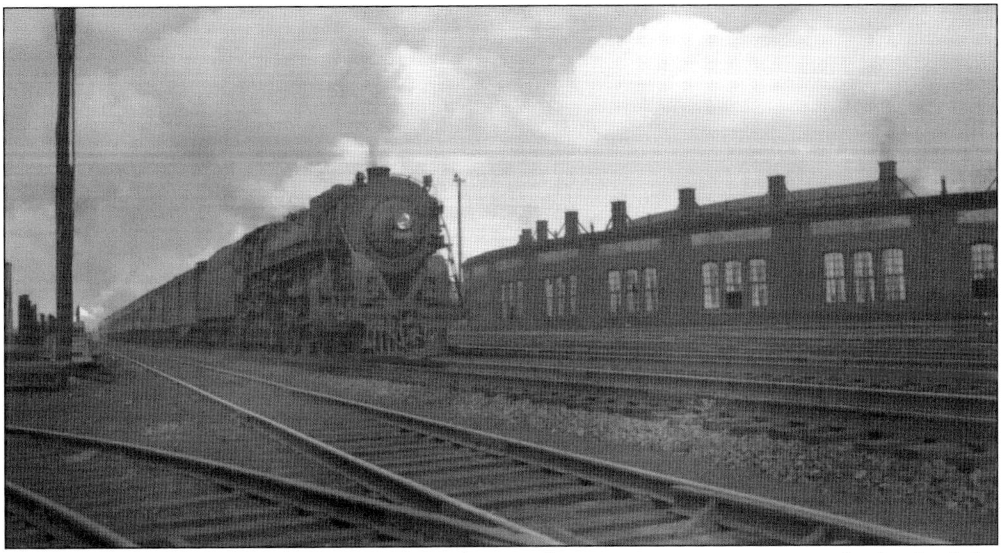

This 1940s photograph shows a NYC J1c class Hudson powering its way past the back of the roundhouse at Goodman Street Yards. The many classes and types of steam engines on the NYC roster made the roundhouse a very busy place. (Photograph by Ed Van Leer, courtesy of Jeff Hands.)

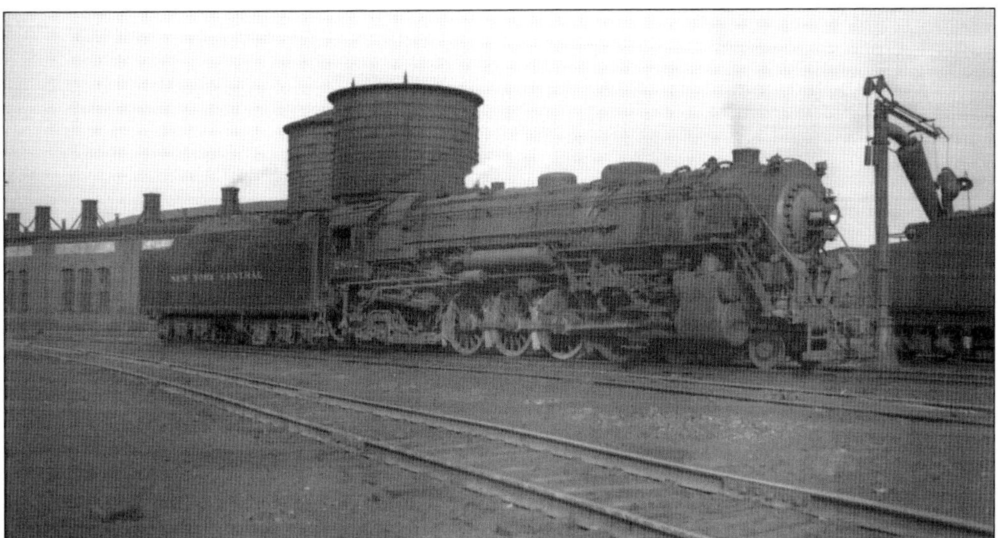

This 1930s photograph shows a L2c Mohawk with its tender full of coal waiting its turn for water at Goodman Street. (Photograph by Ed Van Leer, courtesy of Jeff Hands.)

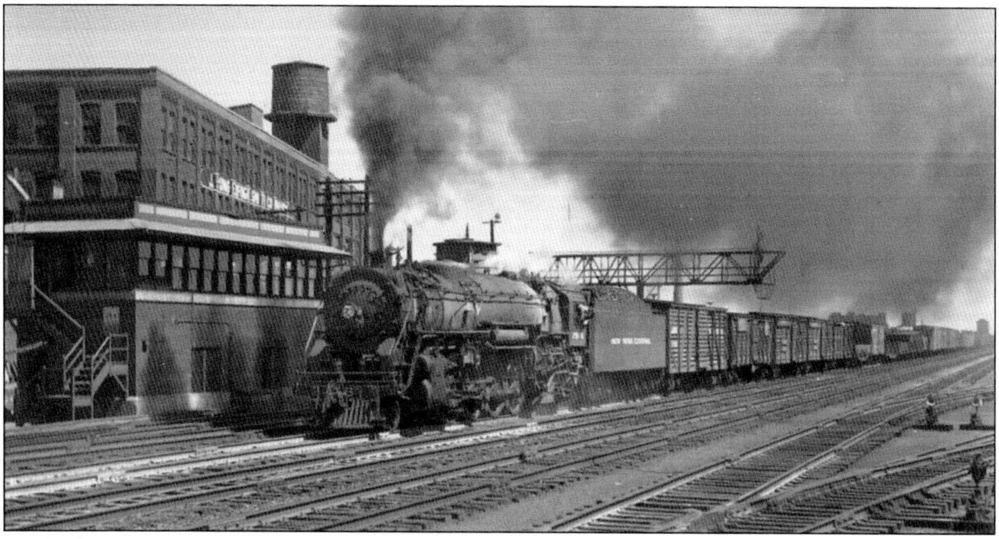

With the Hungerford-Smith food products plant in the background, an eastbound L2d class Mohawk, filled with water and fuel, is shown in this 1950 photograph leaving Goodman Street Yards making its way past Tower 25a. (Photograph by Ed Van Leer, courtesy of Jeff Hands.)

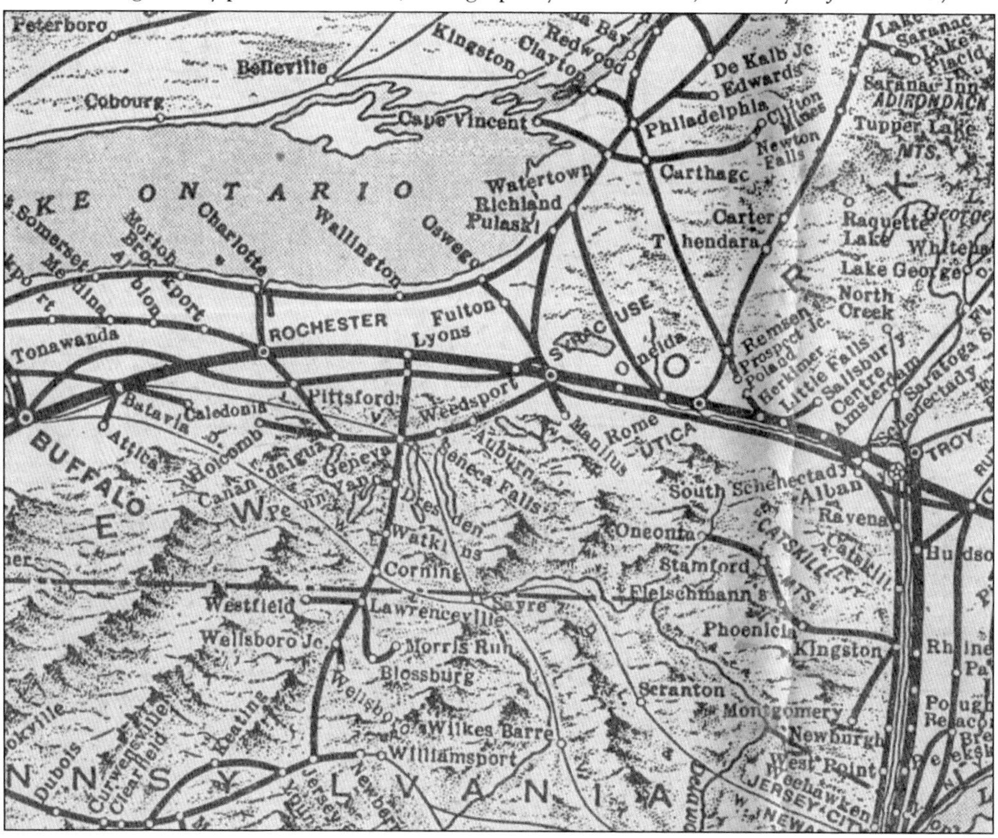

This NYC map shows the Rochester main line as well as important branch lines such as the Auburn Road southeast and then east toward Syracuse, the Falls Road west to Niagara Falls, and the Charlotte branch line north toward Lake Ontario. (Author's collection.)

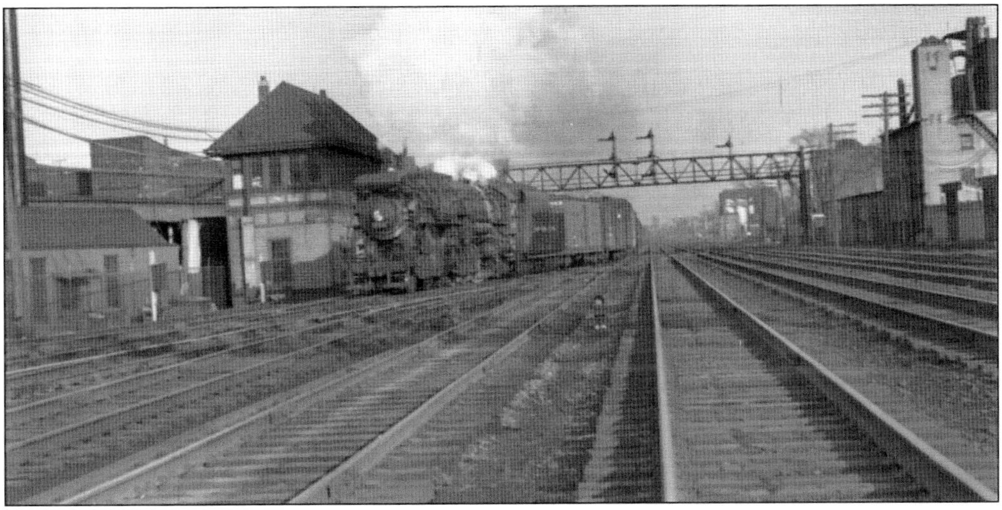

The Falls Road interlocking was located on the NYC main line at Ames Street in Rochester. In this 1951 photograph, a westbound freight powered by a class L2a Mohawk is seen passing the Ames Street tower as it moves onto the Falls Road headed toward the villages of Spencerport and Brockport in the Monroe County towns of Ogden and Sweden, respectively. In the mid-1800s, the line that eventually became NYC's Falls Road replaced the Erie Canal packet boat as a means of more quickly moving farm products to market from these towns as well those from outlying areas of the town of Clarkson, which at that time extended north to Lake Ontario. (Photograph by Robert Carper, courtesy of Jeff Hands.)

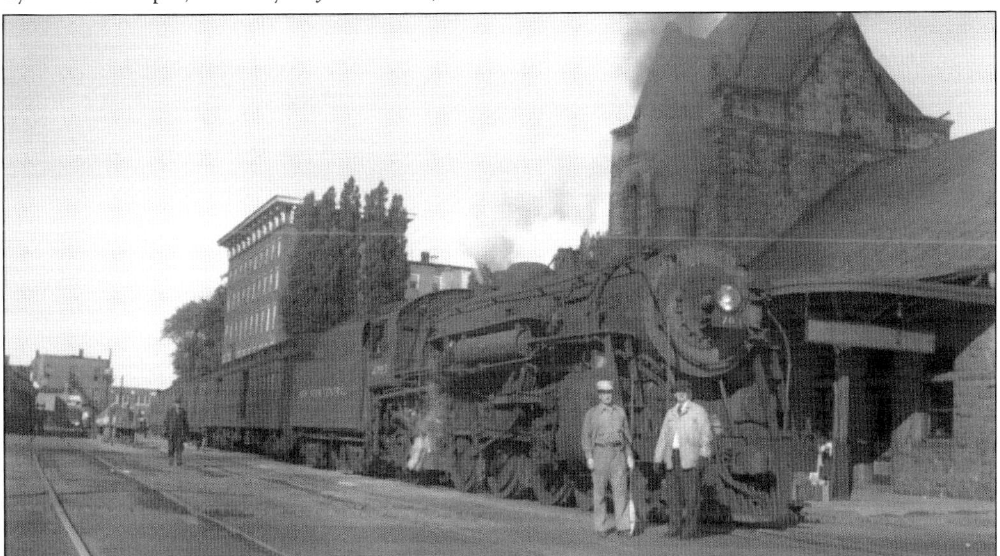

NYC's Auburn Road headed southeast from the main line near Winton Road in Rochester through the towns of Brighton and Pittsford in Monroe County before turning east toward Syracuse. It offered passenger service along the way to cities such as Canandaigua in Ontario County and Auburn in Cayuga County. Before diesels arrived on the scene, reliable 4-6-2 K-class Pacifics were often assigned to Auburn Road passenger trains. Shown in this 1940s photograph is a class K-3p waiting for the highball at the c. 1916 depot in Canandaigua. Passenger service ended on the Auburn Road in 1958. Today, this beautiful building houses a pub and a brewery. (Photograph by Robert Gerling, courtesy of Jeff Hands.)

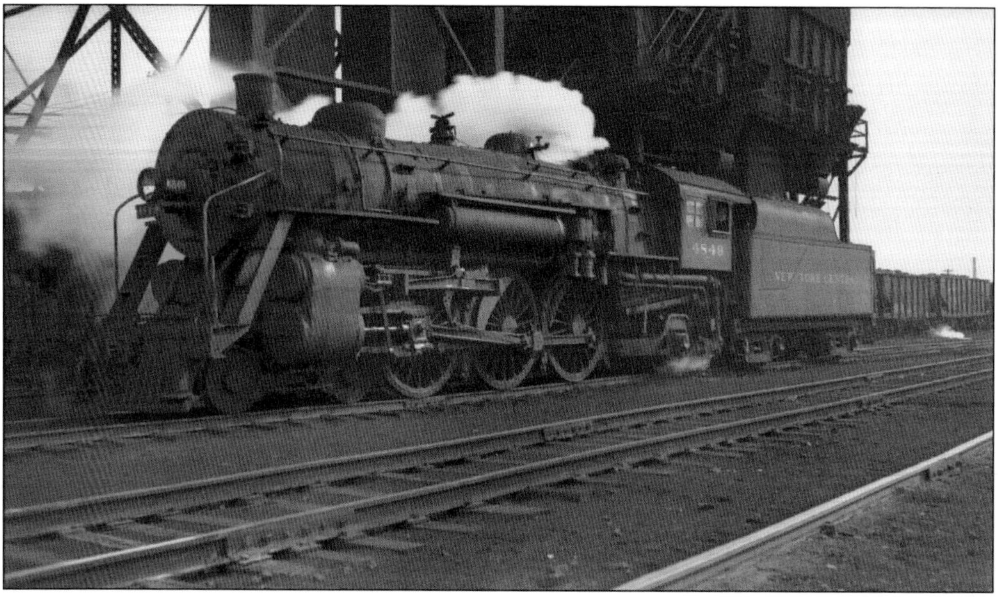

This mid-1930s photograph shows a class K-3g Pacific at the Goodman Street Yards coaling tower prior to possible assignment on the Auburn Road or the Falls Road. (Photograph by Ed Van Leer, courtesy of Jeff Hands.)

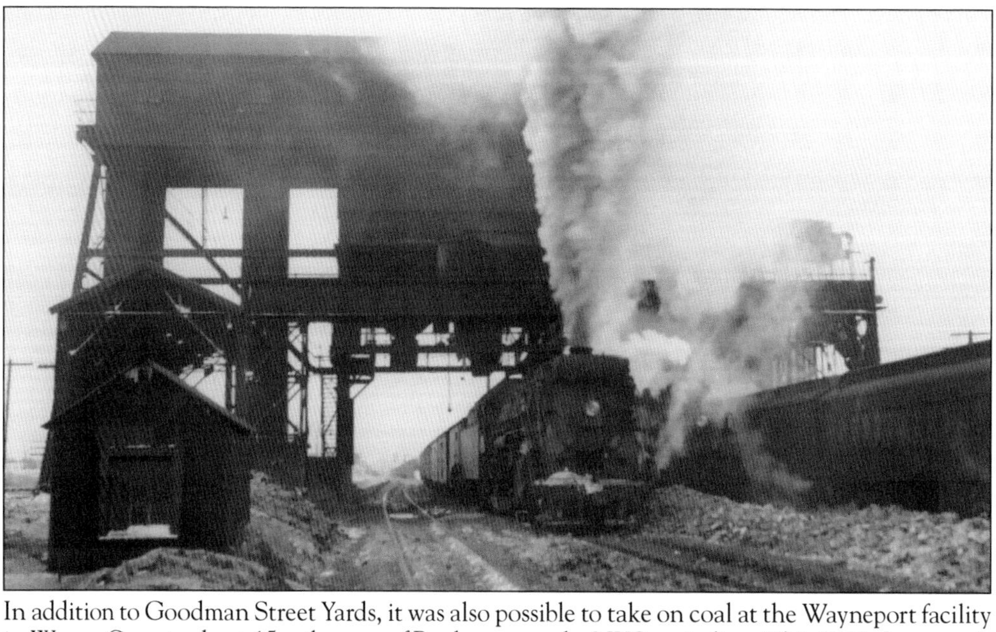

In addition to Goodman Street Yards, it was also possible to take on coal at the Wayneport facility in Wayne County about 15 miles east of Rochester on the NYC main line. This 1945 photograph shows a class L2a Mohawk at the Wayneport coaling tower. (Courtesy of Jeff Hands.)

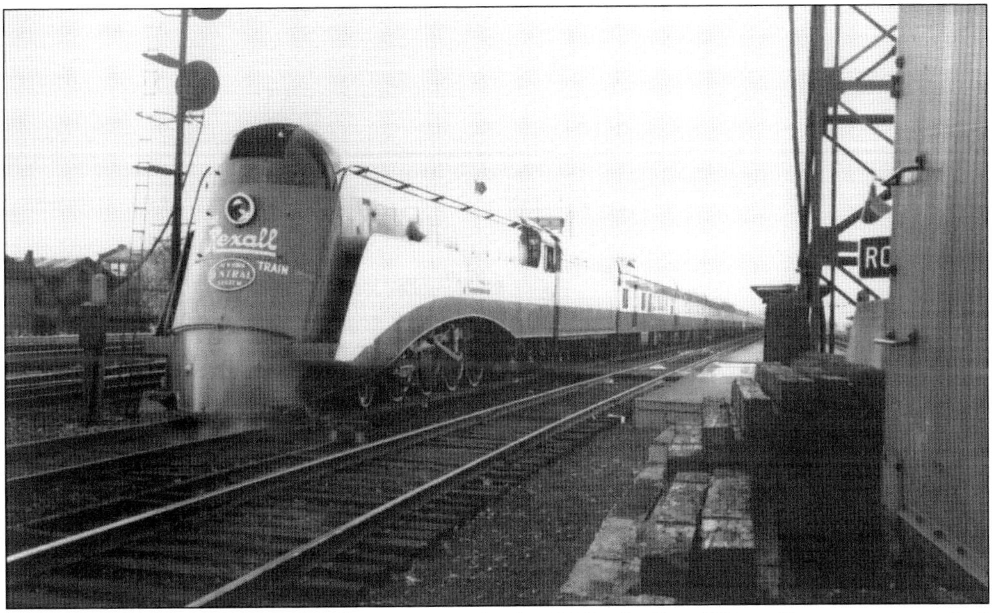

Mohawks were also used for special assignments. In the 1930s, the Rexall Drug Company customized an entire train, which traveled around the country promoting the company. Powered by a streamlined class L2c Mohawk, the "Rexall Train," as it was called, is shown arriving Rochester's Bragdon Station. (Photograph by Ed Van Leer, courtesy of Jeff Hands.)

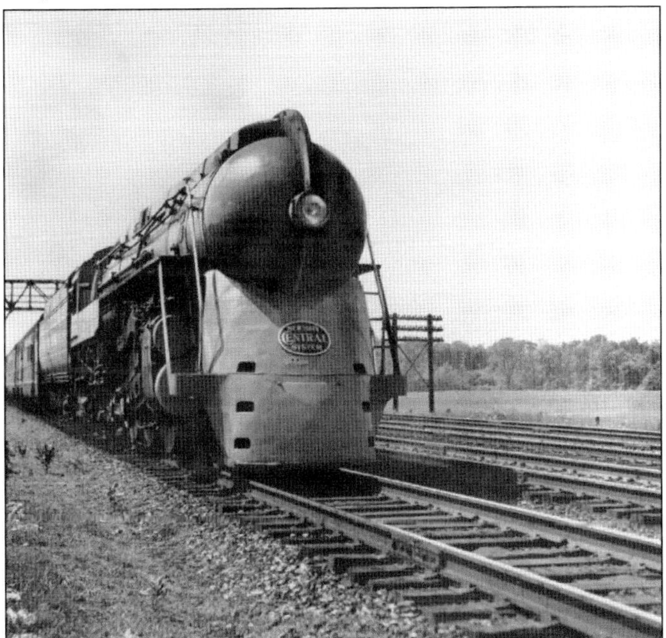

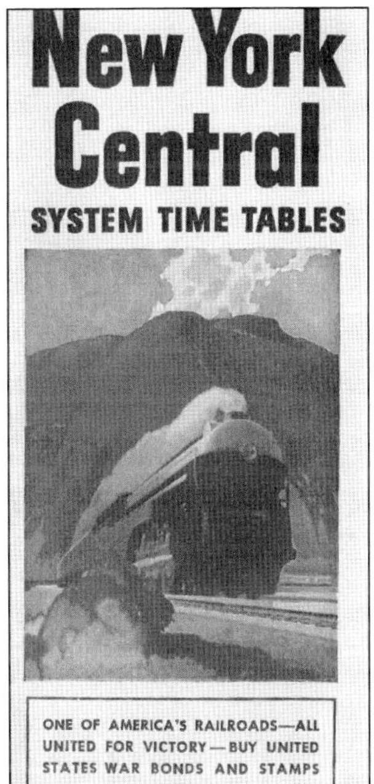

Also streamlined were several class J3a Hudson locomotives for use on NYC's luxury passenger trains such as the Twentieth Century Limited and Commodore Vanderbilt. Shown in the 1944 photograph is a streamlined J3a near Churchville in the town of Riga west of Rochester. The Empire State Express was also powered by streamlined J3as, as shown on the cover of this 1944 NYC timetable. (Left, courtesy of Jeff Hands; right, author's collection.)

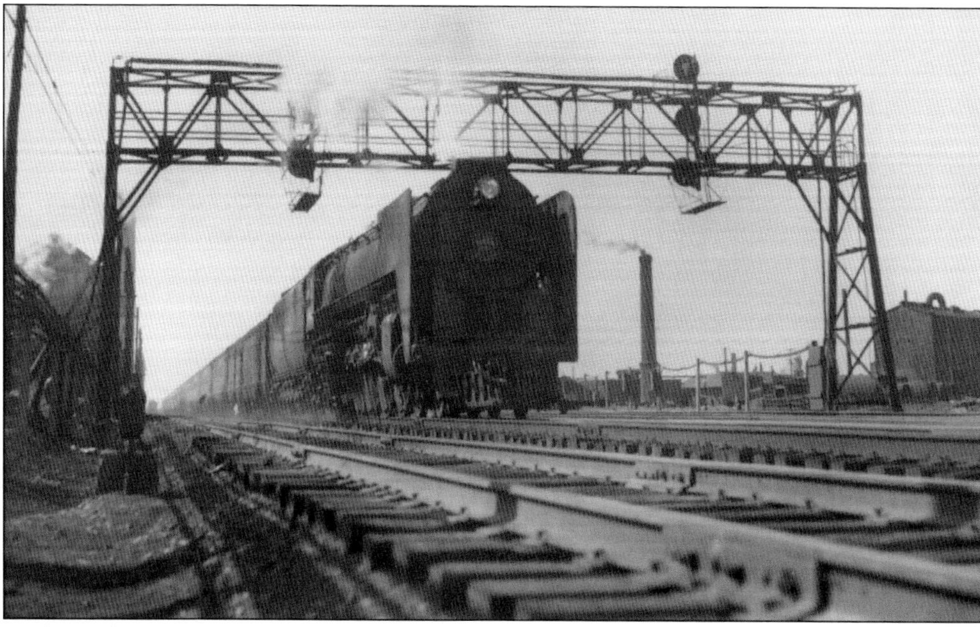

In the mid-1940s, NYC upgraded its steam engine roster by purchasing a handful of powerful 4-8-4 class S1 and S2 Niagara locomotives. These 6,000-horsepower engines, recognizable by their large smoke deflectors, were used primarily for passenger service. At times, they substituted for the streamlined J3a, as shown in this 1946 photograph of a class S1b Niagara on the headend of the eastbound Empire State Express at Culver Road in Rochester. (Courtesy of Jeff Hands.)

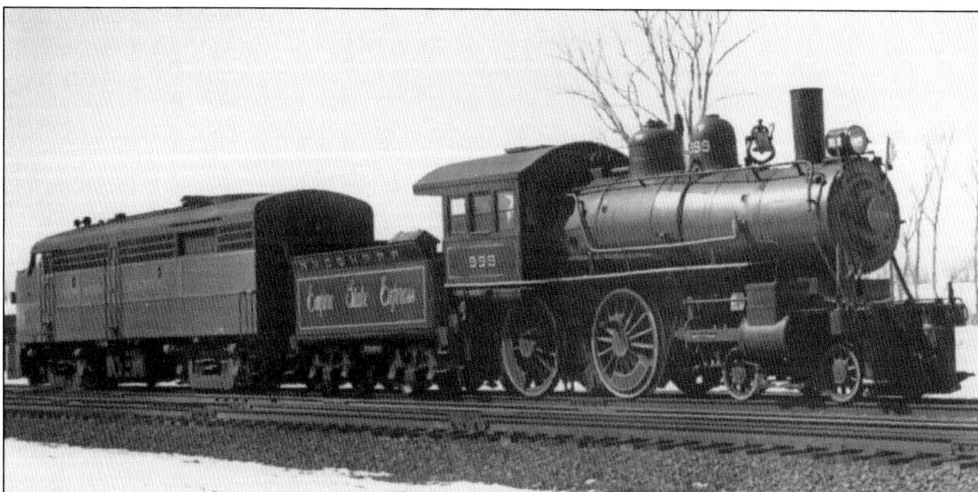

The Empire State Express has been an NYC-named train for many years. In the 1890s, its 4-4-0 engine, the famous No. 999, set a speed record of 112 miles per hour. In this photograph, No. 999 makes an interesting comparison to one of the Alco FA diesel locomotives that was purchased by NYC in the late 1940s. It is interesting to note that in the 1960s, the Empire State Express inspired singer Eddie James to compose a blues song of the same name. This is the same Eddie James who is mentioned in chapter 5 as having worked at the East Rochester carshops. On December 2, 1967, the Empire disappeared into railroad history. Three months later, NYC suffered the same fate when it merged with PRR to form the Penn Central. (Courtesy of *Rochester Images*: Rochester Public Library Local History Division.)

Eight

Watching the Bulldogs, Sharks, and More

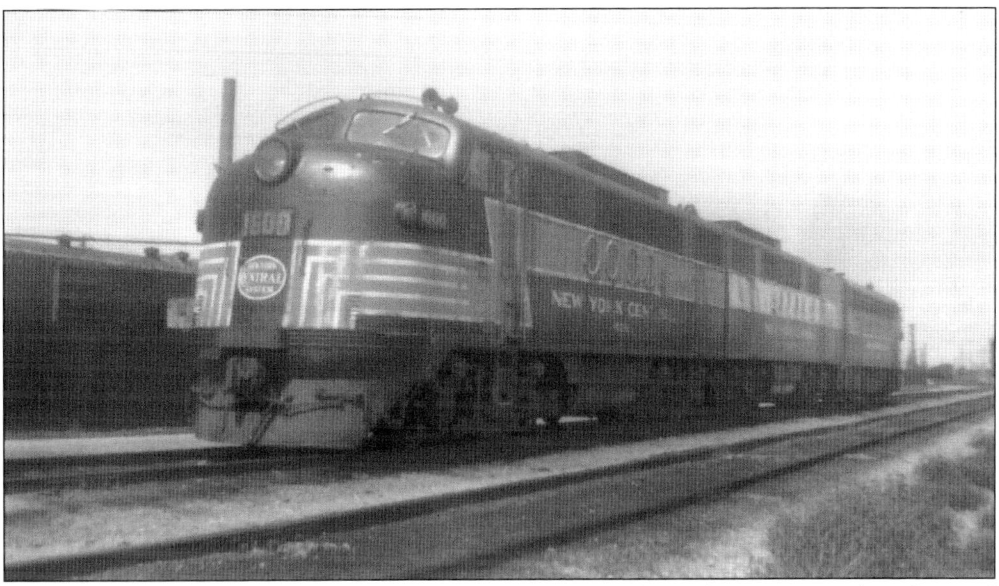

NYC's entered the diesel road freight locomotive market in the mid-1940s. It purchased several EMD FT units from General Motors (GM) for main line freight service. These locomotives were powered by newly developed V-16 diesel engine that provided 1,350 horsepower. The FT was the first in a line of very successful EMD F-units that almost all major US railroads purchased from GM in the post–World War II period. This photograph, taken at NYC's Collinwood Yards in Cleveland, shows the FT with its recognizable four portholes along each side and exhaust stacks surrounded by boxy structures along the centerline of the roof. Also, the cab and cabless booster were part of a combined FT set that provided 2,700 horsepower. They are seen in the photograph as the first and second units. (Courtesy of Charles Bohai.)

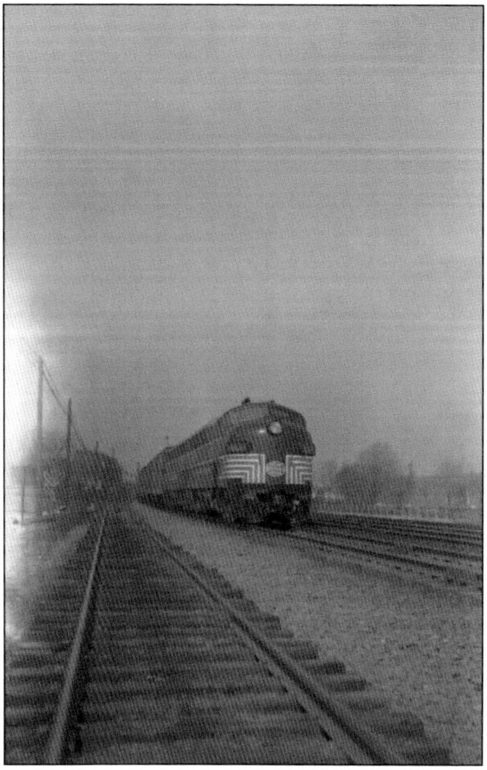

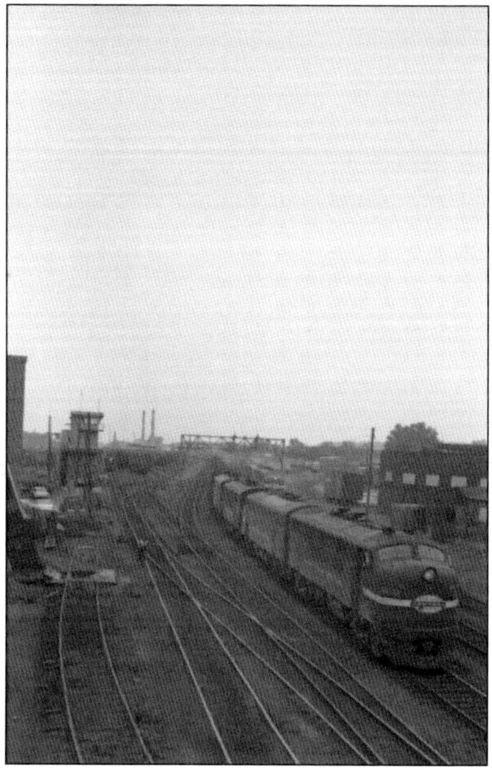

Following the FT, EMD produced the F3 and then the F7 diesel freight locomotive, all with the "bulldog" cab design. The left 1952 photograph shows an EMD F3 underway on the east side of Rochester between Culver and Winton Roads. The higher-horsepower F3 was a worthy successor to the FT. It is interesting to note that many adults grew up with the F3 as it was a popular engine to have as part of their Lionel electric train sets. The right 1967 photograph shows the F3 still going strong on the headend of a freight leaving Goodman Street Yards. Note the new "cigar band" logo that NYC was using at the time. The NYC merger with the PRR to form the Penn Central was about a year away. (Both, photograph by Robert Carper, courtesy of Jeff Hands.)

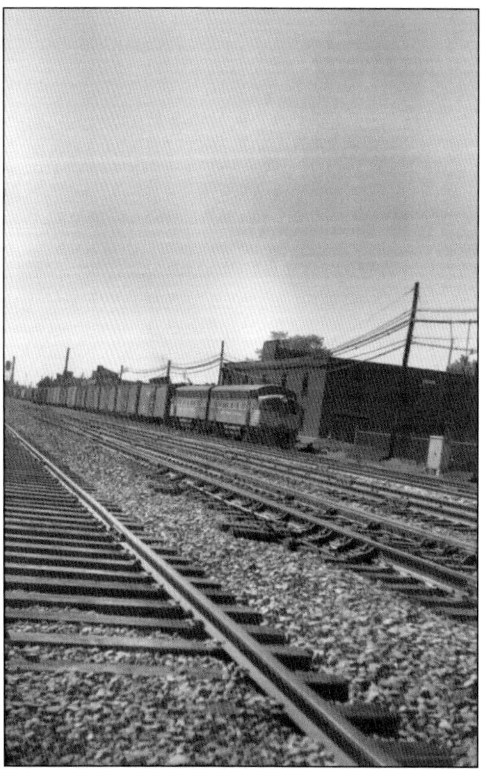

Improved transmission and braking systems led to the production of the EMD F7. The NYC purchased many F7s in the post–World War II period from GM. In fact, the F7 was one of EMD's biggest sellers. Shown in this 1954 photograph is an eastbound F7 near Ames Street in Rochester. (Photograph by Robert Carper, courtesy of Jeff Hands.)

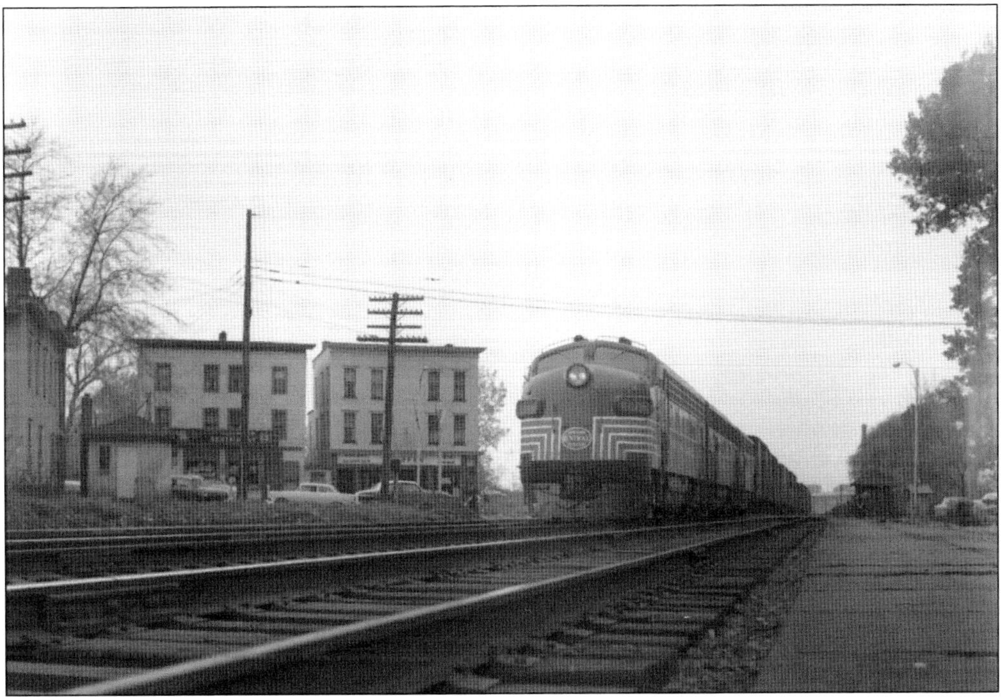

Another 1954 photograph shows an NYC EMD F7 barreling through the village of Fairport in the town of Perinton, southeast of Rochester. Diesel motive power had the advantage of adding more units if needed. Here, three units on the headend provide 4,500 horsepower. (Photograph by Robert Carper, courtesy of Jeff Hands.)

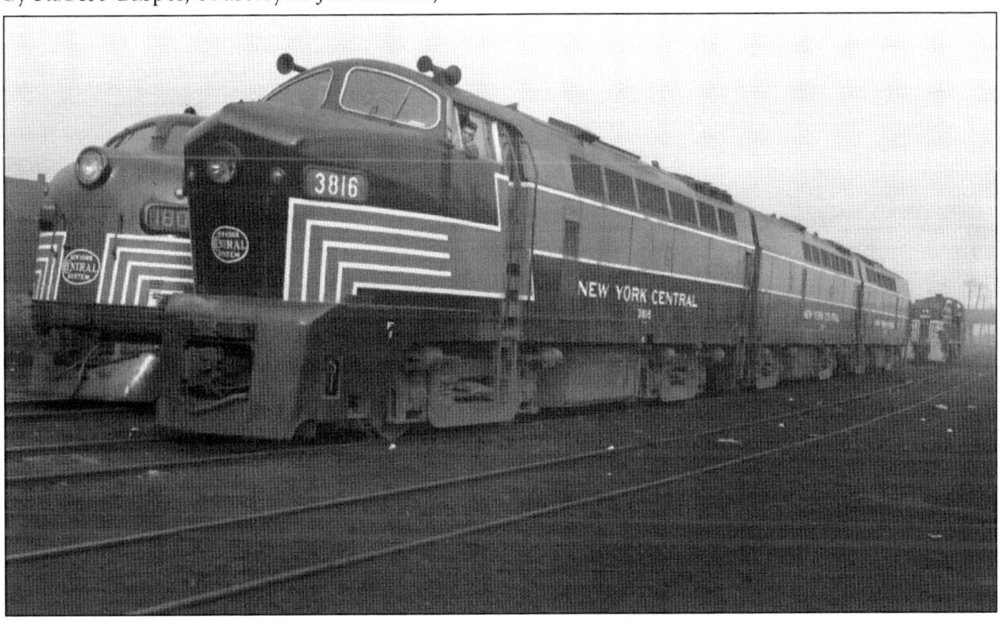

To distinguish itself from the look of EMD F-units, the Baldwin Locomotive Works (BLW) came up with a cab design that was different. Nobody had any trouble differentiating the BLW RF-16 diesel, nicknamed "sharknose" or "shark," from the EMD F7 in this 1953 photograph taken in Buffalo. NYC purchased over 20 of the sharks from BLW. (Courtesy of Jeff Hands.)

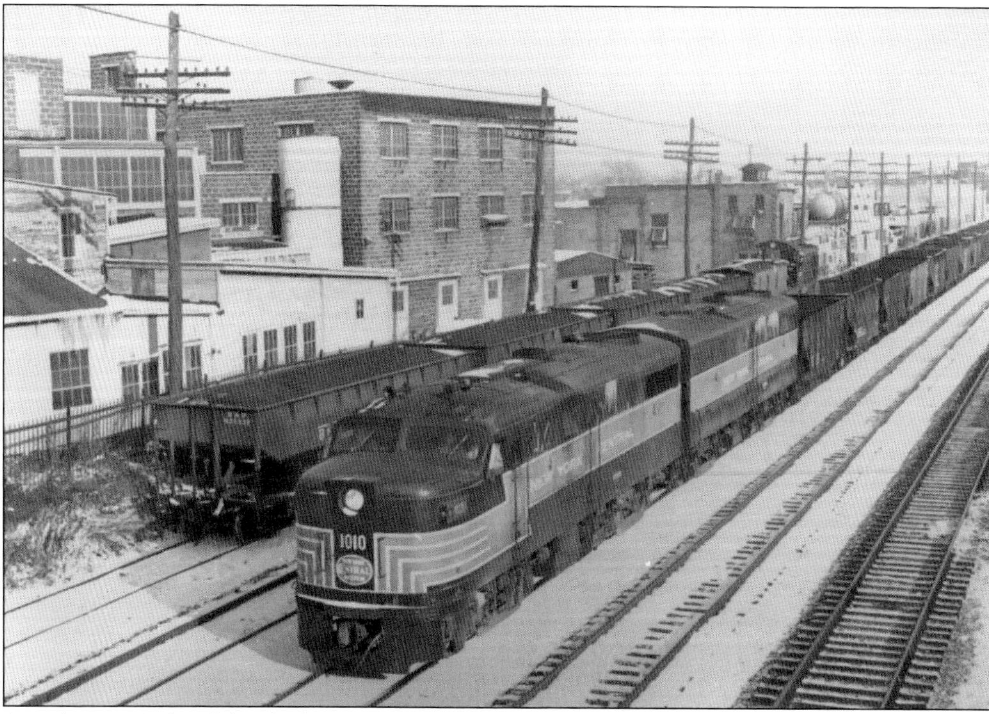

Another NYC diesel freight locomotive with a distinguishing look was the Alco FA-1. With a straight nose and headlight in a square, slotted grille, it was also easy to spot. An FA-1 that NYC purchased in the late 1940s is shown in this photograph on the front end of some empty hopper cars near the former General Railway Signal plant on West Avenue in Rochester. (Photograph by Ron Wright, courtesy of Jeff Hands.)

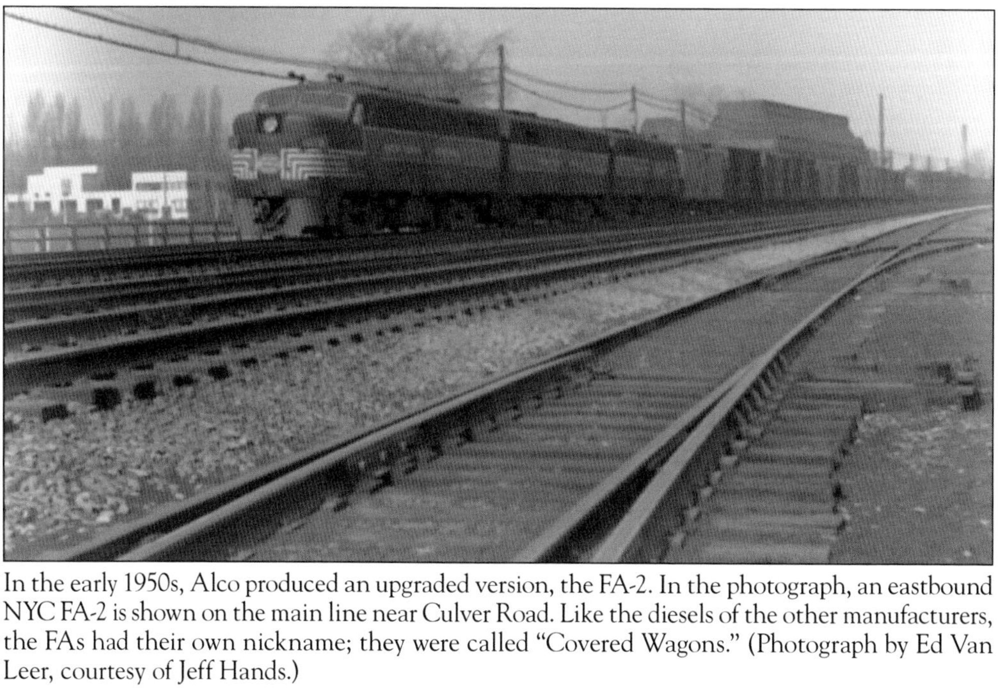

In the early 1950s, Alco produced an upgraded version, the FA-2. In the photograph, an eastbound NYC FA-2 is shown on the main line near Culver Road. Like the diesels of the other manufacturers, the FAs had their own nickname; they were called "Covered Wagons." (Photograph by Ed Van Leer, courtesy of Jeff Hands.)

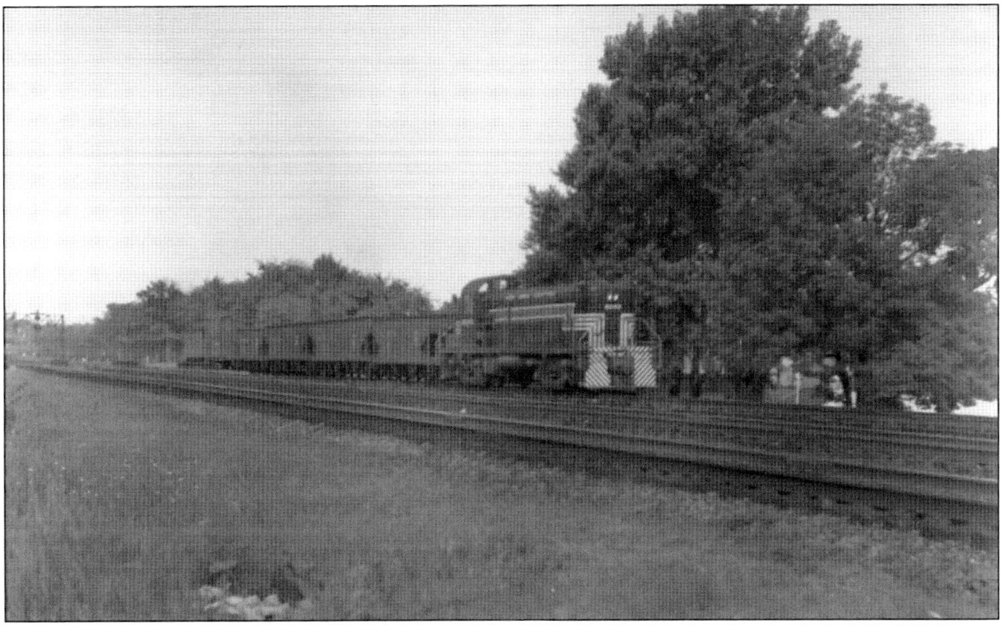

In the early to mid-1950s, Alco also produced a diesel road-switcher locomotive, the RS-3. Starting in the early 1950s, NYC ordered many of these versatile engines that would handle local freight and passenger runs, as well as switching duties. Shown in this 1954 photograph near Ames Street is an NYC RS-3 with rival PRR hopper cars in tow. (Photograph by Robert Carper, courtesy of Jeff Hands.)

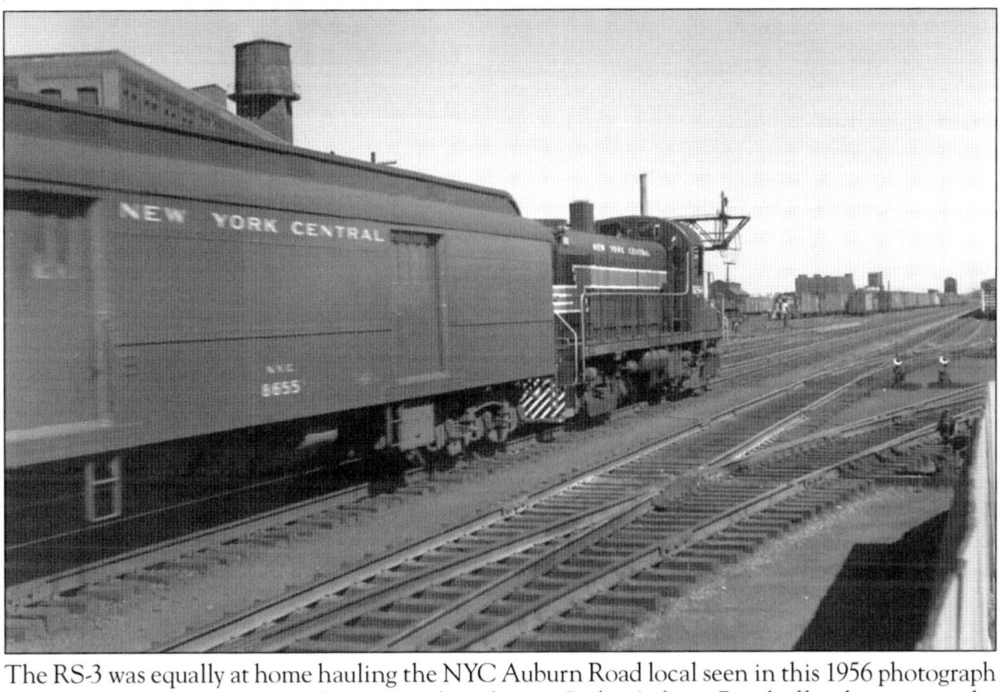

The RS-3 was equally at home hauling the NYC Auburn Road local seen in this 1956 photograph taken at Goodman Street Yards. As noted in chapter 7, the Auburn Road offered service to the major cities in Ontario County and Cayuga County—Canandaigua and Auburn, respectively. (Photograph by Robert Carper, courtesy of Jeff Hands.)

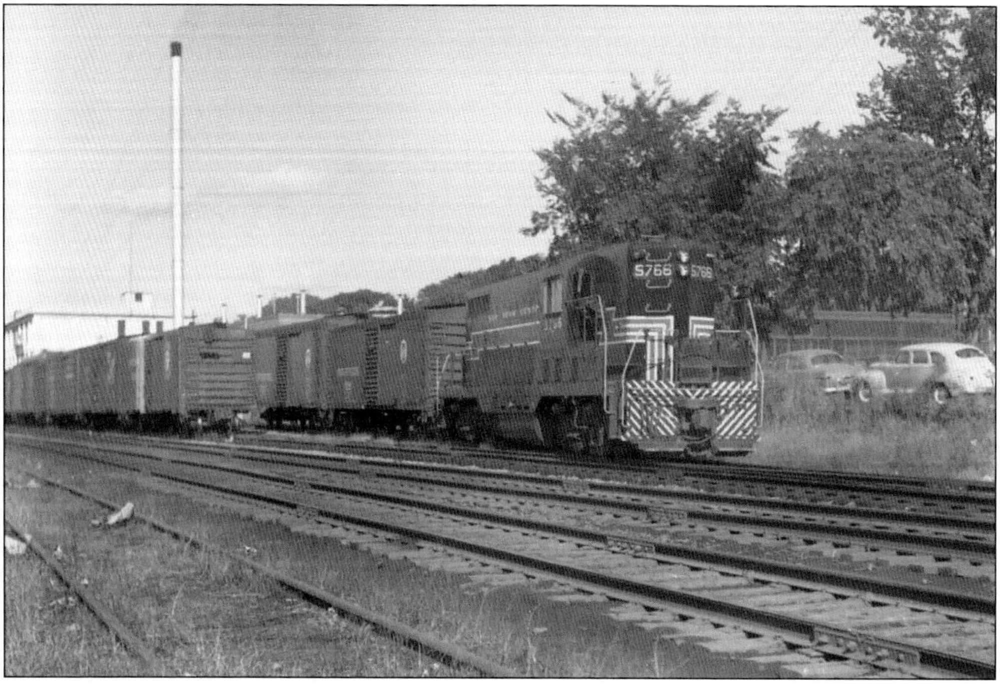

NYC also purchased GM's EMD GP7 and GP9 diesel road-switchers to handle assignments similar to that of the Alco RS-3. This 1954 photograph shows a GP9 handling a switching assignment in Fairport. (Photograph by Robert Carper, courtesy of Jeff Hands.)

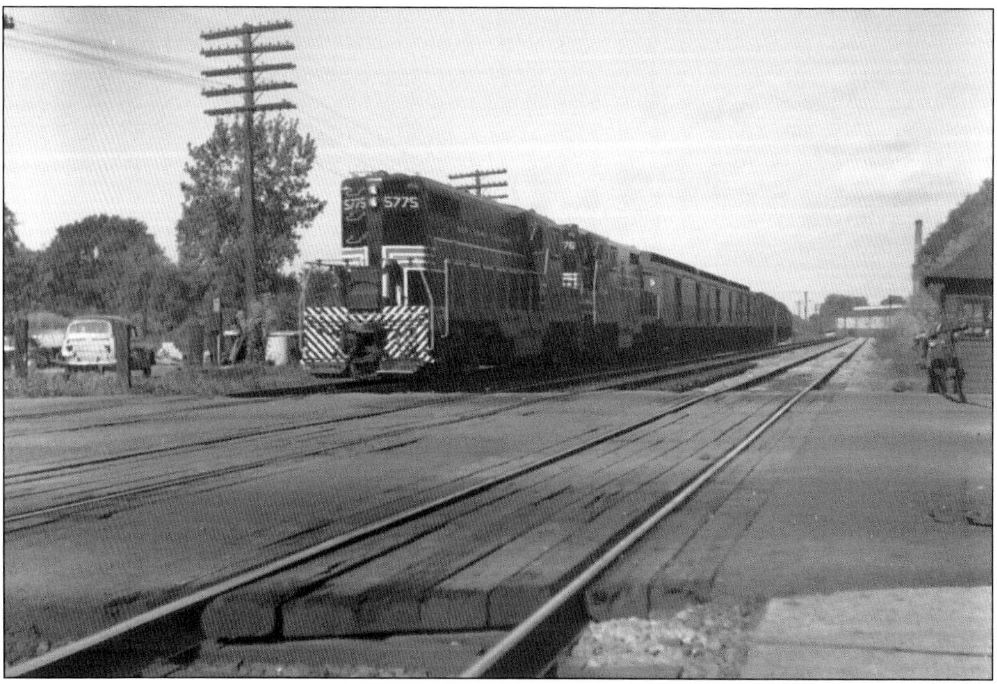

Showing the versatility of the "geeps," as they were called, this 1953 photograph shows two GP9s powering an eastbound mail and express through Fairport on the NYC main line. (Photograph by Robert Carper, courtesy of Jeff Hands.)

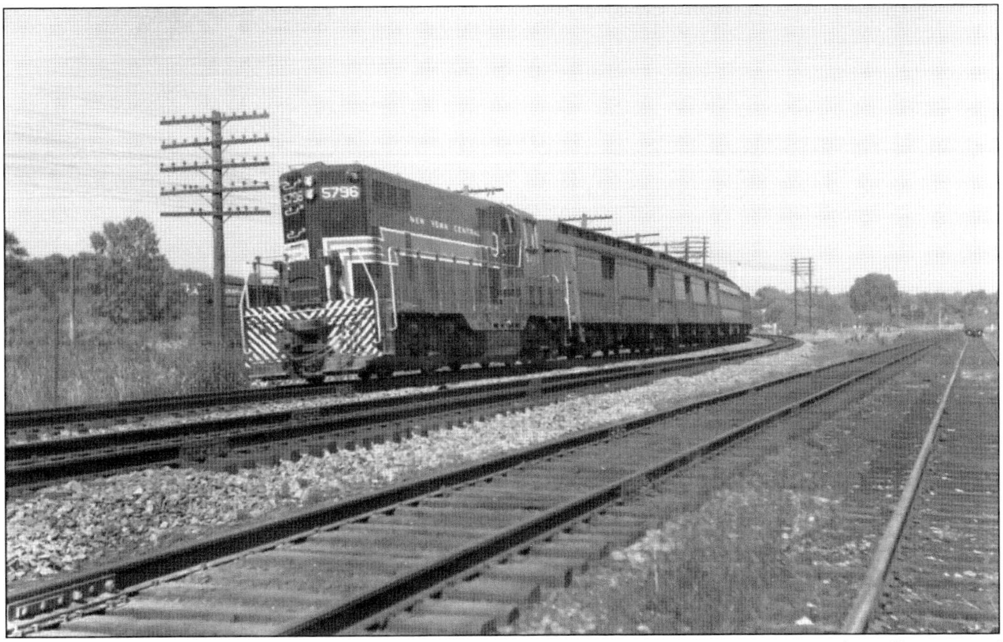

GP9s, with more horsepower than the Alco RS-3, were also given assignments to handle some of NYC mid-distance passenger trains. Shown in this 1956 photograph is the Advance Empire State Express as it passes through Fairport on its way from Buffalo to New York City. (Photograph by Robert Carper, courtesy of Jeff Hands.)

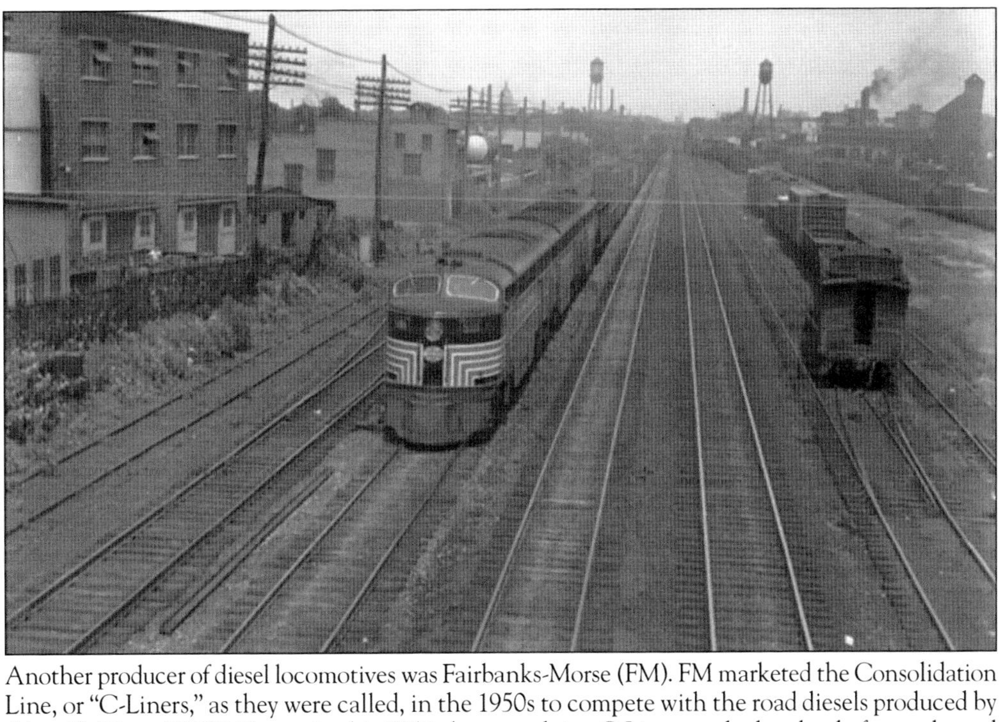

Another producer of diesel locomotives was Fairbanks-Morse (FM). FM marketed the Consolidation Line, or "C-Liners," as they were called, in the 1950s to compete with the road diesels produced by Alco, EMD, and BLW. Shown in this 1956 photograph is a C-Liner on the headend of a westbound freight near West Avenue. (Photograph by Robert Carper, courtesy of Jeff Hands.)

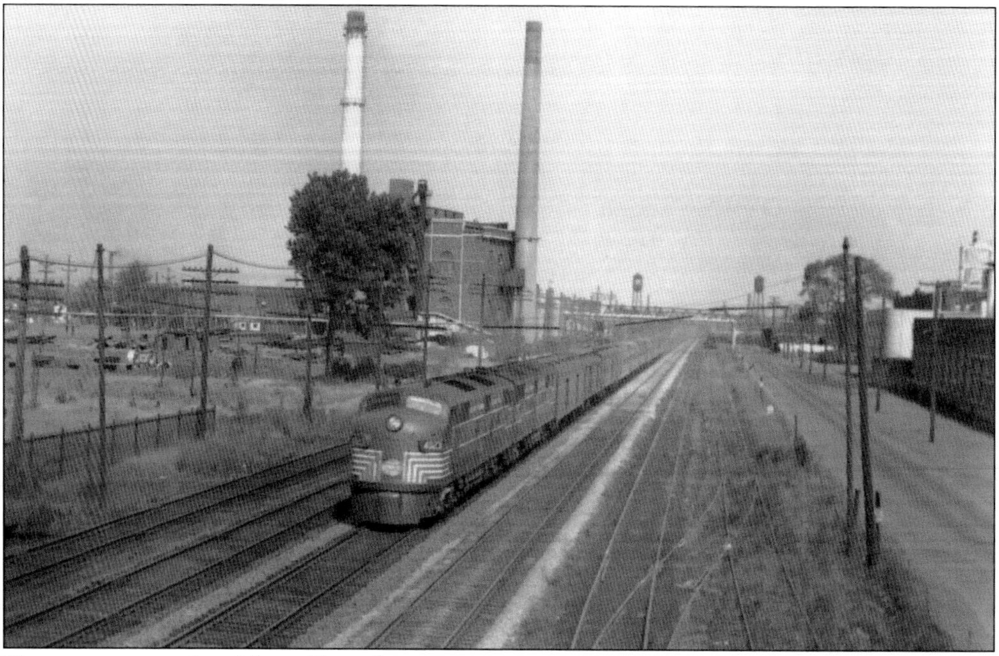

To power its streamlined fleet of long-distance passenger trains in the post–World War II period, NYC purchased EMD E7 diesel locomotives from GM. This 1951 photograph shows E7s on the headend of NYC's eastbound Empire State Express near Rochester. (Courtesy of Robert Pastorkey.)

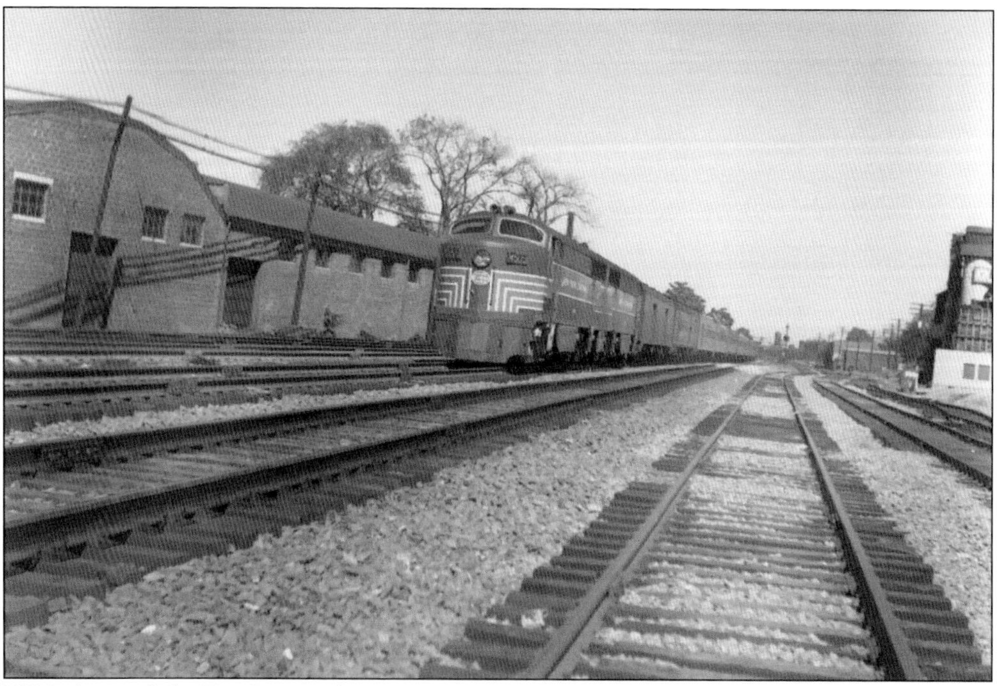

NYC also used the FM C-Liner for its passenger service. This 1953 photograph shows a C-Liner leading the Empire State Express near West Avenue. (Photograph by Robert Carper, courtesy of Jeff Hands.)

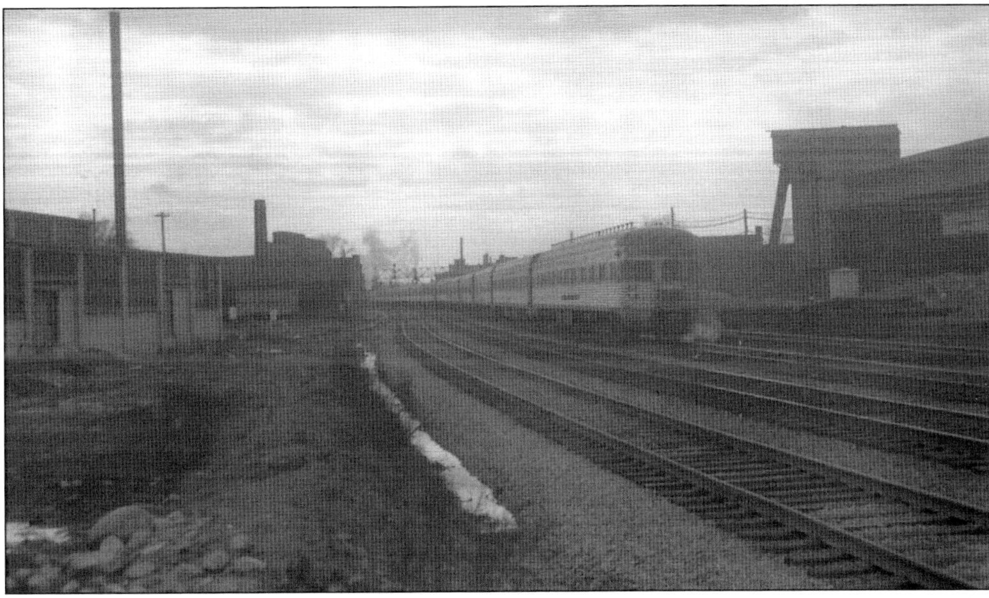

This photograph, taken between Culver and Winton Roads, shows the stainless steel consist that was typical of the Empire State Express and other NYC crack trains of the 1950s. In the NYC timetable of the day, these trains were given the special designation Streamliner. Note the radio antenna along the observation car roof. The antenna provided an opportunity for those passengers in the observation car to enjoy radio programs along NYC's Water Level Route. (Photograph by Robert Carper, courtesy of Jeff Hands.)

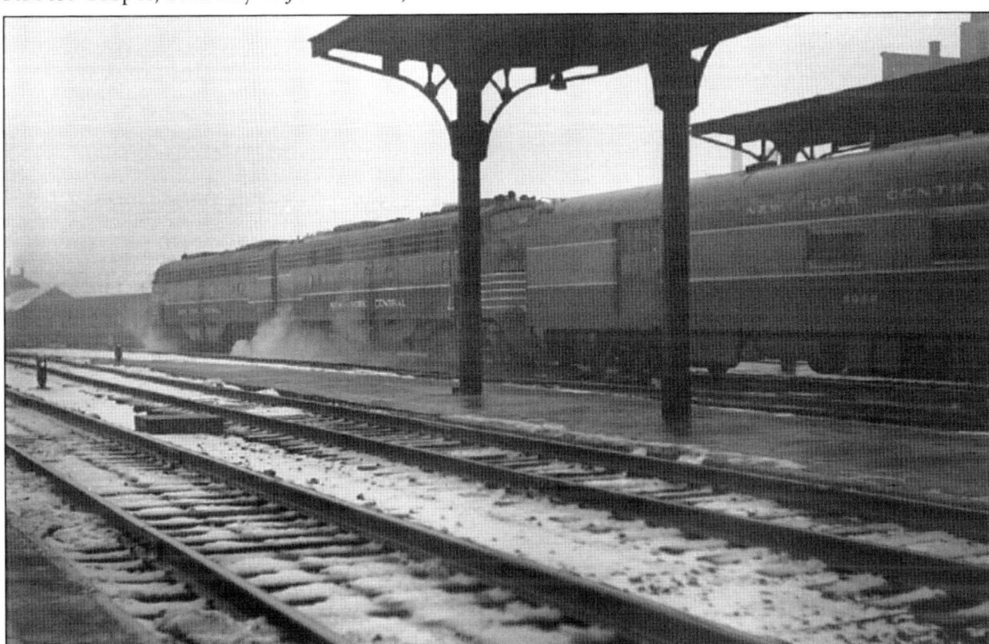

In the 1950s, NYC also acquired EMD E8s from GM. These locomotives were more powerful than the E7s. Shown in this photograph is a pair of E8s about to depart Rochester's Bragdon Station. Like the F-units, both the E7s and E8s had the bulldog cab design. (Photograph by Robert Carper, courtesy of Jeff Hands.)

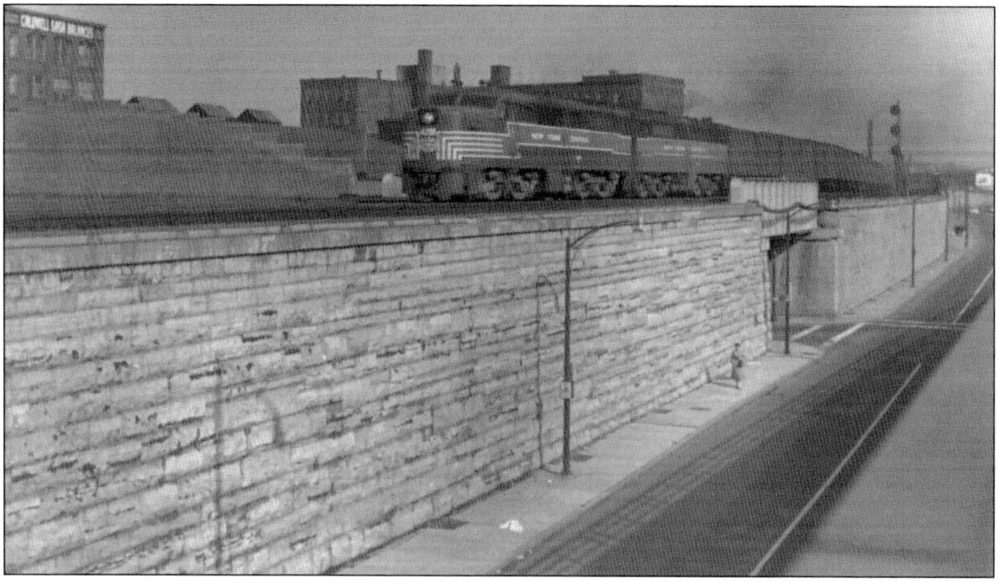

In addition to the EMD E7s and E8s, NYC employed Alco PA diesel locomotives to power its long-distance passenger trains. This 1956 photograph shows a westbound PA-1 having just departed Bragdon Station. (Photograph by Robert Carper, courtesy of Jeff Hands.)

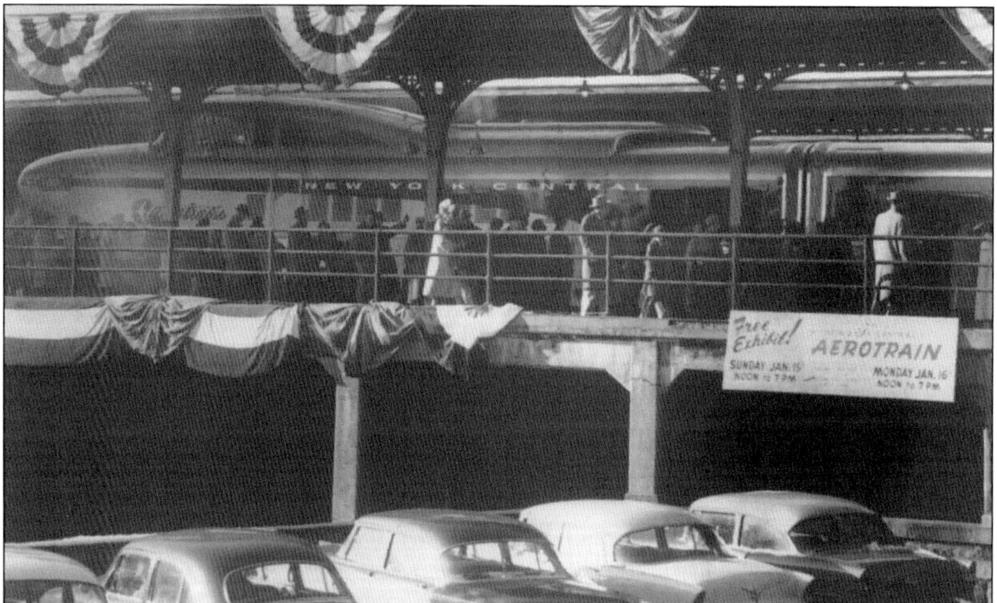

There were attempts for NYC to continue modernization of its passenger service. Shown in this photograph is the Aerotrain during its much publicized 1956 stop in Rochester at the Bragdon Station. It was hoped that the more modernistic look of the engine and 10-car train designed by GM would help improve ridership. It was not to be. Maintenance and passenger-comfort issues shortened its life, not only for NYC, but for other railroads as well. Ridership on the NYC continued to decline into the 1960s, resulting in the creation of the Penn Central in 1968 and then the formation of Amtrak in 1971. (Courtesy of *Rochester Images*: Rochester Public Library Local History Division.)

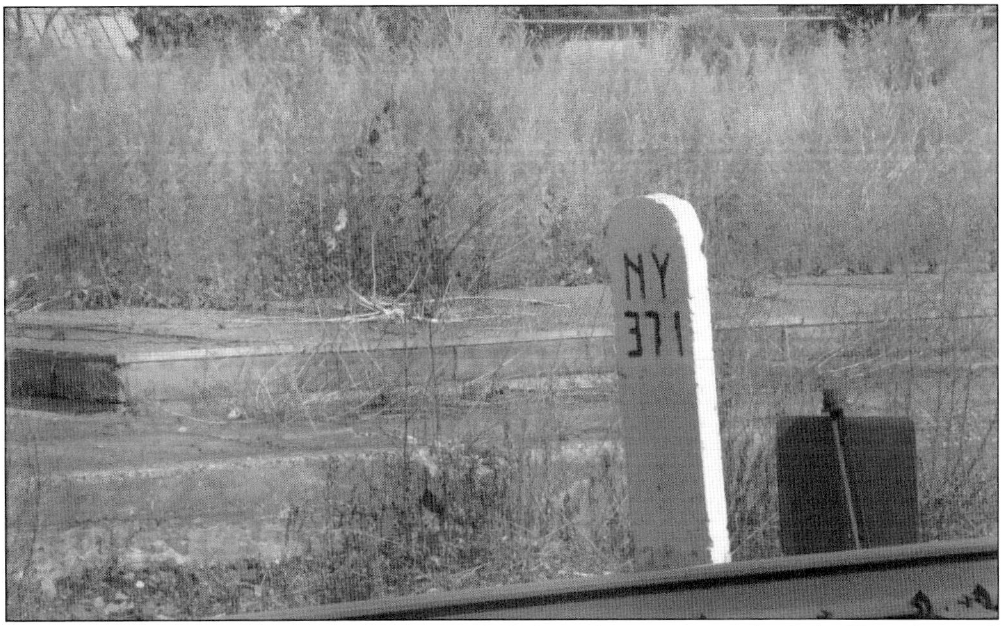

Today, Amtrak provides Rochester with one daily long-distance train, the Lake Shore Limited, and several trains that service New York State. Looking across the CSX main line, Amtrak passengers can see from the milepost that they are 371 miles from New York City. They also see a former Bragdon Station platform. It brings back memories of the days when this platform and several others at Bragdon Station were needed to handle the NYC's many arriving and departing passenger trains that numbered in the double digits. (Author's collection.)

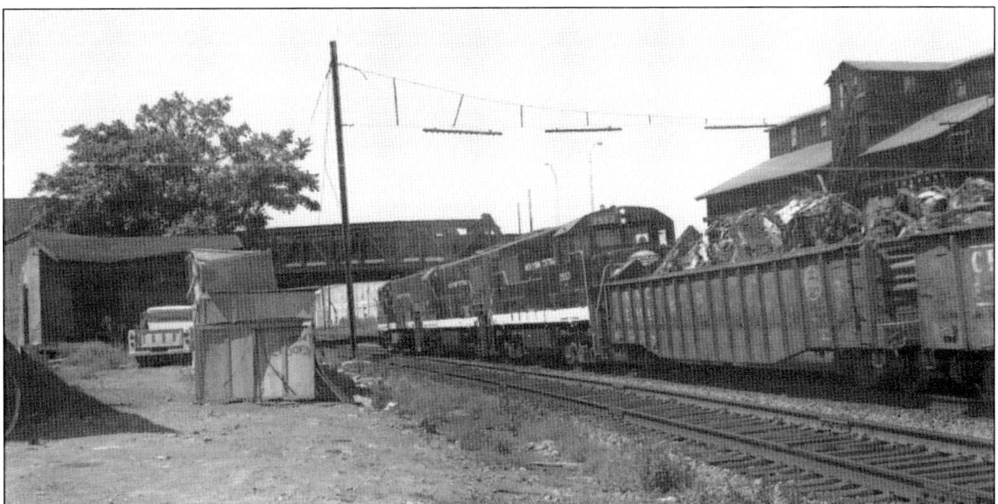

It is interesting to note that, until the mid-1950s, Alco and GE were partners in the design and production of Alco diesel locomotives such as the RS-3, FA, and PA. The U25B, nicknamed the "U-Boat," was GE's first attempt to market a diesel road locomotive after it ended its manufacturing partnership with Alco. The U25B is shown hauling loaded gondola cars in this 1967 photograph taken at the west end of Goodman Street Yards. GE continued with its production of diesel locomotives, and GE diesel locomotives today power many CSX freight trains and almost all of Amtrak's passenger trains. (Photograph by Robert Carper, courtesy of Jeff Hands.)

Consistent with our mission to preserve history on a local level, this book was printed in South Carolina on American-made paper and manufactured entirely in the United States. Products carrying the accredited Forest Stewardship Council (FSC) label are printed on 100 percent FSC-certified paper.

MADE IN THE USA